The Cambridge Introduction to
Theatre and Literature of the Absurd

MICHAEL BENNETT's accessible *Introduction* explains the complex, multi-dimensional nature of the works and writers associated with the absurd – a label placed upon a number of writers who revolted against traditional theatre and literature in both similar and widely different ways. Setting the movement in its historical, intellectual, and cultural contexts, Bennett provides an in-depth overview of absurdism and its key figures in theatre and literature, from Samuel Beckett and Harold Pinter to Tom Stoppard. Chapters reveal the movement's origins, development, and present-day influence upon popular culture around the world, employing the latest research to this often-challenging area of study in a balanced and authoritative approach. Essential reading for students of literature and theatre, this book provides the necessary tools to interpret and develop the study of a movement associated with some of the twentieth century's greatest and most influential cultural figures.

MICHAEL Y. BENNETT is Associate Professor of English and affiliated faculty in Philosophy at the University of Wisconsin-Whitewater.

The Cambridge Introduction to
Theatre and Literature of the Absurd

MICHAEL Y. BENNETT

CAMBRIDGE
UNIVERSITY PRESS

CAMBRIDGE
UNIVERSITY PRESS

University Printing House, Cambridge CB2 8BS, United Kingdom

Cambridge University Press is part of the University of Cambridge.

It furthers the University's mission by disseminating knowledge in the pursuit of education, learning, and research at the highest international levels of excellence.

www.cambridge.org
Information on this title: www.cambridge.org/9781107635517

© Michael Y. Bennett 2015

First published 2015

Printed in the United Kingdom by Clays, St Ives plc

A catalogue record for this publication is available from the British Library.

Library of Congress Cataloguing in Publication data
Bennett, Michael Y., 1980–
The Cambridge introduction to theatre and literature of the absurd /
Michael Y. Bennett.
    pages   cm. – (Cambridge introductions to literature)
Includes bibliographical references and index.
ISBN 978-1-107-05392-2
1. Drama – 20th century – History and criticism.   2. Theatre of the absurd.
3. Absurd (Philosophy) in literature.   I. Title.
PN1861.B43   2015
809.2′04 – dc23   2015021710

ISBN 978-1-107-05392-2 Hardback
ISBN 978-1-107-63551-7 Paperback

To my best friend, Eyal Tamir, with whom I laugh at life's absurdities

In memory of
Robert A. Bennett (1941–2014)

Contents

Acknowledgments   *page* x

Chapter 1 Introduction: Overview of the absurd   1

Martin Esslin's *The Theatre of the Absurd*   3
Common conceptions of the absurd   9
Origins of the absurd: The Greeks through the
    nineteenth century   11
Origins of the absurd: Expressionism, Dadaism, Surrealism,
    and other avant-garde movements of the early
    twentieth century   12
Philosophy of the absurd: Or rather, philosoph*ies*
    of the absurd   14
Challenges to the notion of "absurd"   16
Absurd tragicomedy   20

Chapter 2 Setting the stage   24

Alfred Jarry   25
Franz Kafka   28
OBERIU   31
Antonin Artaud   32

Chapter 3 The emergence of a "movement": The historical and intellectual contexts   35

Post-WWII Europe   36
Post-WWII United States   39
The Existential Front   40
The Camus–Sartre quarrel   40
The emergence of analytic philosophy   44

Why theatre?: How the genre came to be the center
of the "movement"   45

Chapter 4 Samuel Beckett   47

Waiting for Godot   49
Other plays   52
Fiction   57
Poetry   62

Chapter 5 Beckett's notable contemporaries   67

Edward Albee   67
Jean Genet   76
Eugene Ionesco   81
Harold Pinter   84

**Chapter 6 The European and American wave
of absurdism**   92

Arthur Adamov   92
Fernando Arrabal   94
Amiri Baraka   95
Friedrich Dürrenmatt   97
Jack Gelber   98
Václav Havel   99
Adrienne Kennedy   100
Arthur Kopit   102
Sławomir Mrożek   103
Tadeusz Różewicz   104
Sam Shepard   105
N.F. Simpson   113
Tom Stoppard   113

Chapter 7 Post-absurdism?   115

The influence of the absurdist "movement"   115
Dramatic and theatrical conventions following the
absurdist "movement"   116
(Later) female absurdists   119

The multicultural absurd?   122
Absurdism's legacy outside of the theatre: Fiction and poetry
   after the wake of the 1970s   124
Absurdism in pop culture   125

Chapter 8 Absurd criticism   128

Esslin   129
Esslin's contemporaries   129
The lull in absurd criticism   130
The resurgence of absurd criticism in the new millennium   130

Notes   133
Further reading   150
Index   160

Acknowledgments

First, I wish to thank the following people for their feedback and help with the manuscript at various stages of the project: The Fellows at the Institute for Research in the Humanities; William W. Demastes (Louisiana State University, Baton Rouge); J. Chris Westgate (California State University, Fullerton); Robert Combs (The George Washington University); The Samuel Beckett Working Group (IFTR/FIRT 2013) – most particularly, David Tucker (University of Chester and University of Sussex) and Nicholas Johnson (Trinity College, Dublin); and my research assistant, Frederick Hofstetter (UW-Whitewater), made possible by a generous research grant from UW-Whitewater.

Second, I would like to thank my editor at Cambridge University Press, Dr. Victoria Cooper, for her vision and constant support in seeing this book come to fruition. Also deserving of thanks are the anonymous reviewers, for their detailed and constructive feedback.

Third, a few short sections of this book were previously published and graciously allowed to be reprinted here in a slightly modified version: Michael Y. Bennett, *Words, Space, and the Audience: The Theatrical Tension between Empiricism and Rationalism* (2012, Palgrave Macmillan, pp. 82–9, 105–8, 149–55, and 160–2, reproduced with permission of Palgrave Macmillan).

And finally, fourth and most importantly, I wish to thank those in my life who may not have made a direct contribution to the scholarship, but whose indirect contributions made this work possible: my family. My two sons, Max and Julius, show me how to respond to absurdities with love and laughter, and my wife, Kelly, dissolves all absurdities with her love. Kelly is the one thing that always makes sense and where my desires are always fully met by the realities of the world.

Chapter 1

Introduction: Overview of the absurd

Two men have been waiting on a country road for fifty years for a man named Godot. A woman is buried to her waist in the ground, and then buried up to her head, and continually concludes that this is a happy day. The inhabitants of a provincial French town one by one turn into rhinoceroses, until one man, who is by no means a hero, is left to face them. A transient approaches and harasses a well-to-do man sitting alone on a bench in a park and then the transient kills himself by running into a knife the man eventually holds. While still maintaining his love for his wife, an award-winning architect falls in love with a goat. A maybe former concert pianist, who is living at a seaside boarding house, is visited by two maybe unknown men and is interrogated to the point where the pianist is reduced to producing only grunts, at which point, after his supposed birthday party, the men escort the pianist away in a van. An entire novel with no perceivable plot narrated as a fractured and fragmented monologue by an unnamed, possibly immobile man. These are just some of the plots of absurd literature.

What, then, is absurdism? And what does it mean for a literary or dramatic work to be absurd? As some of the most important writers and thinkers of the twentieth century are *associated* with the absurd – writers such as Samuel Beckett, Albert Camus, Harold Pinter (all three being Nobel Prize winners in Literature), Edward Albee (winner of three Pulitzer Prizes and four Tony Awards), and (tangentially) Jean-Paul Sartre (who also *won* a Nobel Prize in Literature, but refused to accept it) – surely, many readers of this book will have some conception as to what is meant by absurdism or absurd literature. And the fact that absurd literature is thought to be a literary response to WWII brings a whole host of assumptions about what it means for something to be absurd. As *The Cambridge Introduction to Theatre and Literature of the Absurd*, the reader might be expecting an answer to these questions in a relatively simple and straightforward statement. Regarding that expectation, though some attempt will be made, this book will have to disappoint. The fact remains that there is no *single* answer – and certainly not a simple, straightforward answer – to these questions: much depends upon who you ask, what decade you asked in, and in what region of the world you posed these questions. But do not lose hope, as this is exactly much of the reason why the absurd has endured and thrived as a "movement," if you will, of extraordinary interest over the past six decades. Absurd literature is elusive, complex, and nuanced: it refuses to be pinned down. And this is precisely why these texts associated with the absurd can be studied over and over, reinterpreted over and over, and have spoken for so long (and continue to speak) so powerfully to so many different generations, cultures, creeds, and types of people.

It is appropriate to introduce the absurd and its literary and dramatic equivalents in much the same way, appropriately (given the perceived overlap between existentialism and absurd literature), that Walter Kaufmann introduces his well-known, long-lived, edited anthology, *Existentialism: From Dostoevsky to Sartre*. Kaufmann starts, "Existentialism is not a philosophy but a label for several widely different revolts against traditional philosophy."[1] He concludes his first paragraph by stating, " . . . it might be argued that the label 'existentialism' ought to be abandoned altogether."[2] A very similar thing can be said about philosophy of the absurd, the "Theatre of the Absurd," and other absurd texts. Absurdism is not a literary "movement," but "absurd" is a *label* placed upon a number of disparate writers (many of whom were playwrights writing in the 1950s and 1960s) who revolted against traditional theatre in sometimes similar and sometimes widely different ways. It might also be appropriate to suggest that maybe the *label* "absurd" (*placed upon* these literary texts and writers) ought to be abandoned altogether, as well.

The fact that the "Existential Front," the only real wave of self-declared existentialism (led by Jean-Paul Sartre and Maurice Merleau-Ponty), found its way to the front of intellectual life (especially in France) following the horrors of the Holocaust and WWII, and the fact that writers such as Jean Genet, Eugene Ionesco, and Samuel Beckett were also writing in France shortly following WWII, may or may not be a coincidence. However, what is important is that the two, almost simultaneous "movements," if you will, were both composed of amorphous, undefined collections of thoughts and practices with none of the writers and thinkers defining themselves by the labels placed upon them (with the exception of Sartre and Merleau-Ponty who self-avowed themselves as "existentialists"). Therefore, when two perceived "movements," neither of which are self-defined or necessarily a conscious "movement," are placed in juxtaposition, there is bound to be utter confusion as to how one is to define them, especially the absurdist literary writers, none of whom ever said they were "absurdists." Despite the challenges posed by these labels, this book will introduce – in a simple, straightforward *manner* – the complex, multi-dimensional, and rich nature of those works and writers associated with absurdism, offering the student of absurdism an inroad to these often challenging but very rewarding works and an in-depth path to continue one's exploration.

There is a common notion, however, that while someone may not be able to define absurd literature, one knows absurd literature when one encounters it. It is this very issue that this book attempts to address. The main difficulty is, *is it possible to discuss absurd literature without re-inscribing the "absurd" as a reductive category?* In order to address this, in this book, I focus less on the *themes* of the texts, but rather on the *techniques and aesthetic forms* that works and writers of absurd literature have in common: it is in this way that it is possible to *group* these disparate writers together without having to impose a straightjacket on what these texts mean or are saying to the reader/audience member. And this, importantly, allows each writer and each of their texts under consideration to simultaneously exist on their own, while still being able to understand the context that there was some organic alignment among a number of writers writing, especially, around the 1950s through 1970s. Ultimately, discussing absurd literature without re-inscribing it as a reductive category – by also placing it within larger literary, intellectual, and historical contexts – gives the student of absurd literature the necessary tools to (re)interpret these absurd texts.

Martin Esslin's *The Theatre of the Absurd*

It may be very unusual to start a book on interpreting literature, especially an introductory text, not with the literature itself and its writers, but with specifically *dramatic* criticism that pre-dated almost half of just the *theatrical* "movement": but such is the legacy of Martin Esslin's 1961 book, *The Theatre of the Absurd*. Christopher Innes, in an article about why Esslin's *The Theatre of the Absurd* is a part of the literary "canon," writes,

> that by explaining and popularizing their work, *The Theatre of the Absurd* directly contributed to that success. This is a book that literally created the movement it defined, changing not only scholarly and public perceptions but also the nature of contemporary theatre.[3]

As implied by Innes, Esslin's reading of the plays in his book is almost as widely known as the plays themselves. And whether or not it is fair to the rest of the literature associated with the absurd – for the "Theatre of the Absurd," while maybe the absurd's most highly crystalized expression, is still just one piece (and one genre) of the absurd – Esslin's vision of these plays permeates through advanced high school and college classrooms, through local and national newspapers' theatre reviews, through just about every English and theatre major's conception of the absurd around the world, and even through academic journal articles and books.[4] Why is this?

We need to step back for a second in order to move forward. Starting in the late 1940s and early 1950s, a few playwrights, most notably Samuel Beckett, Eugene Ionesco, and Jean Genet, had plays produced first in Paris before the plays moved to other countries. Almost immediately, especially with Beckett's *Waiting for Godot* (first published in 1952 and first produced in 1953), these plays became a *sensation*: but a "sensation" is not necessarily because the plays were well loved. Almost on the contrary, with the exception of some of the audiences in the initial productions in Paris, the plays of Beckett, Genet, and later in the 1950s, Harold Pinter and Edward Albee (to name a couple) caused almost an outrage among theatre audiences and critics. These plays were *different*. Despite the interest in seeing a whole new and different type of theatre that was emerging in Western Europe (and the United States soon after), for the most part, audiences and critics alike just simply did not understand the plays: *What was going on? Who are these characters? How can the play end there? What type of dialogue is this? Can you even call this dialogue?* Many critics and viewers even thought that these plays were just displays of intellectual snobbery. Even with the heavy-handed negative critiques, plays doing similar things throughout the 1950s from an ever-growing group of playwrights were simply not seeming to go away.

Then, in 1961, the assistant head of the BBC's radio drama department, Martin Esslin, published *The Theatre of the Absurd*. In short, Esslin suggests that audiences are judging plays by the above-mentioned playwrights (and others) against plays of traditional theatre (presumably, Aristotelian drama and theatrical realism). And this, Esslin asserts, is simply not fair to the plays at hand. In other words, one cannot judge the quality of an orange by comparing it to the taste of an apple. As such, Esslin says that we must judge these plays, which fall into the category he labels the "Theatre of the Absurd," not by the standards of traditional theatre, but by the standards of the "Theatre of the Absurd," which Esslin sets out to define. Importantly, Esslin stresses the fact that the dramatists that make up the Theatre of the Absurd "do not form part of any self-proclaimed or self-conscious school or movement."[5]

Before Esslin defines the "Theatre of the Absurd," he sets out to define "absurd," itself. Esslin turns to the philosophy of Albert Camus, whose *The Myth of Sisyphus* (1942) is about the human sense of absurdity. Esslin states that WWII shattered all hopes of replacing religion with faith in progress, nationalism, and various totalitarian fallacies.[6] Esslin notes that, "By 1942,

Albert Camus was calmly putting the question, why, since life had lost all meaning, man should not seek escape in suicide."[7] Quoting Camus' *The Myth of Sisyphus*, Esslin explains Camus' "[diagnosis] of the human situation in a world of shattered beliefs":

> A world that can be explained by reasoning, however faulty, is a familiar world. But in a universe that is suddenly deprived of illusions and of light, man feels a stranger. His is an irremediable exile, because he is deprived of memories of a lost homeland as much as he lacks the hope of a promised land to come. The divorce between man and his life, the actor and his setting, truly constitutes the feeling of Absurdity.[8]

Esslin continues and suggests, stemming in some ways from its dictionary definition, that the common usage of "absurd" meaning "ridiculous," is not how Camus uses the word nor is it the sense as it pertains to the Theatre of the Absurd. Esslin quotes Eugene Ionesco, from an essay Ionesco wrote about Franz Kafka, to define the Absurd: "Absurd is that which is devoid of purpose . . . Cut off from his religious, metaphysical, and transcendental roots, man is lost; all actions become senseless, absurd and useless."[9]

After defining the "absurd," Esslin begins his discussion of what he sees as the theme of the plays of the Theatre of the Absurd: the "sense of metaphysical anguish at the absurdity of the human condition." Esslin notes that while other writers have the same theme of the "sense of senselessness of life," writers such as Giraudoux, Anouilh, Salacrou, Sartre, and Camus present this same theme in a "highly lucid" manner, using "logically constructed reasoning." The playwrights of the Theatre of the Absurd, on the other hand, write about this same theme – the "sense of the senselessness of the human condition and the inadequacy of the rational approach" – but by matching the new content with a new convention: that is, by striving to express this senselessness "by the open abandonment of rational devices and discursive thought."[10] Thus, while Sartre and Camus express their philosophies in their writing, the Theatre of the Absurd, Esslin argues, does a better job of connecting the similar content with an appropriately matching form.[11] And while Sartre and Camus argue *about* absurdity of the human condition – which is the approach of the philosopher – the playwrights discussed by Esslin "merely [*present* the absurd] in being."

As such, Esslin is then able to move his conversation away from his thematic approach to a structural approach that examines the form of the genre of the Theatre of the Absurd. That is, what are some of the typical devices in this theatre and what is its form and the manner in presenting its theme? Esslin says these plays "[tend] toward a radical devaluation of language . . . what *happens* on the stage transcends, and often contradicts, the *words* spoken by the characters."[12] Earlier in his Introduction, Esslin's characterization of these plays (in relation to traditional theatre) also gives the reader a list of things typically encountered in this genre: "these have no story or plot to speak of . . . these are often without recognizable characters and present the audience with almost mechanical puppets . . . these often have neither a beginning nor an end . . . these seem often to be reflections of dreams and nightmares . . . these often consist of incoherent babblings."[13]

Esslin's book clearly struck a chord with the theatre-going public. Esslin published an expanded edition to include more playwrights in 1969, as well. The books (though the same in their essential arguments) is/are considered arguably the most important book(s) of dramatic criticism in that decade. And the fact that a third edition of the book was published thirty-five years later in 2004 demonstrates the staying power of Esslin's initial readings (which is now in its eighth printing). While this book, *The Cambridge Introduction to Theatre and Literature of the Absurd*, is at times critical of Esslin's book, the importance that Esslin's book had/has in the minds of the general public and academia, and similarly, its importance in popularizing (and almost immortalizing) quite challenging theatrical texts that would have otherwise probably remained removed from the public's consciousness, slipping away into near oblivion as a short-lived avant-garde fad, cannot be overstated. Even Esslin's greatest detractors are highly indebted to Esslin for making these plays not only relevant, but elevating them, in a sense, into high art and philosophy, all the while, making these plays accessible to the general public.

The issue that scholars have had with Esslin's book is not that he places writers together who do not fit with each other: Esslin is rather spot on, in fact, in placing these playwrights side by side. The issue, instead, has been that by naming/labeling and categorizing a group of playwrights together by the theme of absurdity – a theme Esslin very narrowly defines based upon a specific (mis)reading of the philosopher, Albert Camus – the multiple meanings that generally emerge from "great literature" are generally *reduced* to a single theme. Esslin literally placed a *label* on these plays, as he "attaches" the "name,"[14] "The Theatre of the Absurd." Furthermore, in suggesting that these plays and playwrights employ "their own convention," Esslin connotes that there is something formal happening here, as "convention" means, even if these conventions are implicit, that there is general "agreement," "consent," and/or the presence of "rules" to follow.[15] Samuel Beckett's own criticism of the label "The Theatre of the Absurd" is that it was originally constructed as a value judgment.[16] One of Esslin's main stated goals was to create the category of the "Theatre of the Absurd" so that *these* plays were not being evaluated against the norms of *traditional theatre* (which, if they were to be, they were bound to fail). In order to appreciate these plays, Esslin created a label, "The Theatre of the Absurd" which was largely based upon – a theme: the "metaphysical anguish at the absurdity of the human condition." This label, largely, again, by *theme* led to reductionist readings of these plays associated with the absurd, most of these readings still inform our common understanding of these plays and absurd literature as a whole. Despite the fact that Esslin's theme can clearly be seen in these plays, this *reduction to a single theme*, and then labeling a whole group of disparate writers together based on that one main theme, is not fair to the individual plays and especially these playwrights, whose careers span decades and whose plays explore so many other themes and preoccupations, as well. Edward Albee points out the very problems with "labels" (including the absurd label): "I dismiss all labels. Theatre of the Absurd. Angry Young Man. Playwright of Protest. Labels are so facile, and they're a substitute for conscientious analysis so much of the time."[17]

While this chapter will explore the nuances and complex lineage of the absurd, demonstrating the difficulty of classifying it as particularly this-or-that, there, however, *are* ways to *describe* what is happening. But how? Or, stated another way (again), *is it possible to discuss the absurd without re-inscribing the "absurd" as a reductive category?* This has been the elusive quest for scholars since Esslin's book, even by Esslin himself, for much of the rest of his career following the publication of *The Theatre of the Absurd*.

Without any self-declared movement, self-declared name, or literary/artistic manifesto, it is really hard to *simply* "label" or "categorize" these writers (especially the playwrights of the 1950s and 1960s) as "absurdists." While there is just too much variety and too little concerted effort to place a *label* on what these writers were doing, having said that, it is not, however, entirely wrong (and maybe entirely correct) to *group* the playwrights that Esslin associated with the Theatre of the Absurd together, along with comparable contemporary writers of absurd fiction and poetry, *in the same manner* as to how scholars loosely (though not without problems and controversy), but constructively group *modernist* writers and *postmodernist* writers (i.e., both as a loose temporal grouping and one based upon similarities of techniques, forms, and preoccupations). "Grouping" is far less "systematic" than the act of "labeling" or "categorizing." The latter two have connotations that things in the same *class* or *category* are similar in many, if not all, aspects, while instead "grouping" requires only the "presence of *some* common feature or property" (*my italics*). That is, there is room for a lot of *difference* among those placed in a "group," versus much less so, if any difference at all, in a "category" or "class." As it is difficult to get rid of a label that has stuck for fifty-plus years, and then, some term or word – out of the necessity of communicating ideas through language – would need to replace it, suggesting merely *another* "label," I will refer to this loose group of writers and their works as "absurd" (also using "absurd," both as an adjective and as a noun, in uses such as, "absurd literature," "the literary absurd," "absurd theatre," etc.). My use of the word, "absurd," however, also attempts to take into account a far greater sense of the word (both philosophically more diverse and, especially, also capturing the word's sense in common usage) than how Esslin proposes "Theatre of the Absurd" is used in relation to these plays.

Therefore, in order to (re)describe absurd literature without being *reductionist*, I focus not really on the themes or meaning (as Esslin mostly does), but basically just on the techniques and aesthetic forms that absurd literature has in common: it is in this way that it is possible to group these disparate writers together without having to impose a straightjacket on what these texts *mean* or are saying to the reader/audience member (either in the 1950s, now, or fifty years from now). And this, importantly, *allows each writer and each play to simultaneously exist on their own, while still being able to understand the context that there was some organic alignment among a number of writers writing around the 1950s through 1970s.* This book proposes to address this issue by suggesting that by *grouping* these writers according to some common techniques and similarities of literary form, the often wide differences among these absurd writers and their texts remains intact.

Let us take the two example groups above: *modernist* and *postmodernist* writers. If we think of the most iconic modernist writers, some of the first names that come to mind are T. S. Eliot, F. Scott Fitzgerald, Virginia Woolf, James Joyce, and Ernest Hemingway (and this is not an exhaustive list). But while these "modernist" writers, if you will, share certain techniques of expression, wrote around the same time period, and had similar views towards truth, could we say that "The Wasteland," *The Great Gatsby, A Room of One's Own, Ulysses,* and *The Old Man and the Sea,* respectively, are *about* (thematically speaking) the same things? Not at all! It is the same with the metafiction, pastiche, and the time period of postmodernist writers: Thomas Pynchon (*Gravity's Rainbow*), Kurt Vonnegut (*Slaughterhouse V*), and David Foster Wallace (*Infinite Jest*), just to name a few. Are these three books, thematically, *about* the same things? No, of course not. So why would/should we assume/say absurdist literature thematically is *about* the same things? And this is why Esslin's categorization that the playwrights of the absurd share the common theme of "metaphysical anguish at the absurdity of the human condition" is absurd. Can one theme typify Beckett, Genet, Albee, Pinter, and so on? That is where the reductionism of the label, "absurd" (or "Theatre of the Absurd") originates. Yes, it can clearly be seen that the above-named playwrights touch upon this above theme, but to connect writers through a *theme*, or even, maybe more appropriately, through the *meaning* or a *reading* of their texts is typically not done in literary criticism, and for good reasons. Literature, generally, defies a single reading or meaning. Literature almost actively refuses to be *about* this particular thing or that particular thing: it speaks (over the ages) to so many topics, themes, meanings, and so on. Texts like *Hamlet, Ulysses,* and *Godot* are re-interpreted again and again and again, and they are still just as elusive and exciting each time they are read (or re-read). *This book thus aims to give the student of absurd literature the background information, contexts, and the tools to (re)interpret these literary works in varied and exciting new ways.*

Common conceptions of the absurd

There are generally three main ideas surrounding the absurd that float around in the public's imagination. These three common conceptions – that absurdism (1) discusses the senselessness and meaninglessness of life, (2) is existential, and (3) has ridiculous plots – are both kind of on target and also kind of misplaced.

Absurd has long been thought of as a literary response to the horrors of WWII and the Holocaust. In a world that, for the most part, sat by and allowed such horrors to transpire, where was God to be found? How else could the world be anything but senseless and meaningless? The (often misunderstood) widely popular and widely read post-WWII atheistic philosophies of Jean-Paul Sartre and Albert Camus *seemed* to point to the same conclusion. Largely because of the general misunderstandings about Sartre's existentialism and the (generally unknown) fact that Camus revolted against Sartrean existentialism, as Esslin references Sartre and Camus as philosophical backbones of the Theatre of the Absurd, helped the public, both correctly and incorrectly, conflate absurdism with existentialism. Kafka's trials, Godot's absence, the menace of Pinter's dramas, the onslaught of Rhinoceritis, and the general confusion and lack of linearity of thought and logic present in these absurd texts all suggest how senseless and meaningless life is. Esslin's pronouncement that these plays of the Theatre of the Absurd discuss the "senselessness of life" immediately helped theatregoers make sense of these plays. Clearly, these texts can readily be read as dwelling on our "metaphysical anguish."

At the same time, however, these texts also point to the need to make one's own life meaningful. The Samsas learn to live life after Gregor's transformation in "The Metamorphosis," Didi and Gogo are each other's *saviors* and with each other they can "bide one's time," Pinter shows where communication fails in hopes that we (the audience/reader) might not fall into the same traps of silence and conversing without really communicating, Berenger holds on to his humanity and cherishes the revolt despite his absurd situation with the onslaught of Rhinoceritis, and the language of the absurd might mirror the senselessness found in our absurd world, but it also creates fertile ground for making meaning ourselves.

Though Esslin was quick to point out that "absurd" should not be understood in terms of its common usage, "ridiculous," there is clearly an assumption among the general reader that the word, "absurd," is, in fact, used in this way and the plays, especially, are largely perceived (and maybe rightly so, to a degree) as *ridiculous*. Two men waiting on a desolate "country road" for fifty years for a man who never comes, rhinos running through a small provincial French town (and we find out that it is because the townsfolk are the ones turning into rhinos), and a man awakes one morning as a bug, all surely sound like quite *ridiculous* plots.

Esslin expressly states that it is not the "ridiculous" connotation of the absurd that characterized these plays. Esslin suggests that it is the "divorce between man and his life" that constitutes the absurd. This turn to a well-respected and well-read philosopher, Albert Camus, and his philosophy of the absurd, gave Esslin's reading of these plays a very solid intellectual thrust. And while absurd texts have been read (countless times) very persuasively through the philosophies of Sartre and Camus – and the philosophical absurd is absolutely integral to absurd literature – it is also ridiculous to say that there is not an element of the *ridiculous* in absurd literature. The first definition of *ridiculous* is "exciting ridicule and derisive laughter; absurd, preposterous, comical, laughable."[18] While it can be argued that the first part of this definition emphasizes its *ridicul-* root and may not fully apply to the texts of the absurd, "absurd, preposterous, comical, laughable" clearly describes a significant and obvious part of absurd literature. The ridiculousness of absurd literature should not be entirely ignored in order to make these texts simply more philosophical or carry more intellectual weight. The ridiculous element found in these texts not only aptly describes an obvious element of the texts (seemingly more obvious to the general public than academics) and should be cherished for its creativity and inventiveness rather than glossed over *only* in favor of a more intellectually serious notion of the absurd, but the connotations of ridiculous also connect these absurd texts to their lineage stemming from literary nonsense and the hilarity of the *comedy* found within their tragi*comic* texts.

Origins of the absurd: The Greeks through the nineteenth century

The "absurd" cannot be linked directly back to the Greeks, as that would imply that concrete notions of the absurd had been formulated by the Greeks. With that said, however, we can look back and retrace lines of literary influence that appear to have made its way into the absurd's literary expression in the twentieth century. One relatively unexplored area of the origins of the absurd is the history of "tragicomedy." Given that Beckett's *Waiting for Godot* is probably history's most famously billed "tragicomedy," this area of exploration as it relates to the absurd has been sorely needed and, I hope to show, can be enlightening. While the word, "tragicomedy" only came into existence (as far as we know from extant manuscripts) from the Roman playwright, Plautus, in his Prologue to his play, *Amphitryon*, it is very likely that Aristotle, in his *Poetics*, was describing the same phenomenon when he described Greek tragedies with dual endings.

After the fall of Ancient Greece, and the subsequent setting aside of Aristotle's notions of theatre, Roman and Late Antiquity writers looked to Horace for their rules about drama. Horace was primarily concerned with the *rhetoric* of drama, and analysis of drama was judged by rhetorical standards.[19] When the Latin provinces were lost to invaders after the sixth century, it was the East that adopted Greek as its official language (where in the West writers continued to work in the Latin tradition), and thus, the recovery of Aristotle and Greek dramatic traditions began in the twelfth century.[20] It was, however, the Italian Renaissance when Aristotle's *Poetics* became a key starting point in dramatic theory, but it also became a point of contention for playwrights and scholars who departed from the rules set forth by Aristotle.

Much like how *Godot* and its critical response became a turning point in twentieth-century theatre – as plays like *Godot* offended the strictures of traditional theatre and created new directions against traditional theatre – a similar pivotal debate in dramatic theory played out during the Italian Renaissance over the "tragicomic pastoral." Broadly stated, until Giraldi Cinthio (1504–73) and Sperone Speroni (1500–88) challenged the authority of the ancients with their plays and Julius Caesar Scaliger (1484–1558) challenged it with his criticism, much of the theory and criticism of drama up until that point had to do with following the authority of either the Greeks (most notably, Aristotle) or the Romans (most notably, Horace).[21] The "tragicomic pastoral" created a major literary debate as "mixed" plots created a whole new genre not discussed and therefore not theorized by the Greeks or Romans, giving no ground with which to either follow their authority or dispute it.[22] The "mixed" elements of tragedy and comedy, which were so clearly defined (or at least each critic defined their own definitions of tragedy and comedy clearly from a litany of previous critics over the past millennium plus), split the theatre world into a quarrel between the Ancients or traditionalists and the Moderns or modernists. Simply stated, the traditionalists thought that drama should not veer from the prescripts of the ancient theorists, while the modernists thought that drama could have its own independence from the ancients.[23] These debates continued and spread throughout Europe during the Renaissance and well after.

Neil Cornwell, in his detailed and expansive survey, *The Absurd in Literature*, also suggests some appropriate, what he calls, *antecedents to the absurd.* Cornwell identifies a number of "antecedents" from the Elizabethan period to the nineteenth century. Most notable of the antecedents that Cornwell points out are the tradition of English nonsense poetry, the Romantic Grotesque, and the works of individual writers such as Nikolai Gogol and Lewis Carroll.[24]

Origins of the absurd: Expressionism, Dadaism, Surrealism, and other avant-garde movements of the early twentieth century

While the rise of the novel, realism, modernism, and postmodernism dominated much of artistic expression (broadly defined) in the twentieth century, artistic expression in the twentieth century has also been notable for its emergent avant-garde movements, which challenged the status quo of the arts. Many of these movements tussled with the question of how best to portray truth in art. In short, with the rise of naturalism at the end of the nineteenth century and rise of realism at the beginning of the twentieth century, the avant-garde movements of the twentieth century were largely reactions to portraits of realism. Realism seeks to portray life as it is really lived. In a sense, most especially in the theatre, realism is a mirror of life. Theatrical realism – maybe more so than realism in any other art form – best captures humans with all of their virtues and vices; can emulate humans' natural (spoken) language, dialects, and accents; and stages the everyday, lived life, by allowing the audience to view through characters through a "fourth wall." But does putting *real* characters on stage necessarily capture truth most accurately? Many twentieth-century avant-garde movements would have answered this question, no.

At the beginning of the twentieth century, with the flourishing study of human psychology led by Sigmund Freud, there was a new and heightened sense of human interiority. Many of the avant-garde movements of the early twentieth century wanted to outwardly portray the inner lives of humans.

For while realism displayed humans' outward reality extremely well, realism has/had trouble portraying humans' inner life. Expressionism, with its German origins, led the first wave of theatrical attempts to portray an inner reality. While this movement had a clear effect on the German theatre and made its way to American theatres through the likes of experimental plays by Eugene O'Neill, Sophie Treadwell, and Elmer Rice, it is hard to necessarily say that it had an influence on the semi-overlapping movements of Dadaism and surrealism.

While expressionism was clearly a reaction to realism's supposed limitations, Dadaism's expression of nonsense (in direct contrast to the linearity and logic of realism) was a reaction to the perceived failures of logic and rational thought that led to The Great War (WWI). Dadaism was a largely political, anti-war, anti-bourgeois art movement. Surrealism soon grew out of Dadaism. Surrealism thought that liberating the imagination through the examination of dreams, free association, and the unconscious could change the world in a positive way better than by attacking traditional forms (of art, culture, society, etc.) that was advocated by the Dadaists. Surrealists thought that the examination of the above could more realistically portray the actual functioning of human thought.

It should be pointed out that expressionism, with its origins and center in Germany, more influenced German-speaking artists. Dadaism also started in German-speaking Zurich and then moved to Berlin. However, Tristan Tzara and André Brenton (among others) were French speakers based in Paris who created an important connection between Dadaism and surrealism, the latter with its origins and center in France. Interestingly (or appropriately) enough, expressionism made its way (as noted before) to the United States' and English language (with English being a Germanic language) theatrical productions; Dadaism and surrealism had a much larger influence on the French writers. And it should be stressed that the "Theatre of the Absurd" originated largely in Paris, with early plays in French by Genet, Ionesco, Adamov, and Beckett. In an interview in *The Paris Review*, Eugene Ionesco was very clear about the influence that Dadaism and surrealism had on his (and Beckett's) writing: "None of us would have written as we do without surrealism and dadaism. By liberating the language, those movements paved the way for us . . . I was bowled over [by Tristan Tzara] . . . Then I read all the other surrealists – André Breton, Robert Desnos."[25]

There is also a widely held conception that playwrights such as Luigi Pirandello and Bertolt Brecht (and Brecht's Epic Theatre) are absurdists, or influenced the absurd. I think this perception stems from the fact that they were theatrical innovators, much like the writers and playwrights associated with the absurd. In short, these were avant-garde writers, writing against mainstream theatre. However, Pirandello and (even more so) Brecht were experimenting with the *meta-theatrical*, with Brecht breaking the "fourth wall" of theatre. The theatrical absurd, with the exception of mostly two plays (Genet's *The Blacks: A Clown Show* and Jack Gelber's *The Connection*, though Albee also has his moments, too), is neither meta-theatrical nor does it make any attempt to break the "fourth wall" of theatrical realism. In this way, Pirandello and Brecht exert essentially no influence upon the playwrights associated with the Theatre of the Absurd. However, Pirandello and Brecht's willingness to break and experiment with breaking the *conventions* of *traditional* theatre certainly paved the way for other playwrights to break theatrical conventions. (And this is why, as I mention shortly, some absurd writers do see Brecht as an influence of theirs.) It is in this general way that Pirandello and Brecht influenced the absurd.

In fact, much like how Pirandello and Brecht are often thought of as absurdists, the *theatrical avant-garde* – any such movement or isolated instance of the theatrical avant-garde – is so often construed by the public as "absurd." Yes, the mid-century plays of the absurd were influenced by theatrical avant-garde movements – movements such as Dadaism and surrealism – and yes, *the theatrical absurd was avant-garde* itself, as it clearly rebelled against mainstream theatre (and absurd fiction and absurd poetry also rebelled against their, respective, mainstream genres). However, Alfred Jarry's pataphysical avant-garde was not the avant-garde of expressionism, which was not the avant-garde Futurism, which was not the avant-garde of Dadaism, which was not the same avant-garde surrealism, which was not the avant-garde constructivism.[26] And while streaks and elements of these avant-garde movements can be felt in absurd plays, just like the above named avant-garde(s), the theatrical absurd is not Jarry's avant-garde, nor is it the avant-garde(s) of expressionism, Futurism, Dadaism, surrealism, constructivism, nor any other –ism or avant-garde movement. In short, just because a play is avant-garde – rebelling against mainstream theatre – that does not necessarily mean it is absurdist.

Philosophy of the absurd: Or rather, philosoph*ies* of the absurd

The notion of the absurd was made most famous, and most relevant to absurd literature, by Albert Camus, especially with his book, *The Myth of Sisyphus and Other Essays*. But Camus was not the first to express philosophical ideas about the absurd. Søren Kierkegaard significantly dwelled on the absurd many, many years before Camus, as well as Léon Chestov and Benjamin Fondane later, writing in the 1920s and 1930s. Importantly, too, there is a very widely held misconception as to what Camus' philosophy of the absurd actually argues. So, in effect, even besides the philosophies of the absurd from Kierkegaard, Chestov, and Fondane, there are two narratives circling around Camus' notion of the absurd (only one being accurate and, unfortunately, the other – the misreading – being much, much more well known).

As extensive as Kierkegaard's commentary on the "absurd" is, it is vital to remember that he was, above all, a Christian philosopher. True, he attacked the Church, but Kierkegaard's philosophy, at base, was to re-invigorate Christian faith. What Kierkegaard wants for Christians is to not blindly accept faith by rote, but to constantly have to choose faith. Each (existential) choice that a human makes will determine his or her eternal salvation or damnation. This choice is accompanied by anxiety, as the choice contains both the dread of eternity and excitement at the freedom to choose for oneself. However, for Kierkegaard, this choice is not a rational decision. It is in the face of Kierkegaard's "absurd" – the paradox that God is infinite, but Jesus was finite – that humans must renew their faith "by virtue of the absurd," which is beyond the realm of reason. Believing that God forgives sin, even the unforgiveable sin, Kierkegaard suggests that the way to constant renewal is to have faith, despite the difficulty, in an ever-forgiving God.

While Kierkegaard's philosophy of the absurd was aimed only at increasing Christian faith, his conception of freedom and choice became intertwined with the rise of nihilism in Europe in the early twentieth century. Léon Chestov, a Russian emigré living in France in the 1920s, "disclosed the subtle affinity between Russian nihilism and Nietzsche's philosophy."[27] Chestov's philosophy of the absurd was an existential critique of rationality, and as Ramona Fotiade points out, very similar to the nihilistic rejection of mainstream art by the Dada and the Surrealist avant-garde.[28] Furthermore, though few have pointed out the connection, according to Fotiade, Camus' *The Myth of Sisyphus* is, "a barely disguised polemical reply to Chestov's arguments on the absurd."[29] It is Camus' belief and trust in reason that distinguishes Camus' absurd from that of Chestov and Benjamin Fondane, both of whom were critical of a rational method of inquiry and/or knowledge.

Published in French in 1942, Albert Camus' *The Myth of Sisyphus and Other Essays* is the most well-known expression of the philosophy of the absurd. It has commonly been read as an existential outcry of the absurdity of the human condition: humanity lost in a world without God, never getting what is wanted, with humans' only escape being suicide. Especially because of Sartre and Camus' early affiliation and friendship, and the temporal and locational proximity to the outpouring of existential texts during the "Existential Front" both during and after WWII in France, it is quite easy to simply group Camus as an existentialist (though, of course, the above description of Camus' existential outcry is also a simplification of Sartrean existentialism). Esslin's categorization of Camus' absurd – "By 1942, Camus was calmly putting the question why, since life had lost all meaning, man should not seek escape in suicide" – maybe even more so than Camus' own texts, helped further the above reading of Camus.

However, Camus was *not* an existentialist.[30] In fact, Camus revolted against existentialism, particularly against the brand of existentialism of his former close friend, Sartre (and a highly publicized public quarrel broke out between the two of them[31]). Yes, Camus did pose the question, why not seek escape in suicide, but this was on the first page of *The Myth of Sisyphus*. The entire rest of Camus' long essay argues explicitly why one *should not* commit suicide. Camus acknowledges that humans do live in an "absurd situation," but neither the world nor humans are absurd: it is only the union of the world and humans that is absurd. That is, our absurd situation is that the world will never give us what we want. And instead of succumbing to some false illusion of meaning (such as God), Camus suggests that it is better to live *as if* there is no inherent meaning in the world so that humans can contemplate and revolt against the absurd in order to make one's own life meaningful. It is through contemplation and revolt – and especially the use of reason (and reason has been seen as a faulty method of inquiry and acquiring knowledge by existentialists) – that humans, like Sisyphus (who, in Greek mythology, was condemned by the gods to endlessly roll a boulder up a mountain), can create their own purpose and meaning in the world. Despite Sisyphus' truly absurd situation (where very clearly the world does not give Sisyphus what he wants), because Sisyphus contemplates his torments and makes the "rock his thing" and, therefore, becomes the "master of his days," Camus can conclude that "One must imagine Sisyphus happy."

Challenges to the notion of "absurd"

While even to this day the most dominant strain of scholarship surrounding the literary absurd continues on the trajectory that Esslin started, there has been one very recent outright challenge to Esslin's formulation. My 2011 book, *Reassessing the Theatre of the Absurd*, has one main stated goal: "to free the playwrights from the absurdist label placed upon them" (3). After pointing out a couple of perceived misreadings by Esslin, in order to "free" these playwrights, I suggest, *not a term of replacement*, but an "alternative" manner in which to read the plays: that the most common plays associated with the absurd, *structurally*, take the form of a parable. This term, "parabolic drama," is meant to show a structural similarity of aesthetic form between some select quintessential plays, and this, ultimately, lends itself to produce new readings of these canonical plays. In short, by taking the structural form of a parable (i.e., use of extended metaphor, display an agenda of transformation, rely on paradox, move to disorder, audience is left hanging with a contradiction needed to be resolved, and the worlds of the plays are heterotopic with the presence of clashing viewpoints [22–23]), the plays *function* as *ethical parables*, forcing the audience, themselves, to make sense of the contradictions, thereby forcing them to make life meaningful. This is in stark contrast to Esslin's theme of metaphysical anguish. Therefore, should the exact opposite reading of Esslin's exist, then the idea is that the two readings, while they should still stand side-by-side, ultimately cancel each other out, allowing scholars to explore their own paths, not needing to continually go back to Esslin's largely thematic reading of these plays.

There are two other approaches that scholars have taken that are either direct or indirect challenges to Esslin's suggestion that the plays purport the meaninglessness of life or suggest the absurd nature of the works: (1) scholars more or less simply ignore Esslin and discuss *individual* playwrights and writers based upon the merits and varied interpretations of their work (basically ignoring that they are a part of the absurd, and I use the word "ignore" not in a negative way, but suggesting that the ignoring is an active choice made by scholars of this ilk); or (2) scholars (including myself) have pointed to *positive, life-affirming* aspects found in the work of the absurdists. These two above approaches have, ultimately, either directly or indirectly complicated and/or challenged the notion of the absurd. More will be said about these two lines of inquiry in Chapter 8, "Absurd Criticism."

* * *

Without continuing to dwell on the form of the parable found in some of the quintessential absurd plays, I want to draw further attention to some more of the techniques and aesthetic forms that absurd literature has in common. Speaking of technique and form, Esslin says that the playwrights of the absurd "tend toward a radical devaluation of language." Here, though, I could not disagree more. While Esslin is entirely correct in pointing out the "radical" nature of the language, and while they might devalue *realistic* language, *experimentation with language* seems to me to be one of the prime concerns of these writers. Over the course of the first half of the twentieth century, two writers in particular experimented with language: James Joyce and Samuel Beckett.

Beckett, at base – like James Joyce (with whom Beckett had a close relationship in his early years and was clearly heavily influenced by[32]) – even going back to his early 1938 novel, *Murphy*, experimented with language and (lack of) action. If we take a quick survey of the three most critically acclaimed and most widely studied playwrights associated with the absurd – Beckett, Pinter, and Albee – we can quickly understand how their experiments with language were markedly different. In *Godot*, Beckett explores the *non-sequitur*; especially in his later short plays, Beckett plays around with a full range of possibilities and limits of language. Pinter uses both pauses and vapid, everyday, mundane questions to look at what is not said. And Albee explores the precision of language, or rather how the lack of linguistic precision can lead to miscommunication and confusion. Though there was no self-conscious "movement," these writers (particularly in the theatre in the 1950s and 1960s) were profoundly influenced by Beckett and each other. The writers, themselves, were the first to acknowledge their indebtedness to their other contemporary playwrights (especially to Beckett). And so, maybe, *Beckett is the key and the link within absurd literature.*

The influence Beckett had on these other absurd writers was profound and far reaching. Of the playwrights that Esslin characterized as absurd, Albee, Arrabal, Ionesco, Pinter, Havel, Mrozek, Rozewicz, and Stoppard (as well as Shepard) all stated Beckett as a (direct or indirect) influence. The second-degree connections to Beckett continue to tighten the web of influence among absurd writers: Simpson worked with Pinter, Kennedy attended Albee's The Playwrights Unit, and two of Beckett's biggest fans, Albee and Ionesco, shared other influences – Arthur Adamov, Albee, Durrenmatt, and Max Frisch were influenced by Bertolt Brecht; and Adamov and Ionesco influenced by the surrealists.

These 1950s to 1970s playwrights, writers, and poets were writing, like Beckett – not as a reaction to the horrors of WWII – but, rather, writing in a *post-WWII world*. It must also be stated – with emphasis – that the theatrical absurd was not happening all at the same time and in the same place. Yes, between 1948–53 in Paris, the works of Genet, Ionesco, and Beckett were produced. But even 1953 Paris was quite a different place from 1948 Paris: the concerns of Europeans in 1948 were food and shelter, whereas by 1953 the reconstruction of Europe was well underway with the aid of the Marshall Plan. And by the time we see plays emerging from across the Atlantic in the United States, starting in 1958 with Albee's *The Zoo Story*, the United States, which was free (except at Pearl Harbor) from attack, was experiencing a major economic boom. And the political and social situation of Central and Eastern Europeans cannot even be compared almost in any way as a similar situation, as the Soviet Bloc countries were in various stages of being controlled by or rebelling against the Communist influence of the U.S.S.R. Despite its unevenness, the relative speedy (given the length of human history) transition from the "Gay 90s" and *Belle Epoch* – via two world wars – to a rapidly changing modern world, must have produced a feeling of the Kafkaesque. Camus and Sartre, two of the most influential thinkers after WWII (especially in France), clearly understood the almost *surreal situations* that Kafka's characters found themselves in. These situations require a tragicomic response: one must both laugh and cry, sometimes simultaneously, sometimes alternately, and sometimes one is unsure which response is adequate and/or appropriate.

The writers in question in the 1950s, 1960s, and into the 1970s (and even well beyond), then, were experimenting with language and set their plots and characters in "strange" situations (i.e., situations that are simultaneously Kafkaesque, surreal, *and* "ridiculous," in its full sense of the word). And by "strange" – "Unfamiliar, abnormal, or exceptional to a degree that excites wonder or astonishment; difficult to take in or account for; queer, surprising, unaccountable"[33] – situations, I am highlighting the idea of the *uniqueness* of the situation: both in the situation, itself, and the requirement for a unique response to the situation (both by the characters and by the reader/audience). The unique, many times often difficult and "strange" situations lead to a tragicomic response, and these works are appropriately written in the genre of tragicomedy (texts that are "mixed" in their simultaneously tragic and comic natures and plot lines). And I think it is as straightforward as that to group these mostly mid-century writers together: that is, *the four "common threads" found in absurd literature, generally written between the 1950s–70s, are (1) experimentation with language (generally, working against "realistic" language); (2) tragicomedy is the genre; (3) frequently, though not always, experimentation with non-Aristotelian plot lines (where, often, the plots take the structure of a parable);*[34] *and maybe most outwardly noticeable, (4) the literary works are set in "strange" (i.e., Kafkaesque, surreal, and ridiculous) situations.*

In general, though not as a hard and fast *rule*, absurd literature imparts a feeling of absurdity (both in "strange" and tragicomic ways) through two techniques that run counter to Aristotelian arcs: the lack of exposition and the flattening out of the narrative arc. (The experimentation with language, especially experimentation with realistic language, also heightens this feeling and helps further these two techniques that run counter to Aristotelian dramatic/narrative arcs.) First, one of the basic techniques since the Greeks is *exposition*, which is the technique of introducing the backstory, or "subtext," of the characters, the setting, and the situation. In other words, in real life, one does not go around saying things like, "Hello, John Doe, the 35 year old rising star at a bank and son of Jane and John, Sr., the latter of whom wrote a secret will bequeathing his fortune to his mistress." But playwrights, and most novelists, too, generally let the audience/reader know who the characters are and their situation so the characters do not have to speak in the dreadful manner above. *The unfolding of the backstory, or the subtext, is the exposition. In general, in absurd literature, the writer or playwright simply foregoes any attempt at exposition: the characters merely appear and the story proceeds from there.*

Second, Aristotle, in his *Poetics*, specifically describes two types of narrative arcs: tragedy and comedy. The following simple diagram demonstrates the basic arcs of (classic) tragedy and (classic) comedy:

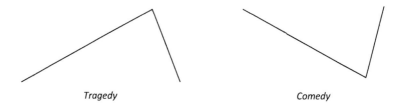

Tragedy   Comedy

On the left, in tragedy, we see the rising tension of a conflict peak at a climax and the subsequent fall of the tragic hero(ine). On the right, in comedy, we see the *seeming* unraveling of the protagonist(s), only we come to a climax where everything ultimately resolves into a happy ending. While Aristotle may have, in passing, suggested the notion of tragicomedy in his *Poetics* (and J. L. Styan anticipates some of these arguments in his book, *The Dark Comedy*[35]), absurd writers – most especially in a play like Beckett's *Waiting for Godot* without an identifiable "conflict," so to speak – have taken the narrative/dramatic arc of "traditional" tragicomedy and flattened it basically into a line; which is also accomplished through the help of having (1) no, or very little, exposition, and (2) an ambiguous and/or hanging ending, as in the form of a *parable*:

Absurd Tragicomedy

Absurd tragicomedy

While absurd writers each use different techniques and write very different plays, while still foregoing most (if not all of) the exposition and flattening out of the dramatic/narrative arc, these common threads, taken together with their individual experimentations with language, mark the "absurd," both capturing Camus' sense of absurdity and the everyday sense of the ridiculous. Besides that, they are all different writers – with different goals, different devices, different themes, topics, and concerns, and different styles.

As will be demonstrated in the following chapters, first the literary and historical lineage of the emerging absurd will be discussed in Chapters 2 and 3. In order to show the complexity, originality, and variation of these writers, peaking with the playwrights associated with the absurd (some of whom also wrote fiction and poetry [e.g., Beckett and Pinter]), discussed in Chapters 4–6, I will focus on the four "common threads" outlined above to demonstrate how these "common threads" manifest into very different texts with very different meanings. This examination of the heyday of absurdism will set the stage for a look at what has followed since the 1950s through 1970s.

As will be shown and has also been suggested by Enoch Brater, the absurd, while not the dominant artistic expression it once was, has not really gone away; rather, the effects of the absurd are still widely felt, and, in some sense, the absurd is so commonplace now that it is seemingly imperceptible despite its wide reach and constant pull.[36] To a large degree, the public has just become used to absurd elements in the literary arts. It is no longer shocking or unusual, unlike for those initial theatre audiences in the 1950s, for "strange" situations to be presented as tragicomedies, often with non-Aristotelian plot lines, and experimental, not-always-realistic language. It is not that the absurd is no longer relevant: rather, the absurd has simply become a part of our literary imagination. Its more avant-garde expression, if you will, in the theatre in the 1950s to 1970s did its trick – did what it wanted and needed to accomplish – by forcing audiences to confront the supposed realism that theatrical realism claimed to present, allowing for something, maybe sometimes less real but often more realistic. Very often avant-garde artistic and literary movements are subsumed into more mainstream traditions. While much of the originality, energy, and experimentation that comes initially with the often organic formation of emergent avant-garde movements fades as it is adopted by more mainstream movements and the public, the tamed fate of those one time cutting-edge movements should not necessarily be seen as a mark of failure, but rather it should be noted how the movement ran its course, with its success marked by the assimilation of its noteworthy elements. After the literary (and, especially, theatrical) absurd ran its course, the public is now constantly presented with "absurd situations" that are "strange" and require unique responses, experimentation with language and non-Aristotelian plots are no longer shocking, and maybe most influentially, tragicomedy has now become the default genre of, generally, the critically acclaimed literary arts. While the more avant-garde and experimental absurd has passed from the literary scene – although we can forever return to and enjoy a large library of now classic literary texts penned by some of the twentieth century's most important writers – the absurd is not going anywhere: the absurd is here to stay. Or – similarly put – as Brater states, "as my colleague Ruby Cohn observes, 'the absurd is around' – I would add here that it is *all* around, even in unexpected corners. There's no *after* after the absurd."[37]

Four short notes about this book

1. Given the nature of this book as an introduction to a subject, many of the chapters do not provide extensive endnotes. Instead, the extensive Bibliography should provide ample direction for further inquiry. However, the endnotes are much more extensive for this Introduction (i.e., Chapter 1) and Chapter 3 due to the contextualizing nature of these two chapters. Also, unlike the writers discussed in Chapters 4 and 5, who are the subjects of many often easily accessible and widely available books, Chapter 6 has more extensive but concise endnotes because it is probably much harder for the average reader to easily find scholarship on these lesser studied writers as most of the scholarship surrounding these writers is found in academic journals (and, thus, much more difficult to locate and usually only accessible through an affiliation with a university library).

2. Since this book covers many different writers, many different editions by many publishers exist. Given that many of these texts were also written in languages other than English, and given the fact that the primary audience of this book is English speakers and readers (as this *Introduction* is written in English), I will be referring to the English translations of the discussed works (though, just a few times, I will discuss [primarily in the endnotes] a passage in its original language). In general, I am using the most widely available English editions, but (also keeping in mind) ones that are also commonly used by scholars. For example, I am using the Grove Press editions for the works of Beckett, Pinter, Ionesco, and Genet (Pinter's works are collected in a multi-volume set by Grove Press.) Since Overlook Press has a recent, multi-volume collected works of Albee, I will use that collection. For some of the other lesser read and lesser studied writers, there sometimes exists just one edition and/or English translation.

3. Why is this book not titled, *The Cambridge Introduction to The Theatre of the Absurd*? First, and most importantly, many of those who were considered to be a part of the Theatre of the Absurd also wrote fiction and poetry. While it is true that absurd literature reached its height in the 1950s to 1970s in the theatre, where it found its most highly crystalized voice and form, to try to isolate just the drama of these writers from their oeuvre is

somewhat misleading, misinforming, and presents an incomplete picture when trying to consider these individual writers as writers. For example, to think about Beckett and his plays without thinking about his important novels, really misses the point of Beckett's lifelong quests in his writing. And, second, while Martin Esslin's label, "The Theatre of the Absurd," has been the dominant term for the plays associated with his book, Esslin's view is still just one person's label. And while "absurd" is still a term that will be closely aligned with Esslin, Esslin was not even the first scholar to use the term "absurd" in reference to these writers. Thus, especially since there has been a recent turn away from Esslin, titling this book *The Cambridge Introduction to The Theatre of the Absurd* would both perpetuate and partly cement Esslin's own individual reading of these plays as *the* reading (in that the nature of this book is an authoritative introductory book from Cambridge University Press). Therefore, while Esslin's reading is persuasive and extremely significant, it is not, and should not be, the *only* reading: literature is only great (and considered great) when it generates many readings and many meanings.

4.   Given that much of absurd literature is found in the theatre, why is there very little discussion in this book about theatrical production and prac-tice? The two-fold answer is space and focus. First, if theatrical production and practice of absurd theatre are to be given their due respect, then I would want to discuss production history and practices associated with each playwright and their individual plays, so as not to lump numerous and disparate productions and practices together. To give the productions and practices the justice they deserve – rather than just a nod of acknowl-edgment (which is almost more insulting) – Chapters 4–6 would need to be almost twice as long, as well as many other needed sections throughout the book. Space considerations simply do not permit this (since I would do it only if I could be thorough). And, second is the question of focus. Again, while the theatre was the absurd's most highly crystalized expres-sion, the absurd was not isolated, by any means, to the theatre. Thus, taking what would need to be so much space (i.e., overall percent of the book) to adequately discuss theatrical productions and practices would skew the focus of the book too much towards theatre. And while I do not want to downplay absurd theatre's importance to the absurd as a whole, I fear that too much focus on absurd theatre would make the discussion of other absurd texts (i.e., absurd fiction and poetry) seem like a side note or an afterthought.

Chapter 2

Setting the stage

It is *possible* to argue that the four writers/movements – Alfred Jarry, Franz Kafka, OBERIU, and Antonin Artaud – discussed in this chapter are a part of the absurd literary canon. On the one hand, these writers *do* form a clear lineage and line of influence *towards* the literary absurd that emerged in the middle of the twentieth century. However, on the other hand, it can be anachronistic to retroactively go back to include these writers as absurdists. In other words, (especially) these writers were writing over the course of decades somewhat in isolation (in that these four did not influence each other). The Theatre of the Absurd, as Esslin calls it, and its contemporary absurd literature in fiction and poetry are clearly indebted to the writers discussed in this chapter, and most of them are indirect influences (maybe with the exception of Kafka, who was a more direct and stated influence). The writers in this chapter are no doubt the *fore*fathers of the literary absurd: stated as an oversimplification (but helpful nonetheless), it can be said that the literary absurd of the 1950s to the 1970s is the combination of the noteworthy elements of each of these writers. In short, each of these writers contributed a key *element* of the absurd to the world of literature: Alfred Jarry rebelled against realism, was really the first *avant-garde* playwright, and created pataphysics that influenced the Dadaists and Surrealists and an indirect line to Genet and Ionesco; Franz Kafka created the "strange," "absurd situation," but told very straightforward stories, and did not experiment with language; the OBERIU poets took up linguistic nonsense to, "[destroy the protocols] of semantic coherence and linguistic realism";[1] and Antonin Artaud's theatre created a theatre of anti-realism in order to shed light on the real. Despite these influences, it would also be a mistake to categorize them or group them together with the literary absurd, as each of these writers also displays so many elements in their respective literary works that the literary absurd of the mid-twentieth century revolted against.

Alfred Jarry

Born in 1873, Alfred Jarry came into prominence in artistic/literary circles in Paris when he was just 23 years old with the premiere of his 1896 play, *Ubu Roi* (translated as *King Ubu* or *Ubu the King*). By far his most notable work, *Ubu Roi* had only two performances: a dress rehearsal, and the next day, the play's premiere. While legend has it that riots broke out during the performances, certainly (and probably much more accurately) there was shouting and arguments throughout both nights. Much of the reaction was to the brutality of the play's farce/satire and the violence and scatology that simply offended both the audience's own sense of their society and the audience's own personal sensibilities.

The play is about Ubu, a caricature of one of Jarry's own professors, whom Jarry clearly detested. Ubu displays all of the (perceived) haughtiness and gluttony of the rising bourgeoisie in France. Playing off of some of Shakespeare's tragedies (most obviously *Hamlet* and *Macbeth*), Ubu leads a revolution against the King of Poland and power grabbing ensues for the rest of the play, as well as the accumulation of corpses. It is not necessarily the plot that is important here (in relation to the absurd), though the plot is certainly important to satirize the perceived abuses of the bourgeoisie's new-found power. After all, if one were to classify *Ubu Roi* as absurd theatre, it would be an anomaly in the absurd canon as *Ubu Roi* is most especially a farcical satire. While absurd literature clearly challenges societal norms and literary and theatrical conventions, in general (with the exception, most notably, of Amiri Baraka's *Great Goodness of Life: A Coon Show*, and *maybe* an argument can be made that also the play that Baraka's play satirizes, Jean Genet's *The Blacks: A Clown Show*, is also satirical), absurd literature is not satire.

Furthermore, Jarry's philosophy and artistic vision of *pataphysics*, while it influenced Dadaism and Surrealism (which in turn, influenced, to a degree, some of the absurd writers, though Genet and Ionesco also acknowledged their own link to pataphysical thought), was too much of a precursor to the mid-century philosophical thought displayed in absurd literature to see that much of a link between Jarry's thought and any philosophical underpinnings that might be in the works of absurd writers in the 1950s and onward. Pataphysics is the term created by Jarry, himself, which Jarry defines as, "the science of imaginary solutions, which symbolically attributes the properties of objects, described by their virtuality, to their lineaments."[2] In short, pataphysicians, as practitioners of pataphysics are called, study what lies outside of metaphysics (i.e., study things and properties that metaphysics either does not address or cannot answer).

It is the language of *Ubu Roi*, however, with its mix of raunchiness and inappropriateness, puns, and awkwardly rhythmed poetic prose that heightens the play's sense of challenging convention and social mores. It is Jarry's experiments with language – away from verse, poetic prose, or realistic prose – that imparts some influence on later absurd writers. The willingness to jettison *theatrical* realistic language in favor of *a combination of awkward speech patterns and (at the time) too-real-for-the-stage banal and crude dialogue*, is what gives Jarry's play the feeling of absurdity.

Outside of Jarry's language, in some ways, *Ubu Roi* has little to nothing to do with absurd literature; in one way, though, his play develops one of the most recognizable features of absurd literature. Actually, the best way to demonstrate this is to recall the words that Jarry, himself, spoke before the curtains were drawn on the night of his premiere:

> The Swedenborgian philosopher, Mésés, has excellently compared rudimentary creations with the most perfect, and embryonic beings with the most complete, in that the former lack all irregularities, protuberances and qualities, which leaves them in more or less spherical form, like the ovum and M. Ubu, while the latter have added so many personal details that they remain equally spherical, following the axiom that the most polished object is that which presents the greatest number of sharp corners. That is why you are free to see in M. Ubu however many allusions you care to, or else a simple puppet – a schoolboy's caricature of one of his professors who personified for him all the ugliness in the world. It is this aspect that the Théâtre de l'Oeuvre will present tonight.
>
> Our actors have been willing to depersonalize themselves for two evenings, and to act behind masks, in order to express more perfectly the inner man, the soul of these overgrown puppets you are about to see...
>
> It seemed very important, if we were to be quite like puppets (*Ubu Roi* is a play that was never written for puppets, but for actors pretending to be puppets, which is not the same thing), for us to have carnival music, and the orchestral parts have been allotted to various brasses, gongs, and speaking-trumpet horns that we haven't had time to collect.[3]

Of the notable marks of this play from the passage above, five elements really stick out as not influencing the absurd: (1) depersonalizing the actor, (2) wearing masks, (3) the expression of the "inner man"/"soul," (4) the idea of characters and/or actors as "puppets," and (5) the use of music. These five elements point, rather, to two playwrights who have already been discussed in Chapter 1: Luigi Pirandello and Bertolt Brecht. Maybe because so many of the techniques and preoccupations that we observe in Jarry's play are taken up by Pirandello and Brecht – and Pirandello and Brecht have so often (mistakenly) been thought of as absurdists or precursors to the absurd – that Jarry's play is so often called the first absurd play.

First, the idea of depersonalizing the actor is maybe more central than any other technique to the theatre of Bertolt Brecht. In developing what he called "Epic Theatre," Brecht trained his actors – not to be the character – but to be an actor commenting on his/her character. For Brecht, the biggest problem with traditional theatre was that the audience goes through an emotional journal; thus, if the audience's emotions take over, then the audience's critical mind ebbs into the background. Therefore, in order to prevent the audience from being emotionally drawn into the fate of the character, Brecht sought to ensure that the audience is aware (due to the actor being self-aware) that the audience is watching an actor. This move always keeps the audience from relating to the character and instead makes the audience fully aware that he or she is watching a piece of theatre.

The second and third elements are both characteristic of Pirandello's most famous play, *Six Characters in Search of an Author*. Pirandello's play, like Jarry's, was wildly ahead of its time and shocked many audiences. In fact, Pirandello revised his play multiple times over a number of years until audiences finally appreciated his play. Pirandello's play is about exactly what the title suggests: six characters interrupt a play rehearsal, looking for a playwright to write down their story they carry within them. The Father, usually considered the protagonist of the play, suggests that the characters are more real, or at least truer, than any human. This line of thought by Pirandello forces the audience to confront their inner selves, and maybe even question whether they have some type of essential soul, as The Father argues that human reality changes from second to second, and that humans change with that reality. The fact that this is stated by a character is so shocking (and deep) that – to go back to the second element – Pirandello in his later versions of the play, put the characters in masks to both make it obvious that these characters really were characters and not humans, and to highlight the characters' essential features.

Fourth, Brecht discussed at length in his theoretical writings how his characters were puppet-like, in that Brecht wanted to expose the strings of the puppets to the audience. In short, going back to Brecht's desire for critical assessment (taking a social and political lens, too), if Brecht could show that a play was, in fact, a play, not a real story emerging in front of an audience, then the audience would be alienated from the play, allowing them moments of critical reflection. This metatheatrical self-awareness is the hallmark of Brecht's theatre. And fifth, for the very same reasons as above, Brecht frequently inserted music and songs into his plays. But unlike the music in *melo*drama that sets the mood for the audience and suggests to the audience how they should/do feel, Brecht's theatre segments off the music so that the songs disrupt the narrative and its flow, giving pause for critical observation and ensuring that the audience does not get too attached to the dramatic narrative, and thus the characters and story.

But while the above five elements very clearly influenced Pirandello and Brecht – who besides promoting avant-garde theatre, did very little to influence absurd literature – the idea about Jerry's characters as "rudimentary creations" versus the "most perfect" (creations) is extremely important for absurd literature. One of the most recognizable elements of the absurd is, what Richard Schechner called of Pinter's theatre, its "conceptual incompleteness."[4] Whether or not they are round characters (as opposed to flat characters), there is usually no backstory attached to absurd characters. And without this sub-text/backstory, it is hard to pin down absurd literature to mean this or mean that. Paraphrasing Jarry, this is why you are free to see in, for example, Godot, however many allusions you care to.

Franz Kafka

Franz Kafka was born in Prague in 1883. A child of Jewish parents who spoke both Czech and German, Kafka was sent to the German University where he received a doctorate of law in 1906. Kafka spent most of his adult life working for the state insurance agency, writing on the side. Publishing only one collection of short stories before his early death in 1924 of tuberculosis, Kafka asked his friend to destroy all of his unpublished manuscripts. Kafka's friend could not bring himself to do it, and the rest of Kafka's writings were published after Kafka died.

Much has been made of his relationship with his own father as the troubled father–son relationship fills the pages of Kafka's works. Also, there has been much discussion concerning why Kafka chose to write in German despite his living in Czech-speaking Prague. Though important to scholars and students of Kafka, neither of these subjects will be discussed here: instead, relevant to absurd literature, this section will examine the situations that Kafka put his characters in. The adjective, "Kafkaesque," in fact has become almost standard English to describe such situations that resemble those found in Kafka's fiction.

Kafka is perhaps best known for his short story, "The Metamorphosis." This is a story about Gregor Samsa, who one day wakes up as a bug. While much of the story is about how Gregor's (especially) parents relied too heavily on

Gregor, and it took Gregor to turn into a bug (and stop being able to work and support the family) for the family to seize life again, what is most notable is the characters' situation: for an unexplained reason, Gregor finds himself as a bug. But this is not the remarkable thing! What is remarkable, rather, is everyone's (especially Gregor's) reaction to the situation that is "Kafkaesque." Instead of worrying about the fact that Gregor is a bug, everyone, including Gregor, is more concerned with the fact that Gregor is not able to go to work. The mark of the Kafkaesque, and really (subsequently) absurd literature, is the (non)reaction to a strange and unique situation. "The Metamorphosis" recalls a play like Ionesco's *Rhinoceros*: one by one the townsfolk of a small French town turn into rhinos and instead of freaking out, life (and especially the gossip) goes on as normal (except for a couple of characters). Or in Beckett's *Godot* and *Happy Days*, one wonders, (1) why Didi and Gogo simply continue to go on waiting (for fifty years) for a man they probably never met named Godot, and (2) why there is no comment, struggle to get out, or concern that Winnie finds herself buried in the ground. Again, it is not just the situation that produces the Kafkaesque (or the Kafkaesque situations found in absurd literature), but the feeling of the Kafkaesque is produced by the disconnect between how one would, presumably, normally act when in a bizarre and unique situation and how Kafka's (or absurd) characters react or do not react.

This disconnect between finding oneself, or finding someone else in a strange situation, and what is a normal human reaction defines Kafka's two other most notable works. His short story, "In the Penal Colony," is about a presumably Western and highly educated traveler visiting a (seemingly remote) colony. This traveler is held in high esteem and is introduced to the Officer, who continues the work of his idol, the now dead Commandant's precepts in running a machine that enforces justice. The machine in question is made up of a bed that the condemned are strapped to and from above, a set of sharp harrows oscillate up and down and in different directions to spell out, on the condemned person's body, the lesson they need to learn for their (supposed) crime. In short, the multiple harrows dig into the flesh and produce multiple tattoos (not with ink, but with their blood) that spell out a phrase. This effectively kills the condemned, who bleed to death.

On the day of the story, the condemned man fell asleep on his job and, without knowing his sentence, he was given over to the Officer, who is the judge, jury, and executioner. The Officer explains to the traveler that "Honor thy superiors"[5] will be written on the condemned man's body. This whimsical and entirely disproportionate punishment is, essentially, torture. However, this traveler is supposedly so worldly that he deems wise and respectful the fact that he does not interfere with or protest against the ways of life of another foreign culture. Here though, the finger is pointed at us, the reader, for any admiration we might have for the traveler. This worldly traveler was held in high esteem and his thoughts and words would have been considered, but the fact that he watches an essentially innocent man be tortured to death, without even a simple word of protest, is almost more inhuman than the actions of the Officer. The Officer is clearly power hungry and mad (eventually killing himself on the machine), and while no one can condone the Officer's actions, they at least make sense. But the supposedly level-headed traveler's inaction is what is horrifying and is utterly inhuman.

In Kafka's most well-known novel, *The Trial*, the reader is equally exacerbated because nobody in the novel is seeing the injustice done to the main character, K. In this novel, K. finds himself one day simply under investigation and faced with a trial, for reasons entirely unexplained (to both K. and the reader). Unlike in "The Metamorphosis," K. is at least semi self-aware of the oddity of his situation. But the Kafkaesque in this is that nobody that K. approaches thinks anything of this bizarre predicament and the *status quo* remains intact and goes unchallenged.

Part of the Kafkaesque is due to Kafka's narrators, who, while they may (though the reader does not know) be omniscient, present their stories with a matter-of-fact straightforwardness. *There is no "questioning voice" in Kafka's stories, neither by the narrator nor by the vast majority of his characters*; the absence and/or destruction of a "questioning voice" is a theme that Pinter discussed concerning his own writings.[6] Without inquiry, things remain *status quo*. However, in addition, the background story, or subtext, never (fully) emerges in Kafka's stories. *Without sufficient context, then, the reader of Kafka's stories and Kafka's characters are left reeling in a nonsensical world, trying, but failing at rational enterprise to make sense of what is happening.*

This last idea *is* the absurd situation, and especially the situation that Camus deals with in his book/essay, *The Myth of Sisyphus*. And that is why Camus instructs his readers to contemplate their situation and revolt. One must, for Camus, confront the absurd, and Camus turns to Kafka's writings in his Appendix to *The Myth of Sisyphus* to make his case. Kafka, himself, confronts the absurd by writing his stories, showing how difficult it is for the world to confront absurdity. These situations come to the forefront after the horrors of the Holocaust and WWII for many writers in the 1950s–70s. But absurd writers, while they incorporated the Kafkaesque situation into their plots, also experimented with language and narrative arcs, while Kafka wrote in very straightforward prose and had traditional narrative arcs. While Kafka's work does produce the occasional giggle, it would be hard to call his fiction tragicomedy in the traditional sense of the term. Kafka writes more dystopic fiction, and his stories have much more of a horrified, worrisome, exasperated, and/or frustrated tone. But it would also be a mistake to assume that Kafka is writing tragedy. Kafka's fiction is more like Beckett's simultaneously a-tragic and a-comic later novels and even later short plays.

OBERIU

OBERIU was a group of Russian poets that lasted from 1927 to 1930. Two Russian writers, Daniil Kharms and Alexander Vvedensky, founded this group to distance themselves from Russian Futurists, as the work of Kharms and Vvedensky lacked the utopian teleologies that were characteristic of the Russian Futurist modernist poetry.[7] Vvedensky coined the neologism, "*chinar*," to further the gap between them and the Futurists: Vvedensky calling himself, "*chinar*, authority on nonsense" and Kharms calling himself, "*chinar*-observer."[8] Writing plays, short stories, and poems, this group (made up of a few other members, as well) broke and scrambled narrative by, "presenting parts of narrative as autonomous with respect to the whole."[9]

Frequently called "Russian absurdism" in Western academia, the creative works that came out of this group do remind us of absurd literature from the 1950s to the 1970s. Self-described as keeping with "the poetics of meaningless," OBERIU writers not only discredited normative language, but sought to generate nonnormative statements.[10] These "poetics" and the jarring nature of the non-normative language certainly recalls much of the common notions of absurd literature. But especially the latter technique of generating nonnormative statements recalls many of the *non-sequiturs* that fill many of the pages of Beckett's plays.

However, their influence on absurd literature was essentially naught: the works of OBERIU did not leave the Soviet Union until after its fall and were not translated into English until the 1990s. However, despite there being no direct influence, OBERIU clearly did some things typical of absurd literature well before the 1950s. Most similar is the work of Daniil Kharms. Kharms has a touch of the Beckettian flair for destroying generic norms. Kharms' poetry had characters and was written somewhat like a play; his theatre was poetic; and his fiction mixed in poetry and theatre.

It was Kharms' *fragmentation* of narrative structure that really reminds us of Beckett's novels. Kharms' "The Saber" is divided into nine sections, each semi-related to the whole, but also totally separate. For example, section "5" reads.

The three pairs of our edges are as follows:

1. arm – arm.
2. shoulder – shoulder.
3. head – heels.[11]

And then section "8" is the "APPENDIX," even though it is followed by a final section, "9."

In a different vein, Kharms' short story, "Anton Antonovich Shaved Off His Beard," is a straightforward narrative, but it – despite its levity – feels Kafkaesque in that nobody either recognizes or believes Anton that he is Anton, simply because of the fact that he shaved off his beard. Kharms' (and OBERIU) creativity is mixed with a playfulness that despite its Kafkaesque nature is more tragicomic in feel. And the more experimental works (e.g., "The Saber") are almost without recognizable tragic or comic elements, reminding us of Beckett's later experimental plays that are tragicomic in the sense that they are simultaneously a-tragic and a-comic.

Antonin Artaud

Antonin Artaud was a French writer and actor. Born in 1896, Artaud died of cancer in 1948, barely known outside of readers of Surrealism. In the decades following his death, Artaud has come to be known as a theorist of theatre, though exactly what his theories are remains somewhat debated. His writings are numerous (and his writings are collected in five volumes), but Antonin Artaud is most well known for his book, *The Theatre and its Double*, containing his famous manifesto, "The Theatre of Cruelty," which, through suggesting a mix of strange and jarring techniques, aims to shatter false illusions so that theatre can better represent reality. In short, it is not that the reader of Artaud does not know what Artaud wants to do in the theatre, it is just that Artaud is never quite able to say exactly how one is to go about accomplishing Artuad's desires for the theatre. I think Adrian Marfee best explains Artaud's writings:

> he is always gesturing towards something he cannot quite
> state . . . Artuad does not build theories but theorizes, his work is
> directed not towards creating objects, either aesthetic or theoretical, but
> towards the activities of thinking and writing. His is a writing of
> intellectual energy, not intellectual fruits. What matters to Artuad is not
> structures, but the dissolution and reconstitution of structures.[12]

This remark about Artaud helps us understand not only Artaud as a writer, but Artaud's project in the theatre. In short, Artaud was something of a poet whose language was not about direct communication but invoking thought. What connects Artaud to absurd literature is that his influence in Surrealism, in turn, influenced some absurd writers.

Like the Surrealists, Artaud was deeply concerned with truth. But theatre, or *traditional* theatre, seemed to shackle truth in Artaud's eyes. Artaud writes, "Our petrified idea of the theater is connected with our petrified idea of a culture without shadows."[13] For Artaud, truth is in the "shadows," and confronting and bringing to life these "shadows" (possibly, of our metaphysical beings and souls), in some way exorcizes the "shadows" and allows us to live. As Artaud suggests, ". . . the theater, not confined to a fixed language and form, not only destroys false shadows but prepares the way for a new generation of shadows, around which assembles the true spectacle of life."[14] For Artuad, theatre is not a "thing," but something that is done using things from everyday life, such as "gestures, sounds, words, screams, light, darkness."[15] These "things" were to be used to re-engage modern theatre with the "metaphysical fear of ancient drama."[16] Creating a type of "psychotherapy," Artaud wanted to provide his audiences with "physical stimulation" and appeal to "fears and carnal desires" using myths to reawaken the body.[17]

Artaud's influence on the absurd is hard to precisely discern because, especially, absurd theatre does not (in general) break the fourth wall and is written down in formal theatrical language. But Artaud's influence on a wide range of, especially, theatrical directors, and "happenings" (e.g., John Cage read Artaud at Black Mountain College in 1952) in the 1950s and 1960s clearly influenced the theatrical avant-garde (and avant-garde art in general). And while the absurd in the theatre in the 1950s to 1970s was in no way the same avant-garde as the avant-garde occurring with Jerzy Grotowski's Laboratory Theatre or The Living Theatre, absurd literature was clearly *an* avant-garde organic movement happening at the same time as an upsurge in avant-garde movements in the arts. Artaud's writings helped create an environment where the avant-garde could flourish.

* * *

Again, it is extremely important to note possible (and even some stated) influences or precedents to the absurd literature that emerged in the 1950s: rarely, if ever, does something entirely new emerge without lines of influence. However, as demonstrated in this chapter, it would also be a mistake to categorize these writers as absurdists, not just because it is anachronistic to go back and imagine that some organic thought and literary expression was present way before it ever emerged, but because the writers above also display so many characteristics that were antithetical to writers of absurd literature. Also, while absurd literature was not happening exactly all in the same place at exactly the same time – 1952 Paris was not 1958 New York City, which was not the 1960s in Eastern Europe under the communist control (whether official or unofficial) of the USSR – there were clear connections and stated lines of influence that loosely tie most of the absurd writers together (most commonly, Beckett is the link). And, while these three above "places" were in very different situations, the situation of all three derived from the consequences and after effects of WWII: 1952 Paris was rebuilding after WWII, 1958 USA was thriving as *the* new superpower (both militarily and economically), and 1960s Eastern Europe was experiencing a power vacuum after WWII that was being filled by an eager and hungry USSR that was vying to challenge the USA as the world's superpower.

If we perform the same type of juxtaposition with the writers discussed in this chapter, we see "places" that are nothing alike. Jarry was writing in fin-de-siècle Paris; Kakfa was writing at the beginning of twentieth-century Prague; OBERIU writers were writing in post-Revolution Russia after The Great War (WWI); and Artaud was writing after The Great War and into the beginning of WWII in France. These are obviously drastically different "places" with drastically different circumstances.

Chapter 3

The emergence of a "movement": The historical and intellectual contexts

As discussed in Chapter 1, absurd literature developed in a post-WWII world. While it is commonly thought to be a *response* to the Holocaust and WWII, the comedic elements in absurd literature's tragicomedy and the enduring element of hope really embodies a post-WWII reality: aided by The Marshall Plan, with the massive efforts of rebuilding Europe underway by the time the plays of the absurd began to be written and emerge in public, there was a renewed sense of optimism in Europe and the beginnings of an economy that propelled a decade-plus era of economic prosperity on both sides of the Atlantic. Much of absurd literature was, in fact, written during this economic boom.

Unable to forget the horrors of the Holocaust and WWII, but also hopeful of the future, the *tragicomic* view took hold. Within the possibilities of a better future Europe and better future United States, there must have been – as first described in Kierkegaard's absurd – the "dizziness of freedom" and then, as suggested during and after WWII in Camus' absurd – the need for a return to rationality in a world that itself is not absurd, but where humans endure an absurd situation where the world does not give humans what they want. The need for a true realism that Camus' absurdity offered in a post-WWII world (as opposed to the belief in illusion or not accepting the reality of our absurd situation) mixed naturally with the comedic element of tragicomedy to also create ridiculous plots and characters.

It must also be stated – with emphasis – that the theatrical absurd was not happening all at the same time and in the same place. Yes, between 1948–1953, in Paris, the works of Genet, Ionesco, and Beckett were produced. But even 1953 Paris was quite a different place from 1948 Paris: the concerns of Europeans in 1948 were food and shelter whereas, by 1953, the reconstruction of Europe was well underway with the aid of the Marshall Plan. And by the time we see plays emerging from across the Atlantic in the United States, starting in 1958 with Albee's *The Zoo Story*, the United States, which was free (except at Pearl Harbor) from attack, was experiencing a major economic boom. And the political and social situation of Central and Eastern Europeans cannot even be compared almost in any way as a similar situation, as the Soviet-Bloc countries were in various stages of being controlled by or rebelling against the Communist influence of the U.S.S.R.

Post-WWII Europe

On June 5, 1947, US Secretary of State George C. Marshall announced what was later to be called the Marshall Plan that was to change not only the economies of Europe but fundamentally changed the attitudes of Europeans. The Marshall Plan's psychological benefit to Europeans was palpable:

> *The Times* was not so very wide of the mark when it stated, in a leader on January 3rd 1949, that "(w)hen the cooperative efforts of the last year are contrasted with the intense economic nationalism of the inter-war years, it is surely permissible to suggest that the Marshall Plan is initiating a new and hopeful era in European history."

> The real benefits were psychological. Indeed, on might almost say that the Marshall Plan helped Europeans feel better about themselves. It helped them break decisively with a legacy of chauvinism, depression and authoritarian solutions. It made co-ordinated economic policy-making seem normal rather than unusual. It made the beggar-your-neighbour trade and monetary practices of the thirties seem first imprudent, then unnecessary and finally absurd.[1]

The path to feeling better began with an economic plan, which included aid through annual requests.[2] The USA also poured in American dollars to furnish a credit pool which came to be the Bank of International Settlements. This "Bank" offered lines of credit to each country proportional to their trading requirements: "contribut[ing] not merely to the steady expansion of intra-European trade but to an unprecedented degree of mutually advantageous collaboration."[3] This liberalized trade created a post-war economic boom stemming from, not the pre-war emphasis on "protection and retrenchment," but on "sustained commitment to long-term public and private investment in infrastructure and machinery."[4]

The Marshall Plan set the stage for recovery, but what really created economic interdependence was, as Alan S. Milward argues, the establishment of the European Payments Union in 1950, which was essentially a huge European currency exchange.[5] The Marshall Plan poured US dollars into Europe, but that created only bilateral trade between the United States and a particular European country. The European Payments Union allowed for multilateral, intra-European trade. The Marshall Plan and then the European Payments

Union made trade possible, but it was also the fact that – totally separate and independent – each European nation, especially up until 1950, had their own national reconstruction policies.[6] In short, each Western European country following the end of WWII had a separate economic boom, which then continued and picked up steam, first with the Marshall Plan, and then, especially, with the establishment of the European Payment Union.[7]

But the changes following WWII were not just economic in nature. The political landscape of the world was changing. With the Korean War and the Cold War, especially, building up between the USA and the USSR, always in the background, new colonial and post-colonial concerns arose. In France, for years, French schoolchildren saw "France" as extending well beyond its natural borders, where the, "cultural attributes of Frenchness were open to all."[8] After the liberation in 1945, France's colonial reach was vast. But the loss of Indo-China was a "political and military catastrophe."[9] North Africa later became the center of France's attention. However, the attention was not always there: the French government simply quashed an Arab uprising in the Kabylia region east of Algiers in May 1945, demonstrating that France was indifferent to Arab sentiment.[10] It took the November 1, 1954 Algerian insurrection and the formation of the Algerian FLN (*Front de Libération Nationale*), followed by eight years of civil war, to get France to focus on North Africa.

By the year that *Waiting for Godot* was published in 1952, France, and particularly Paris, was also undergoing a cultural upheaval. Part of this cultural upheaval had to do with the increase of an automobile culture. With the introduction in 1947 of the first French car to be mass produced and affordable, the "people's car," the Renault 4CV, production could not keep up with demand as there were thousands times more buyers than cars. Culturally, as Ross suggests, automobiles offered people a new mobility that allowed them to break with the past and gave them a new attitude towards mobility and displacement.[11] But this cultural upheaval also had to do with the "generalized postwar atmosphere of moral purification, national cleansing, and literary laundering."[12] In a sense, Ross suggests, the new focus on actual hygiene in France derived its power from the fact that France and its women needed to be clean so that it could maintain its metaphorically clean role in its colonies. But with the continual loss of the colonies, the French must turn inward to the home, "as the basis of the nation's welfare."[13] Though Milward suggests that the economic boom was a phenomenon of the 1950s that started in 1950 and wound down in the 1960s, which is not to say that Europe, and especially France, was economically in the clear.

Maybe the result of these lingering economic struggles or the result of cultural shifts, the leading topic of the day in post-war France then centered round the pro-Communism/anti-Communism divide and the use of political violence.[14] Many youth were attracted to the "leadership, direction, discipline and the promise of action in harness with 'the worker'" that characterized the French Communist Party, also known as "PCF" (and hereafter referred to as such).[15] But the realities of the crimes committed in the name of Communism were not easily ignored by all.[16] Among the intelligentsia, the debates in public raged mostly through those *categorized* as "existentialists." Maurice Merleau-Ponty suggested that the new dilemma was "being versus doing" and that one must engage in History.[17] In this respect, the French claimed to have learned about the inevitability of political violence.[18]

The United Kingdom, which also started its boom in 1950, possibly suffered less internal turmoil than France because, unlike the massive political Communist/anti-Communist division in France, as Pauline Gregg surmises about the success of post-War Britain,

> perhaps the most significant conclusion to draw from internal post-War politics is that the party in office makes little difference to the fundamental principles of government. The Welfare State is acknowledged by Labour, Liberal and Conservative alike ... The principles of social service, of nationalized basic industries, of the planned allocation of national resources, are accepted.[19]

In addition to the establishment of the Welfare State, the economic boom in Britain also represented the changing face of the world economy. Employment of basic occupations steadily declined after WWII, as the move away from heavy industries gave way to the increasing trend of an ever-expanding *service* economy.[20] In the rest of Western Europe, much of the stability and economic expansion had to do with the success of Western Germany, whose own recovery combined with intra-Western European trade circuits, created a vigorous export market for all of West Germany's neighboring countries.[21]

But while Western Europe, for the most part, was seeing a unified economic boom beginning around 1950 and lasting well into the 1960s, Central and Eastern European countries faced an entirely different set of problems. Politically and economically, the USSR swept in and/or influenced the Central and Eastern European countries through communist regimes, creating the Soviet Bloc: that is, a block of countries aligned with the Soviet Union. While each country had their own unique set of circumstances, for the most part, these Central and Eastern European communist countries were ruled by dictatorial heavy hands, were economically impoverished, and politically and culturally oppressive.

Post-WWII United States

Crucial to understanding the historical contexts of absurd literature in the United States of America is that (arguably) the first American absurd play (Edward Albee's *The Zoo Story* in 1958) came out ten years after the first wave of French absurd plays (1948). So not only was the absurd in the United States based in a country that, besides Pearl Harbor, was free from being bombed and, thus, was able to mount a quicker economic recovery, 1958 was also ten years further removed from the horrors of the Holocaust and WWII. The American literary absurd really got going in the early- to mid-1960s.

The JFK-led period that began the decade of the 1960s was largely a reaction to the Eisenhower-led late 1950s. The seeds of the 1960s may have been sown in the cultural rumblings of the late 1950s. Classically, the late 1950s were seen as a period of "blandness" and "optimism" as public opinion polls at the time seemed to suggest; however, James T. Patterson and some other scholars cite evidence of "cultural unease": the "Beats;" early rock n' roll (Chuck Berry and Elvis); the comedians Lenny Bruce and Tom Lehrer; the widely discussed 1957 essay by Norman Mailer called "The White Negro," celebrating a "hip," loose lifestyle; and various political dissenters.[22] This view is furthered by the fact that opponents of the conservative status quo (especially after the recession in 1958) began making headway in politics, with Democrats capturing many seats in the 1958 election and the emergence of John F. Kennedy.[23] But it was not only at home where Americans started to sense unease. The landing of *Sputnik* in 1957 caused Americans to react, "with an alarm approaching a panic."[24]

However, even with the intensification of the Cold War, Kennedy's presidency was celebrated. Of course, though a beginning-to-boom economy may have been a huge factor in Kennedy's popularity, even more so than the 1950s – where upwardly mobile Americans were able to rejoice at the thriving economy that brought material comforts along with it – the 1960s was the longest period of uninterrupted economic growth in United States history.[25] Industries such as electronics, which fueled the boom in the 1950s, continued even more growth in the 1960s, while businesses and professionals became used to a world of high-speed air travel, credit cards, and expense accounts, all in a world being transformed by explosively growing suburbs and the designing and construction of high-rise buildings.[26]

The Baby Boomers, as they came to be known, were growing up in a United States where they were personally unaffected by the Depression or WWII; their numbers breeding more self-conscious and more self-confident individuals.[27] Many now attending colleges and universities, "their brimming 'can-do' certitude stimulated grand expectations about the capacity of government to solve social problems," changing attitudes about what were perceived as entitlements (which were privileges just a generation earlier) and about "winning 'wars' against contemporary problems, ranging from poverty to cancer to unrest in Vietnam."[28]

The changing world and attitudes around them were reflected (or furthered) by a number of provocative and influential books that questioned conventional notions about American society and culture: Jane Jacobs' *Death and Life of Great American Cities* (1961), Joseph Heller's *Catch-22* (1961), Rachel Carson's *Silent Spring* (1962), and Michael Harrington's *The Other America* (1962).[29] These anti-Establishment books reflected also the emergence of groups of protestors. The year 1962 saw the SDS radicals' Port Huron Statement – the manifesto of New Left activism; James Meredith's attempt to attend the University of Mississippi as its first black student (and subsequent retaliatory violence by segregationists, which forced Kennedy to send in the army); and the formation of the National Farm Workers Association organized by César Chávez and other migrant workers.[30] Of course, needless to say, much of the late-1950s and early-to-mid-1960s had to do with Civil Rights, most particularly for African–Americans.[31]

The Existential Front

Jean-Paul Sartre was *the* French intellectual in post-war France.[32] David Drake, in *Intellectuals and Politics in Post-War France*, notes that *Being and Nothingness* (1943) established Sartre as a philosopher; *The Flies* (1943) as a playwright; the first two volumes of *Roads to Freedom* (1945) confirmed him as an author; writing with the underground press as a literary critic and then later as a journalist; thus, following the war, there was no one in France who paralleled Sartre's literary reputation.[33] Thus, with the co-founding and subsequent success of *Les Temps modernes* (first published in October 1945), Sartre was at the center of the postwar intellectual world.[34] And Sartre's prominence was highlighted by what Beauvoir later called the "existentialist offensive": in addition to *Les Temps modernes*, 1945 saw the publication of two existential novels – Beauvoir's *The Blood of Others* and Sartre's *The Age of Reason*.[35]

The Camus–Sartre quarrel

Maybe because of Sartre and the fame of the members of the "Existential Front," intellectuals, following the waning of *épuration* after the Liberation passed and German capitulation, positioned themselves in relation to existentialism and/or the Marxism of the French Communist Party (PCF).[36] The PCF, until Sartre's *rapprochment* with the PCF in 1952, viewed Sartre with a great deal of suspicion. Sartre, in the PCF's eyes, "was a degenerate *petit bourgeois* writer, the epitome of idealism and individualism [which contrasted with hierarchical discipline of democratic centralism and the cult of the leader of the PCF] who rejected the materialistic 'scientific' truths of Marxism, and who was a friend of the 'traitor' Paul Nizan to boot."[37] Sartre's individualism, in the mind of the PCF, contrasted with the ideals of Marxist theory in that, as Marxist historian Auguste Cornu writes, that the Sartrean individual is, "an absolute subject with his *raison d'être* in himself."[38]

While Sartre was upset and wanted the support of the PCF, Camus, on the other hand, feared a PCF take-over and supported Malraux, who, in 1946 saw the USSR as the principle danger to world peace. Writing in *Combat* in November 1946, Camus delivered a harsh critic of Stalinism.[39] Though there was a period up to 1951 when these two friends shared some ideas (both participated in the *Rassemblement Démocratique Révolutionnaire* [RDR] and the two became closer during the rehearsal of Sartre's play, *The Devil and the Good Lord*, which opened in June 1951), the publication of Camus' *The Rebel* (*L'Homme révolté*) in October 1951 opened up a furious debate which divided the two from there on out.[40] This was on top of the always-building tension between Camus and Sartre owing to their different social and cultural backgrounds (Camus came from working class roots in Algeria while Sartre came from a, "literary Parisian *petit bourgeois* household").[41]

In hopes of sidestepping the need to define Camus' philosophy of the absurd and rebellion and Sartre's existentialism (as the purpose of this book is not to explore these philosophies, per se),[42] I hope that examining the differences, rather, between Camus and Sartre will sufficiently give the reader an overall sense of both philosophies. The opening pages of Camus' *The Rebel* offer a strong rebuttal to nihilistic existentialism, of which Sartre is the principle philosopher. Camus' *The Myth of Sisyphus* (1942) argues that in order to make life have meaning, humans must confront the absurd: a situation where one's desires are contradicted by the realities of the world. Suicide, Camus argues, cannot be a legitimate answer, for suicide makes revolting against and contemplating the absurd impossible.[43] In *The Rebel*, Camus continues his idea of revolt with the idea of rebellion, where, "with rebellion, awareness is born."[44] As opposed to existentialist nihilism, where, "if [Camus'] age admits, with equanimity, that murder has its justifications, it is because of this indifference to life," Camus' essentialist view that humans are good leads to the idea that "from the moment that life is recognized as good, it becomes good for all men."[45] Camus' sense of humans as essentially good derives from Camus' sense of the existence of human nature. Royle describes the difference, what he calls "perhaps more fundamental than any," between Camus and Sartre's sense of the existence of human nature:

> Camus continues to believe in the existence of human nature, Sartre denies that there is any such thing: for him there is neither human nature in general nor anything natural in individual human beings. This is, of course, in part what he means by his dictum that for man existence precedes essence: nobody is born a coward – a person makes himself a coward through his actions, which he always remains free to change.[46]

For Sartre, since God does not exist, humans are the only thing whose existence comes before its essence. As Sartre bluntly states in "Existentialism is a Humanism," "Man is nothing else but that which he makes of himself."[47] On the other hand, in recognizing that "Man is the only creature who refuses to be what he is," Camus' rebellion, unlike that of the nihilistic existentialists, does not justify universal murder, but rebellion, "can discover the principle of reasonable culpability."[48] In fact, rebellion finds its justification in human solidarity in that suffering (which in absurdism is an individual suffering) is a collective experience in rebellion, for one must realize that he or she, in suffering, suffers like the rest of humanity: from the distance that separates human reality from the universe.[49] Camus, like the existentialists, may argue that life has no inherent meaning, but unlike the existentialists, life is not made meaningful through experience/actions that affirm and define existence (the central tenet of the existentialists where *existence precedes essence*), but through the use of human reason (where reason justifies the statement, *essence precedes experience*). Camus literally plays off of the rationalist *par excellence*, Descartes, in forming the creed of rebellion and ethical revolt: "I rebel – therefore we exist."[50] In other words, my suffering proves that we are all human, for we all suffer. In short, Camus is primarily concerned with the meaning of existence, as opposed to Sartre who focuses on the philosophical sense of being and the existentiality of existence.[51]

I used mostly *The Rebel* to bring these two philosophers into greater relief because it was, in fact, the publication of Camus' *The Rebel* (*L'homme révolté*) in October 1951 that set off the public intellectual debate in mid-1952. The key texts of this public debate, which appeared in *Les Temps modernes*, were (1) the review of Camus' *The Rebel* by Sartre's colleague, Francis Jeanson, in the May 1952 issue of *Les Temps modernes*, and (2) Camus' rebuttal in the August 1952 issue, which also contained responses by Sartre and Jeanson. As

Ronald Aronson, in *Camus and Sartre: The Story of a Friendship and the Quarrel that Ended It*, put it: "For fifty years The Rebel has demanded of those who read it to take sides. And for good reason. Between the middle of October 1951 and the summer of 1952, Sartre and Camus dramatically took positions concerning the Cold War."[52] These philosophers and their philosophies were not immune to the realities of post-WWII French (and European and world) history.

Jeanson's initial review takes aim at Camus' metaphysical rebellion, which Jeanson claims is abstract in the fact that Camus ignores history and how real history affected real people. Camus' metaphysical rebellion, in a sense, is so metaphysical that it turns Camus into a "passive atheist" who never denies God and sets the rebel up in opposition to God in "a pure metaphysical conflict in which there is no role for men and their history":

> The rebel . . . is the victim who presents a permanent challenge and who does not give God the satisfaction of contemplating failure – because he plans nothing and therefore cannot fail.[53]

Because Camus, Jeanson argues, has relegated rebellion to the intellect without the context of a real historical event, Camus has created an illusion by projecting a pure rebellion only based upon itself.[54]

Camus' response was equally as harsh and personal in its impersonal tone, as he referred over and over again to Jeanson, not by name, but as a "your collaborator." Camus accuses the "collaborator" of having, more or less, criticized him through a very selective reading that ignores much of what Camus actually wrote: "against all evidence, [Jeanson turned my book into] an antihistorical manual and the catechism of abstentionists":

> He has, in fact, adamantly refused to discuss the central theses to be found in this work: the definition of a limit revealed by the very movement of rebellion; the criticism of post-Hegelian nihilism and Marxist prophecy; the analysis of the dialectical contradictions concerning the end of history; the criticism of the notion of objective guilt; etc. On the other hand, he has discussed in detail a thesis that is not to be found there.[55]

Camus largely examined the flaws of Jeanson's argument, saying that Jeanson was criticizing what was not there and ignored what was there.

If the tone of Jeanson's review and Camus' response was harsh, Sartre's tone and subject matter was violently personal. In essence, Sartre accuses Camus of taking it personally owing to, as Sartre argues, Camus' "struggle within [his] own heart."[56] Sartre continues on this personal psychological attack:

Your personality, which was real and vital as long as it was nourished by events, became a mirage. In 1944, it was the future. In 1952, it is the past, and what seems to you the most intolerable injustice is that all this is inflicted upon you from the outside, and without your having changed.[57]

Though Sartre echoes Jeanson's idea that Camus rejects history, but he does so in the utmost of personal ways by calling Camus himself, "an abstraction of a rebel": "You became violent and a terrorist when History, which you rejected, rejected you in turn."[58] Sartre's closing line prophetically sealed their relationship: "But whatever you may say or do in return, I refuse to fight you. I hope that our silence will cause this polemic to be forgotten." After this article was published, the two never spoke again.[59]

In a large sense, the public exchange of letters was nothing more than the airing out of dirty laundry between friends owing to building tension from their more and more divergent philosophies. In this sense, from a philosopher's standpoint, these letters did little to shed new light on their respective philosophies. However, the soap opera that unfolded in print in mid-1952 Paris fascinated the public by showing the two philosophers and their philosophies at such odds that they would sever a friendship. However much or little the letters revealed about their philosophies, the fact was that this battle thrust the two thinkers (and their battle) into the national limelight. Aronson puts the importance of these articles in context. *Les Temps modernes*, a Paris journal, had a circulation of just over 10,000. When the August 1952 issue came out, it immediately sold out, reprinted, and sold out again. Outside of *Les Temps modernes*, the exchange of letters was republished in *Combat*, the paper Camus once edited and discussed in over a dozen newspaper and magazine articles with sensational headlines. As Sartre's friend Raymond Aron said, these articles, "immediately assumed the character of a national dispute."[60]

The emergence of analytic philosophy

While the "Existential Front" captured the public's attention, particularly in the 1940s and 1950s and especially in Europe, existentialism, also known as a "Continental" philosophy, was fading out of fashion especially in academic circles by the late 1950s and certainly by the 1960s. What was taking its place was what has come to be known as analytic philosophy. However, while analytic philosophy dominated philosophy in the 1960s in particular, the seeds of analytic philosophy were sown much, much earlier: in the 1890s, in fact.

In a sense, both existentialism and analytic philosophy grew out of the 1890s, as the same questions were being asked by two philosophers: Edmund Husserl and Gottlob Frege.[61] In a simplified sense, the answers to the questions of the 1890s diverged into two different schools of thought: in two long, non-linear processes, existentialism grew out of Husserl's response to the questions, while analytic philosophy grew out of Frege's response. In short, Husserl influenced Heidegger, who influenced Sartre, while Frege influenced Russell, who influenced Wittgenstein. The line started by Husserl took a phenomenological approach to understanding the world (focusing on the subjective), while the line initiated by Frege took an analytical, logical approach to understanding the world (through a much more objective lens).

Much of analytic philosophy grew out of the study of *reference*: that is, what does a word *refer* to? Gottlob Frege was the first to note that a sentence has a *sense* (i.e., the thought expressed) and a *reference* (i.e., what the word denotes).[62] Years later, Bertrand Russell, in his famous essay, "On Denoting," focuses on definite descriptions (e.g., "*the* man" versus "*a* man") and how a denoting phrase *denotes* one and only one entity. Russell was questioning the validity of sentences and whether they were true or false. Therefore, if the definite description does not refer to an entity, then the sentence, Russell claims, is false.[63] From Russell's work, and a 1921 book by Ludwig Wittgenstein, *Tractatus Logico-Philosophicus*, logical positivism became one of the leading schools of philosophy in Europe. The logical positivists attempted to make the study of language into a science, believing that an ideal language could be created to explain, in a scientific manner, the questions philosophy posed. It was Wittgenstein, himself, years later, in his *Philosophical Investigations*, who deflated the work of the logical positivists. Wittgenstein's book was written as a refutation of (mostly) his own earlier work, *Tractatus Logico-Philosophicus*. Wittgenstein's *Philosophical Investigations* was written throughout the 1940s and published posthumously in 1953. Wittgenstein suggests that instead of studying ideal notions of language that philosophy study how language is actually *used*. This book, considered maybe the most important and greatest book of twentieth-century philosophy, opened up the philosophical exploration into ordinary language, which dominated philosophy in the late 1950s and 1960s.

Why theatre?: How the genre came to be the center of the "movement"

It is not every day that a piece of literature comes along that has the impact of a play like Samuel Beckett's *Waiting for Godot*. In fact, one could probably count on one's hands and toes all of the works throughout the past millennia that had as much of an *impact as Godot*. While the early to mid-twentieth century saw a string of American novels that helped create the idea of "The Great American Novel" starting with *The Great Gatsby* (and subsequently, *Catcher in the Rye*, *Heart of Darkness*, *Catch-22*, *East of Eden*, and *The Old Man and the Sea*, to name a few) and novels like Marquez's *One Hundred Years of Solitude*, stories found in Borges' *Ficciones*, and poems like Ginsberg's "Howl," these previously mentioned classics still did not have nearly the same impact that Beckett's *Waiting for Godot* (and Kafka's *The Trial*, Joyce's *Ulysses*, Eliot's "The Wasteland," and Pirandello's *Six Characters in Search of an Author*) had.

And it might just be simply because of this – that *Godot* was written as a theatrical text – and for no other reason that the absurd flourished in the theatre in the 1950s and 1960s. It is not even that Beckett chose theatre as his sole medium of literary expression: Beckett's first publication was a poem, "Whoroscope," and his first novel, *Murphy*, preceded the publication of his first published play (i.e., *Godot*) by fourteen years. And certainly, too, Beckett's fiction (especially his novels) is held in the highest esteem. But while Beckett was publishing novels (i.e., his "Trilogy") that at the same time were similar to his experiments on stage (though very different due to the generic differences), the absurd elements found in, especially, his novels never quite spurred a large group of writers and novelists to follow Beckett's lead. Besides Beckett's theatrical works, in his other works, Beckett was similarly asking the same questions, experimenting with language, content, and form, and re-inventing literary form. Despite his success and acclaim in his fiction, for whatever reason (or the combination of a whole host of reasons and historical, intellectual, and social contingencies), the distillation of Beckett's literary genius just came together in *Godot*; it also appeared at the right place and time in history, where it struck an unnerving, poignant, and unforgettable chord with the theatre public. It may just be that absurdism found its home in the theatre in the 1950s and 1960s really simply due to the worldwide success of (or stunning curiosity about) *Godot*.

Chapter 4

Samuel Beckett

Samuel Barclay Beckett (1906–89) was born in the Dublin suburb of Foxrock, Ireland. Son of middle-class Protestant parents, Beckett attended Portora Royal School (where Oscar Wilde also went) and then Trinity College Dublin. After graduating, Beckett took lecturer posts at École Normale Supérieure and then back at Trinity College Dublin. Giving up his career in academia, and after being a part of the French Resistance in WWII, Beckett spent most of his adult life in Paris writing plays, short stories, novels, essays, and poetry. Best known for his play, *Waiting for Godot*, Beckett won the Nobel Prize in Literature in 1969. Samuel Beckett died in 1989.

One of the primary challenges in discussing a writer in relation to the absurd, as mentioned earlier, is that these writers associated with the absurd were not a part of a self-proclaimed movement; rather, the "movement" was thrust upon them as a somewhat after-the-fact categorization. The analysis of Samuel Beckett's work maybe most clearly typifies this conundrum for both the scholar and the student. Samuel Beckett is one of the most written about authors of the twentieth century. And while Beckett has been the *poster boy* of absurdism, and in some ways defines how the general public and academics alike understand absurdism, it must be stressed (and this cannot be overstated) that Beckett should not be (and is not) understood *only* through the lens of the absurd. The absurd is a catchall concept that functions almost as mental shorthand for connecting writers who, while doing some similar things, are also each creating their own literary paths. Therefore, it is vital to understand how Beckett does not just fit in with other absurdists, but transcends and departs from them. As such, it is worth noting that Beckett studies, especially in the last number of decades, has followed its own leads, not defaulting to Beckett as an absurdist to make sense of his work. Beckett studies, reinvigorated even more so in 2006 for the centenary celebration of his birth, has (as characterized very well by Linda Ben-Zvi in 2008), in recent years, followed five trajectories of inquiry: historicizing and particularizing Beckett's work; locating Beckett in a suitable "-ism"; investigating the relationship between Beckett's work and other art forms; honing in on which of Beckett's text is most appropriate for our current time (*Krapp's Last Tape* seems to be the consensus); and examining Beckett's influences and impacts.[1] To this list, since the time of this categorization and, especially, with the publishing of Samuel Beckett's large collection of letters by Cambridge University Press, Beckett studies have also begun to examine Beckett's archives.

It is important to remember how much Beckett influenced the writers associated with the absurd. Beckett's looming legacy, as well, did not just extend its reach to his immediate contemporaries, but is still felt today. And we also must not forget the influence, especially, James Joyce had on Beckett. In Beckett's first published work, an essay entitled, "Dante . . . Bruno. Vico. Joyce," noted Beckett scholar Ruby Cohn rightly observes that (discussing Joyce's *Work in Progress*) Beckett's "primary enthusiasm is language as form *and* content. And it is by language that Beckett yokes Joyce to Dante, for he contends that they both invented a distinctive ideolect, spoken by no one."[2] Beckett, as suggested in the Introduction, much like Joyce, destroys the Aristotelian plot line and places his characters and objects in his literary texts in an "amoral and arbitrary" (rather Kafkaesque) world, while bringing "form *and* content" together through an equally "amoral and arbitrary" language – with the effect that Beckett invents his own "distinctive idiolect, spoken by no one." This language "spoken by no one" unites the omnipresent motifs found in Beckett's work: the inability to express, the offstage presence, faltering memories, pain, immobility, and the relationship of mind to body.

So how did Beckett end up being labeled an absurdist? And what should we do about the absurd (both in relation to Beckett and to writers as a whole) now? The first question is answered easily because, especially *Godot*, was featured prominently in Esslin's *The Theatre of the Absurd*. As I propose in the Introduction, I think it best to see how the "common threads" found in absurd writers manifest themselves very differently, and this is how I think the absurd (like *modern* and *postmodern* literature) should be considered *now* (to answer the second question). While the following two chapters (on the other major absurdists [Chapter 5], and on the minor absurdists [Chapter 6]) will focus on a selected play at a time, I think it best, since so much of the absurd is influenced by Beckett, except for starting with a separate analysis of *Waiting for Godot*, to examine and organize Beckett's corpus of plays and novels around these four "common threads": *(1) experimentation with language (generally, working against "realistic" language); (2) tragicomedy is the genre; (3) frequently, though not always, experimentation with non-Aristotelian plot lines (where, often, the plots take the structure of a parable);[3] and maybe most-outwardly noticeable, (4) the literary works are set in "strange" (i.e., Kafkaesque, surreal, and ridiculous) situations.* Given that poetry is such a different genre, and – in a sense – naturally displays the first and third "common threads," a close read-ing of Beckett's first, and most notable, 1930 poem, "Whoroscope," will bring the chapter back full circle. Given that this book examines absurd *literature,* this chapter will include neither analyses of Beckett's television plays nor his non-fiction.

Waiting for Godot

Perhaps the most famous response to Beckett's most famous work, his play *Waiting for Godot* (published in French as *En attendant Godot* in 1952 and produced in Paris in 1953, and then translated by Beckett into English in 1954), comes from an early theatre critic who took a line from the play itself to summarize this critic's own thoughts about the play: "nobody comes, nobody goes, it's awful." Mirroring this critic's response, especially English-speaking audiences wallowed in the play's action (or lack thereof), the seeming despair, and the fact that Godot never comes. In short, *Waiting for Godot* is a play about two tramps, Vladimir and Estragon (nicknamed Didi and Gogo, respectively) who, simply, over the course of two days, are waiting on a "country road" for someone (or something) named Godot to arrive. In their seemingly endless wait (and it is hinted at that Didi and Gogo may have been doing this for fifty years), the two spend the day in idle discourse about wide-ranging topics (some deep and some mundane), interrupted each day by the arrival and departure of Pozzo and Lucky (who, together, have some sort of master–slave relationship). Each night, a boy arrives and delivers a message that Godot will not come today, but will surely come tomorrow.

Perhaps, though, the play's most common response comes in the form of a question: *Who is Godot?* very well could be (along with the question, *does Hamlet go mad?*) one of theatre's (two) most enduring questions about a specific play. It is hard to even estimate how many pages have been written, directly or indirectly, answering this question. Some of the most common answers are Godot is God, Godot is hope, and Godot is death.[4] But for each scholar who has thought one of these three, there are scores who have their own interpretation. In other words, since "Godot is everything and nothing, and everything in between that"[5] (and given Beckett's famous remark, if I knew who Godot was, I would have said so), maybe it is even better to ask, does Godot exist, and, if so, how? If we are to believe the boy, and the boy certainly appears to exist (though his reappearance in Act II, saying this is his first time coming, does throw some doubt on this question), the boy not only talks on a regular basis to Godot (as apparently Godot tells the boy to tell Didi and

Gogo that he will not be coming, but will surely come tomorrow), but the boy can also describe what he looks like. And the fact that Vladimir and Estragon mistake Pozzo for Godot certainly suggests to us that Godot is human (or at least that Didi and Gogo think Godot is human). As for what Godot represents, that is another question altogether, but Godot does *affect* the play (regardless of who, precisely, Godot is). Whether or not they are "tied . . . ti-ed" to Godot does not matter. As Didi and Gogo *could* easily succumb to the abyss, in a Sisyphean manner, the two tramps have made purpose out of their seemingly absurd situation (that is waiting for Godot, and life, in the larger sense), both in its ridiculousness and how their desires are not met by the reality of the world:

> VLADIMIR: . . . What are we doing here, *that* is the question. And we are blessed in this, that we happen to know the answer. Yes, in this immense confusion one thing alone is clear. We are waiting for Godot to come – . . . We have kept our appointment and that's an end to that. We are not saints, but we have kept our appointment.

Vladimir riffs off of Hamlet's "To be or not to be, that is the question" and suggests that instead of merely existing (being), the question is, since we exist (in a world of "immense confusion"), what are we to do?[6] And waiting for Godot – no matter how seemingly futile or meaningless that wait is, nor how irrelevant Godot, himself, is – provides some type of purpose, some structure, some goal, something to hope for.

When I was a child, I wanted to play basketball and be the center for the New York Knicks. My mom is 5'5" and my dad is 5'4½". Was I going to be the center for the New York Knicks? No, of course not (I ended up *towering* over them at 5'9")! But was it, say, as crazy as Vladimir and Estragon waiting for a man named Godot? Were the countless hours of dreaming about taking over for Patrick Ewing once he retired pointless? Were the hours upon hours playing basketball in my backyard with my childhood best friend, Scott Pinney, a waste of time? What child does not dream? What adult does not need to dream? How many of our goals do we accomplish? Do we not constantly set mundane, seemingly pointless goals that help us make it through the days, weeks, months, and years? How many of those New Year's Resolutions fade into next year's resolution? And the ones after that? But *our* "Godots" are necessary in this world of "immense confusion," where we have no inherent guideposts, nothing telling us how to move forward, where to go, or what to do (i.e., *what are we doing here?*)?

In a different vein, *Waiting for Godot* is something of the post-WWII version of the Italian Renaissance "tragicomic pastoral." The "pastoral," as was discussed in Chapter 1, was where the first "mixed" plays were found. The "shepherds" of the Italian "pastoral" are a different kind of "savior," leading a different type of flock. In Act I, Pozzo leads Lucky, in that Pozzo directs where Lucky goes; in Act II, Lucky leads Pozzo, in that Pozzo is blind. Though in *Godot*, Estragon always "compare[d] himself to Christ his whole life," Vladimir saved Estragon fifty years before the time of the play and tends to be the leader of the two, but as Vladimir says of Estragon, "You're my only hope." In this modern "pastoral," as can be attested above, there is confusion between "shepherd" and flock. Yes, time – "accursed time" – will go on, but where does one go? Whom does one follow? Yourself? Another? Why go at all? And what direction does one take where there is but one "country road" and only two logical directions to take? Is one mired by the choices or the lack thereof?

These two companions offset each other's weaknesses. Thus, this is why they get frustrated and quarrel with one another, as the other brings his own weaknesses into greater relief. However, this is also why they need one another and function well together. Especially because of the repetition of language in the play, it is easy for a reader/audience member to mix up Vladimir and Estragon. But if one looks at Didi and Gogo's subjects of attention, then it becomes more clear as to how the two are quite different characters. Estragon's focus is on his sensations and the needs of his own body: his hunger, how he needs sleep, his safety from his nightly tormentors, and his pain. Vladimir, on the other hand, focuses on his thoughts and lives in his own mind, pondering universal, intellectual questions: his questions are about life in the most general sense and his comments take the form of impersonal aphorisms. And it is in this mind–body duality that Vladimir and Estragon are complementary and in need of one another: Vladimir needs Estragon to bring him out of his mind and into his own body, into the moment and the present; Estragon needs Vladimir to escort him out of the present needs of his body and into his mind to see the bigger picture. By making the two semi-dependent upon the other, Beckett suggests in this play that neither (nor anyone else for that matter) can live only in the mind nor only in the body. But together, as Estragon says, "we don't manage too badly, eh Didi, between the two of us?"

That is not to say, by any means, that Didi and Gogo's life is not depressing (to themselves and to the audience/reader). It *is* horrible! But the point is, if they can – *every* day – actively decide against the obvious and easy way out of their absurd lot in life (i.e., hang themselves from the tree), then why can't we make do on "this bitch of an earth"? If Didi and Gogo can *go on*,[7] why can't we? It is in this way, they are *our* "saviors," too.[8]

I clearly do not want to give the reader the impression that Beckett is a happy-go-lucky, optimistic writer. He is certainly not. However, it would also be misguided to suggest that he is necessarily the opposite, that is, a pessimistic writer. Beckett – as he once returned to his dormitory at Trinity College Dublin posted a sheet of aluminum on the wall on which he wrote, "PAIN, PAIN, PAIN" – did not, by any means, see the world as a joy ride. But just because his world was filled with misery that does not mean that he had a necessarily *bleak* outlook on the world and life. As Camus writes, "I rebel – therefore, we exist." But like Beckett, just because Camus saw through illusion and saw how *suffering* (and the need to "rebel" from it, and it is in this suffering and rebelling that humans are connected) is an inescapable part of reality that does not mean that there cannot be hope and meaning when we decide to choose to *go on*. Like Edward Albee's pronouncement (that we will explore in more depth in the following chapter) that their theatre is a more "realistic theater," Beckett strips down all of the falsities and illusions that we create to comfort ourselves and presents a world of struggle. Just think: minus humanity, the natural world is a cruel place where only the strong survive and the weak die (out). But humanity, like Vladimir, can think. And it is in this, that we can still find purpose, even in a world where the only guidepost may be a silly commitment to waiting every day for an unknown man named Godot.

Other plays

Experimentation with language (generally, working against "realistic" language)

While much of the jarring nature *of Waiting for Godot* comes from dialogues that *are* hard to follow because of the frequent *non-sequiturs*, Beckett's body of work seems to hold together coherently through Beckett's *quest* to test the limits of communication through his constant experimentation with language. The language in his plays range from spewing language "out" of the "Mouth" and "into the world" in *Not I*, to a single, sustained breath in *Breath*, to no language and miming in his *Act without Words I* and *Act without Words II*. But the amount of words or amount of silence does not quantify how much is being said. It is, rather, as if Beckett realized that *realistic* language could not express the inexpressible, so Beckett needed to destroy language, making it inexpressible, to adequately express the inexpressible.

While thoroughly revolting against traditional realistic language, Beckett's earlier plays (let us say, the ones that came out in public in the first ten years since *Godot* was published in 1952) – *Godot* (1952), *Endgame* (1957), *Act without Words I* (1957), *Krapp's Last Tape* (1958), *Act without Words II* (1959), and *Happy Days* (1961) – still displayed a certain amount of *causality* due to language. Despite frequent *non-sequiturs*, the conversations and plot lines do meander back, usually in some type of circular fashion, and communication is had. In a sense, whether the language is verbal or not (as in the case of the two "mime" plays), the audience sees how communication, while utterly ineffective, does produce some type of results that do make some sense.

For example, even in the plays without "language" in *Act without Words I* and *Act without Words II*, there is a sense of communication that leads to causal action between the offstage presence and the body or bodies on stage. For example, *Act without Words I* shows a cruel game between the offstage presence that controls, presumably, the objects on the stage. Each movement of the objects produces a logical reaction by the "mime." When a "carafe" is dangled down with a "rope," the "mime," for example, tries to climb the rope to reach the carafe. This is the logical thing to do in a "Desert." What is illogical in this short play is the mindset and the cruelty of the offstage presence. Why tempt the man? Why not help him? The continuing struggle of the man to best the actions of the offstage presence also make sense: in the desert, the man is, presumably, fighting to survive, willing himself to "go on," in the words of *Godot*. The fact that he continues to react to the offstage presence communicates to the offstage presence that the game can continue. It is only when the man makes the decision to stop playing the game that the offstage presence wants him to play (wants him to fail at) that the audience sees the offstage presence lose its power, with the man regaining his own power to choose his own actions, even if it may lead to his ultimate demise. Once the man actively decides non-action, the actions of the offstage presence are logical reactions: losing its control, the offstage presence tries to tempt the man back into the game where the offstage presence has the upper hand. While "language" may never be spoken, actions, reactions, and gestures clearly set up communication and causal behavior. *Act without Words II* also has a similar pattern, with the offstage presence wielding a "prod" that never threatens the bodies in the sacks into action, but "prods" them, allowing the two bodies to each express themselves in their own way. This communication is less malevolent than in *Act without Words I*, and are almost-encouraging gestures, as the repeated pattern of the "prod" stopping short assures the bodies in the sacks that the "prod" will not actually inflict any bodily harm.

In his other longer plays, *Endgame* and *Happy Days*, the earlier *Endgame* is stylistically filled with *non-sequiturs*, much like *Godot*: there are bursts of monologues and dialogues that are perfectly logical and causal in communication, mixed with illogical leaps between topics and statements. *Happy Days*, on the other hand, is essentially one giant monologue: Winnie not only converses with herself, as we see in *Krapp's Last Tape* (a conversation, in a sense, between an old man and his younger [previously-recorded] self), but her pronouncements affect her behavior in the first act, when she still has the ability to move her arms and pick up objects, and then her reasoning in her conversation (throughout both acts) leads her to constantly conclude that "this is a happy day." Ultimately, while Willie never speaks to her until the final moments of the play, and thus the audience feels as though Winnie really is only talking to herself, the pronouncement of "Win" by Willie demonstrates that Winnie was successful in communicating, both with herself and with Willie, having her repeated line, "this is a happy day," justified by the single word of recognition that Willie utters at the end of the play.

The later he gets in his career, the more distrust, or lack of faith, Beckett seems to have in (particularly spoken) communication. And this is, largely, why he turned to radio plays and music as his theatre career progressed. Beckett had many philosophical problems with language, and thus other forms of art, especially painting and music, spoke to Beckett in ways that language could not. Discussing music, Michiko Tsushima discusses a tension between materiality and immateriality in Beckett's radio plays, where, "for Beckett, music is an ideal other of language which can move beyond the materiality of language"; Tsushima suggests that Beckett's use of radio was an attempt to attack language, despite this "paradoxical attempt to immaterialize language that can never be free from its own materiality."[9] The radio plays – *All That Fall* (1957), *Embers* (1959), *Words and Music* (1962), *Cascando* (1963), *Rough for Radio I* (1976), and *Rough for Radio II* (1976) – more obviously than his other later plays take the physical body and its gestures out of the equation, leaving only sounds and words, exposing how words devoid of the body can be both understood and communicative, and also, at times, decontextualized and uncommunicative.

In his later short stage plays – for example, in *Come and Go* (1966), *Not I* (1972), *Footfalls* (1976), *Quad* (1982), *What Where* (1983) – Beckett's carefully constructed notes on movement take a diagram/picture form. Where spoken language is only one abstractly poetic element of Beckett's later plays, communication borders on pure movement, almost creating a series of paintings or tableaus, communicating stories about relations between bodies and objects that cannot be comprehended by spoken language. It is the fact that language cannot communicate successfully that demonstrates the complexity of relationships (between bodies, within a body, between bodies and objects, and between objects).

Tragicomedy is the genre

Waiting for Godot is self-billed by Beckett as a "tragicomedy": the play's comedic moments are punctured by moments of tragic realizations, and visa versa; or, sometimes, one does not know whether to laugh or cry; and the action of the play is cyclical, barely rising or falling. But *Godot* is not unique in Beckett's oeuvre as his only tragicomedy. Far from it, (absurd) tragicomedy is the mode of expression for Beckett's worldview. Beckett's tragicomedy expresses both tragic and comedic insights, but – maybe even more noticeable – Beckett's opposing generic elements often seem to cancel each other out, cancelling out the movement of tragedy and/or comedy, resulting in dramatic and theatrical stasis. Even with the subtle changes between Act I and Act II of *Godot* (most notably the leaves on the trees that were not there in Act I) and between both acts of *Happy Days* (most notably Winnie goes from being buried up to the waist to up to the head in the ground), there is a sense of circularity that results in going nowhere in *Godot* and despite the gradual march to further physical immobility, the same thought patterns are unchanged in *Happy Days*.

In his early one-act plays, especially in *Act without Words I* and *Act without Words II*, there is movement and a dramatic arc building from the beginning of the play. However, the end of both of these above-named plays, for example, disrupts the dramatic arc by deflating the rising action with (a return to) inaction. In his later one-act plays, especially the ones with diagrammed movement (e.g., *Come and Go*, *Not I*, *Footfalls*, *Quad*, and *What Where*), there are complex movements and complex patterns. But like the humorous chess game in Beckett's early novel, *Murphy* (and Beckett, himself, was an avid chess player), the movement in these plays does not really go anywhere or lead somewhere. *Come and Go* best epitomizes this through the metaphor of the "Oh," spoken in different ways: signifying both "zero" and the circular and infinite "O" shape of "rings" that are not "apparent": an exercise in nothing and in movement that goes nowhere except back to its original place.

Frequently, though not always, experimentation with non-Aristotelian plot lines (where, often, the plots take the structure of a parable)

To a large degree, Beckett's early and longer plays, *Godot* and *Happy Days*, most resemble something of a play with an Aristotelian plot line. It is possible that these two plays only feel as though there is some Aristotelian arc primarily because there are two acts in each of these plays. While subtle, there is something of a change between these two acts: there are now a small number of leaves on the dead tree at the beginning of the second act of *Godot*, and the ground, which was up to Winnie's waist in Act I, is now up to her head in Act II of *Happy Days*. Along with Beckett's other early plays, *Endgame* and *Act without Words I*, these plays, despite maybe never satisfying the audience's expectations, do contain a tension that needs to be resolved or a dramatic direction: there is hope that

Godot will come (*Godot*); the enveloping of Winnie by the ground seems to be progressing and swallowing her up until she is completely underground (*Happy Days*); there is a movement towards escaping and seemingly inevitable death (*Endgame*); and there is the increasing tension of the "mime's" escape from the "Desert" (*Act without Words I*). As is clear from the end of these previously mentioned plays, Beckett disrupts the Aristotelian arc by never fulfilling the expectations of where these plays appear to be heading. And these hanging endings, ones without clear resolutions, are typical of the form of the parable, where the reader/audience is forced, him- or herself, to make sense of the unresolved conflict(s).

As Beckett moves through his theatrical career, however, his plays become shorter, his plot lines become less defined, and there is little-to-no dramatic/theatrical arc to speak of. In his later plays, Beckett destroys both causality and linearity in plot. In the plays that appeared in the last ten years of his life – *A Piece of Monologue* (1979), *Rockaby* (1981), *Ohio Impromptu* (1981), *Quad* (1982), *Catastrophe* (1982), *Nacht und Träume* (1982), and *What Where* (1983) – *A Piece of Monologue* is a rambling four and a half page monologue uttered by a presumably old man named, "Speaker"; *Rockaby* is basically a poem uttered by a woman on a rocking chair; *Ohio Impromptu* has a "reader," "R," reading the last pages of a book with no real perceivable plot to "L," a "listener," with R frequently interjecting, "Little is left to tell" and then, later, "Nothing is left to tell"; *Quad* is a somewhat randomly and somewhat artistically choreographed play of movement, lights, and sound by "four players" numbered "1, 2, 3, 4"; *Catastrophe* has characters that seemingly go together – a director, a female assistant, a protagonist, and lighting director – but the dialogue, always ultimately eludes the context of the characters; *Nacht und Träume* is a short almost-mime of a play featuring humming, singing, and the playing of Shubert's *Lied, Nacht und Träume*; and *What Where* is choreographed something reminiscent of *Quad*, but has dialogue like *Catastrophe*, in that each time a question and answer seem to have a causal connection, the conversation ultimately yields talking that is seemingly arbitrary in the lack of causality.

Setting the literary work in "strange" (i.e., Kafkaesque, surreal, and ridiculous) situations

From just a sample of simple plot summaries, the settings and situations especially in Beckett's earlier plays certainly are "strange": a woman buried up to her waist and then up to her head in the ground, who always concludes that "this is a happy day" (*Happy Days*); a bare, gray, and lifeless interior with four characters, two of whom sit in "ashbins," who want to leave the "endgame," presumably, of life (*Endgame*); and an offstage presence repetitively extends a prod at two bodies in sacks until each comes to life (*Act without Words II*). As these simple plots demonstrate, Beckett's early plays are set in situations that humans (except metaphorically speaking) do not really ever encounter or find themselves in.

In his earliest plays, *Godot*, *Endgame*, and *Act without Words I*, the characters appear, at times, to be self-aware that they are in an unusual situation, as in the aforementioned plays, the characters realize that they cannot leave. This self-awareness of their surreal and unique situations reminds us a lot of K. in Kafka's *The Trial*, who, himself, understands that his situation is unique, absurd, ridiculous, and surreal. But as his theatrical career progresses, Beckett's characters do not seem to really realize that they are in "strange" situations, much more like Kafka's Gregor Samsa's (non)reaction to being a bug in "Metamorphosis." The best example of this initial turn in the (lack of) self-awareness of Beckett's theatrical characters is Winnie in *Happy Days* who seems to be essentially unaware, or at least mentally unaffected, that she is buried in the ground.

As Beckett gets later in his theatrical career, the settings and situations are more removed and decontextualized in their relation to bodies and objects: a stage filled with rubbish, a cry, then an inhale, and then an exhale (*Breath*); a radio play with music and little, if no, indication, of the situation of the speakers (*Cascando*); and a rambling monologue out of a "Mouth" (*Not I*). These later plays are much more dreamlike (or surreal) in the way that these plays are hyper-focused on unusual subjects and/or objects, and the world of the play does not make a *coherent* whole (or complete picture of a world). In these later plays, it is the audience who must wade through these situations: the where, when, who, and whats are constantly eluding any attempt at placing and fixing the play in some understandable and coherent world.

Fiction

Experimentation with language (generally, working against "realistic" language)

While Beckett is most well known for his earlier plays, Beckett's tremendous experimentation against realistic language was on display much earlier and, arguably, to a much greater extent in his fiction. By the time that *Godot* was published in 1952, Beckett had already published three full-length novels – *Murphy* (1938), *Molloy* (1951), and *Malone Dies* (1951) – in addition to other published works of fiction, non-fiction, and poetry.

Murphy is Beckett's most traditional novel, if there is any way to call *Murphy* "traditional." There is a recognizable story with recognizable characters in recognizable settings. *Murphy* is a novel about a "solipsist" named Murphy, who often ties himself naked to a rocking chair as a seeming means of sensory deprivation to clear his mind, much like Murphy's mentor, Neary, who has the ability to stop his heart. Celia, Murphy's lover (who is a prostitute), convinces Murphy to find a job. In response, Murphy finds work in an insane asylum, something he enjoys because the patients do not experience a normal conscious life: something – like Murphy's pleasure in his rocking chair habit – Murphy desires. Having withdrawn into the world of the asylum, Neary and a host of other eccentric characters pursue Murphy for their own various reasons.

The language in this early novel in some ways echoes the plot: the story is offbeat and the language reflects that. Like the characters of *Murphy*, the language is awkward (in relation to anything traditional), but confident in itself. While the characters' behaviors are unusual, much like the language in the novel, they are casual and understandable. The first line of *Murphy* demonstrates the unusual-but-understandable awkwardness of Beckett's writing style perfectly: "The sun shone, having no alternative, on the nothing new." (1) The frequently profound, but un-rhythmic and jarring, modifying clauses found in *Murphy* disrupt, but do not destroy, the sense of normalcy. Much like the title character, who weaves in and out of his life that sits on the edge of just being eccentric to being mentally insane (i.e., an outlier, in his mental state[s]), the language of the novel often hints at jumping off of the deep end, but is often reeled back to simply being eccentric and whimsical:

> The moon, by a striking coincidence full at the perigee, was 29000 miles nearer the earth than it had been for four years. Exceptional tides were expected. The Port of London Authority was calm.[10]

Just like Murphy – who always seems like he is headed into a world of insanity but somehow he manages to come back and solidify his relationships – as in the preceding passage, the language yolks the movements, first towards insanity, in its disconnect with rational and linear thought patterns, and then, the retreat from that insanity into simple eccentricity, imparting a feeling of randomness, but still demonstrating very clear, purposeful thought.

However, as time passes for Beckett, once he gets to his mid-to-late forties, Beckett's experimentation with language rapidly increases. Over the course of just two years, the language in *Molloy*, *Malone Dies*, and *The Unnamable*, successively, becomes less and less *causal.* Here are the opening passages of these three successive books:

> I am in my mother's room. It's I who live there now. I don't know how I got there. Perhaps in an ambulance, certainly a vehicle of some kind. I was helped. I'd never have got there alone. There's this man who comes every week.[11]   *– Molloy* (1951)

> I shall soon be quite dead at last in spite of all. Perhaps next month. Then it will be the month of April or of May. For the year is still young, a thousand little signs tell me so. Perhaps I am wrong, perhaps I shall survive Saint John the Baptist's Day and even the Fourteenth of July, festival of freedom. Indeed I would not put it past me to pant on to the Transfiguration, not to speak of the Assumption.[12]
> *– Malone Dies* (1951)

> Where now? Who now? When now? Unquestioning. I, say I. Unbelieving. Questions, hypotheses, call them that. Keep going, going on, call that going, call that on. Can it be that one day, off it goes on, that one day I simply stayed in, in where, instead of going out, in the old way, out to spend day and night as far away as possible, it wasn't far.[13]
> *– The Unnamable* (1953)

From the awkwardness of prose in *Molloy* and the increasing randomness of thought in *Malone Dies*, by *The Unnamable*, punctuation, character, speaker, and really almost everything, lacks linear cause and effect. By *The Unnamable*, it is almost as though language has no bearing on either shaping or representing a world of cause and effect. This increasing distrust of language's ability to communicate, demonstrated by Beckett's extreme literary output of fiction writing in the early 1950s as indicated above, in a sense, presages Beckett's movement away from causality in language and plot that defines the later stages of Beckett's theatrical career.

Tragicomedy is the genre

In *Murphy* (1938) and *Watt* (1953), Beckett's (absurd) tragicomic vision is much more like we see in *Godot*: the story is filled with comical moments, but the setting is, if one steps back, somewhat depressing. In these two novels, the comedy and tragedy spring from the same source: the reader laughs at Murphy and Watt's eccentricities, but it is also these very eccentricities that are the cause of Murphy and Watt being left out on the margins of society. Murphy, who does have friends – however eccentric they are, themselves – feels a need to retreat into the confines of and company of the patients at an insane asylum. Of course, the combination of an eccentric and the mentally insane makes for some quite hysterical episodes, producing moments reminiscent of many sketches by *Monty Python*, whose sketch comedy is filled with "twits" and/or eccentrics coming into contact with each other and/or society. But unlike *Monty Python*'s non-stop hilarity and almost-slapstick raucousness, which really leaves no time or space for reflection, Beckett's *Murphy* and *Watt* provide enough pauses that the reader realizes the two title characters' saddening states.

As I wrote earlier about the narrative arc of Beckett's dramatic and theatrical version of (absurd) tragicomedy – how the generic elements of tragedy and comedy often cancel each other out, which yields a type of dramatic or theatrical stasis – much of the same can be said for Beckett's "Trilogy," *Molloy, Malone Dies*, and *The Unnamable*. Unlike *Murphy* and *Watt*, where tragedy and comedy co-exist to create the net overall effect of (absurd) tragicomedy, in his "Trilogy," the comedy and tragedy are so closely intertwined and, thus, are almost a-comedic and a-tragic; this results in tragicomedy, but a different brand of tragicomedy – one that evokes more of that feeling of stasis.

Frequently, though not always, experimentation with non-Aristotelian plot lines (where, often, the plots take the structure of a parable)

To relate to the previous section on tragicomedy, in a large sense, the clearer the comedic and tragic elements are in Beckett's novels, the more closely the novel has some feel of an Aristotelian structure. That is, it is almost as if the greater the outwardly perceivable comedy and tragedy, the more the reader observes the Aristotelian narrative arcs of comedy and tragedy. Thus, *Murphy* – Beckett's funniest and silliest novel – has something of the Aristotelian arc of comedy, while *Watt* – which is funny, but is much less obvious in switching back and forth between more subtle comedic and tragic elements – has less of an identifiable plot, though Watt's journey, though filled with a number of often-lengthy tangents, is traceable.

Beckett's "Trilogy," however, has an entirely different trajectory – or, rather, lack of trajectory – because while there are lines and passages that are funny or sad, it is hard to say that especially, by *The Unnamable*, where there are no plot lines to speak of, the "Trilogy" takes a comedic and/or tragic arc. Thus, without a clear arc of tragedy and/or comedy, it is almost as if there is nowhere for the plot to go. Appropriately, maybe it is the other way around: that is, because there is nowhere *to go* (an omnipresent theme in Beckett's work), one and/or the world can only simply *be*. Without direction then there is no arc to follow, be it comedy or tragedy; language simply spews forth.

For Beckett, then, movement dictates language and language dictates movement. Thus, as books progress in his "Trilogy," the less causal the language gets in his subsequent novels, the more arbitrary the movement or narrative arcs, resulting in a feeling of going nowhere. By *The Unnamable*, there are simply no signposts to guide movement. That is, without the normal sense of cause and effect displayed in language, it is harder to follow, or go from, point A to point B; all that is left is stasis.

Setting the literary work in "strange" (i.e., Kafkaesque, surreal, and ridiculous) situations

Continuing the train of thought from the previous section, when the reader encounters comedic and tragic elements in Beckett's novels – and thus, as stated before, the more the novel follows an Aristotelian arc – there are clear, though clearly "strange," settings and situations found in these novels. On the other hand, when the comic and tragic elements start to disappear, and the Aristotelian arc fades, the "strangeness" comes, not from what is happening, but because not much, if anything, happens: all of the reader's expectations of plot, setting, characters, and situation are subverted, and the reading experience – itself – is what becomes "strange," Kafkaesque, surreal, and ridiculous.

In *Murphy*, Beckett's funniest and most Aristotelian novel, the setting and situations are zany, as the world, happenings, and inner life of eccentrics are to the rest of us: Murphy tying himself naked in a rocking chair and rocking himself into a frenzy in order to free his mind, or Murphy playing a ridiculous game of chess with a patient in an insane asylum. Or in *Watt*, the reader laughs at the awkwardness of the epically stated journey within Mr Knott's house with Watt trying to make sense of basic things such as Mr Knott's pot:

> Looking at a pot, for example, or thinking of a pot, at one of Mr Knott's pots, of one of Mr Knott's pots, it was in vain that Watt said, Pot, pot . . . For it was not a pot, the more he looked, the more he reflected, the more he felt sure of that, that it was not a pot at all. It resembled a pot, it was almost a pot, but it was not a pot of which one could say, Pot, pot, and be comforted.[14]

What is "strange" is not that Watt finds himself confronted by a pot in Mr Knott's house. What is "strange," and it speaks to the "strangeness" in Beckett's "Trilogy," is that something so mundane is not at all mundane; rather, Beckett estranges the reader from the mundane, producing a much more surreal world. That is, if Watt encountered an alien, Beckett would clearly be putting Watt in an absurd situation. But by making Watt befuddled in encountering an everyday object, the reader, much more so than Watt, is the one who feels like he or she is in some Kafkaesque, surreal world, for it is much harder to imagine unlearning and/or forgetting reality and what one knows than to imagine encountering something new.

Thus, when one reads through Beckett's "Trilogy," with signposts to reality in each novel subsequently becoming less and less clear, again, it is the reader who is largely in the "strange" situation. It is almost as though the novel is to the reader what Mr Knott's pot is to Watt: *it resembled a novel, it was almost a novel, but it was not a novel of which one could say, Novel, novel, and be comforted.* In short, Beckett makes the reader un*comfort*able with language, feeling as though he or she is encountering something new and novel, so that the reader must dwell on *language*'s "strangeness," making sure the reader does not take the language – and language's limits – for granted.

Poetry

Beckett's first published poem is "Whoroscope" (1930), published as a result of winning a small literary prize. "Whoroscope" is somewhat based on the biography of René Descartes (1596–1650), considered the father of modern philosophy, and a writer who Beckett was reading at the time when he was encouraged to submit a poem to this literary competition. Given the subject of this poem and since Beckett's *oeuvre* does discuss the mind and body at length, over the years there has been much speculation by scholars as to whether Beckett was a Cartesian (i.e., devotee of Descartes) or not. While I, myself, have waded into this debate in the past,[15] my purpose here is not to discuss Beckett as a Cartesian or as an anti-Cartesian, but to demonstrate that ever since Beckett's early days of writing, he was fascinated by the same *questions* that Descartes pondered about the relationship between mind and body (i.e., whether or not they had similar or different answers to the same questions, Beckett and Descartes did share the same preoccupations); these questions, then, laid the groundwork for the rest of Beckett's writing career.

"Whoroscope" is a long poem filled with allusion after allusion to great thinkers and notable people throughout the ages: Galileo, Descartes, Augustine, Bacon, and Christ are just some. While the act of reading the allusions and discerning precisely why they are there and what they mean for the overall meaning of the poem is a very useful task, it has been done countless times before and does little for the present discussion. Instead, thinking about the "egg," and the "chicken" and the "egg," motif(s) in a poem that brings up

Descartes, Bacon, and Christ is important for establishing the preoccupations that Beckett would revisit for the rest of his career.

In a particularly loaded passage in the poem, Beckett dwells on the transubstantiation of Christ:

> So we drink Him and eat Him
> and the watery Beaune and the stale cubes of
>   Hovis
> because He can jig
> as near or as far from His Jigging Self
> and as sad or lively as the chalice or the tray asks.
>   How's that, Antonio?
>   In the name of Bacon will you chicken me up
> that egg.
> Shall I swallow cave-phantoms?

Referring to the act of drinking wine ("watery Beaune") as drinking Christ's blood ("we drink Him") and the act of eating a wafer ("stale cubes of Hovis") as ingesting Christ's body ("and eat Him") during a Catholic Mass, Beckett ponders how Christ can be anywhere and/or everywhere at once ("because He can jig / as near or as far from His Jigging Self"). Beckett turns to Francis Bacon, the first great modern empiricist and father of the Scientific Method, to dive into the debate based upon empirical evidence instead of just blindly "[swallowing] cave-phantoms," which (alluding to Christ's resurrection) are ethereal.

This allusion to Bacon is significant given that much of the poem alludes to René Descartes, the first great modern rationalist. The division between rationalism and empiricism was renewed by Descartes and Bacon, but goes back to Plato and Aristotle. In short (and, for the purposes of brevity and simplicity), rationalism espouses that some objective truth can be developed through a rational mind, while empiricism relies on the senses and the realities presented to a body to develop some subjective truth.

The whole reason that the chicken and the egg debate is alluded to in this poem is that both rational and empirical solutions to the problem are common. And, moreover, the *idea* of the chicken (as a future product of an egg) is a rational line of thinking, while the presence of the chicken as evidence of its primal existence comes from an empirical line of thinking. In this poem, Beckett not only splits the chicken from the egg, but in doing so, he splits not the mind and the body, but the two sides of the debate into two different people. Descartes is associated with the egg (and the rational vein of thinking, where the thoughts of the mind take precedence over the stimuli received by the senses of the body); Bacon is associated with the chicken (and the empirical vein of thinking, where the body's reception of external stimuli takes precedence over the thoughts of the mind).

"Whoroscope" does not create a clear allegiance to either Descartes or Bacon. Instead, the presence of both of these philosophers, and the metaphorical splitting of the two, suggests that Beckett was clearly thinking about the issues that divided Descartes and Bacon: the issue of whether the mind or the body takes precedence in our ongoing search for truth. This is the very issue that I argue preoccupies Beckett throughout his career.

* * *

On the first page of Ciaran Ross' recent book, *Beckett's Art of Absence: Rethinking the Void*, Ross recalls two quotes by Samuel Beckett. First, after confiding to Patrick Bowles, "There are many things I don't understand in my books," Beckett quoted Democritus, "Nothing is more real than nothing," concluding, "They are a positive statement of a negative thing."[16] And second, in a letter to Aidan Higgins in 1952, Beckett, "realised that his writing resembled more of a journey 'in gathering thinglessness.'"[17] Ross uses these quotes to set up his psychoanalytical readings of Beckett's major postwar writings. Ross argues for a Beckettian version of a "negative sublime"[18]:

> The Beckettian negative is potentially positive: the negative of remembering, speaking, and loving is about the only "real" thing in Beckett's work. The Godot that is not there is more real than the Godot who might eventually come.[19]

While Ross suggests that the absent Godot is more real than an actual Godot, I read the two above quotes by Beckett as Beckett's predilection for *gathering thinglessness* into rather *thinghood*, making what is negative an existent positive. Beckett explores Being through exploring nothingness, demonstrating how nothingness gives Being its shape. In this sense, turning nothingness into Being fills nothingness' void.

In his "Three Dialogues," Beckett discusses the painter, Pierre Tal-Coat, and how Tal-Coat's painting captures nature, which is "a composite of perceiver and perceived." (138) The expression of nature (or may we say, reality) that Tal-Coat *creates* and *liberates*[20] is,

> B – The expression that there is nothing to express, nothing with which to express, nothing from which to express, no power to express, no desire to express, together with the obligation to express.[21]

While this statement by B would appear to reify the typical reading of Beckett's elevation of nothingness, it is important to note that this expression of nothingness – which is discussed earlier in "Three Dialogues" – is an "expression of natural experience":

> B – In any case a thrusting towards a more adequate expression of natural experience, as revealed to the vigilant coenaesthesia. Whether achieved through submission or through mastery, the result is a gain in nature.[22]   (Disjecta 138)

The significance here is that by expressing nothingness ("natural experience"), "the result is a gain in nature." Implied by the phrase, "a gain," something is added (as "opposed to *loss*"[23]) to nature as a result of expressing nothingness.

Beckett's nothingness is clearly not a Sartrean vision of it, where nothing is the opposite (or absence) of Being. And while it may at first appear that this project by Beckett is based upon the model developed by Heidegger, where Being springs from nothingness,[24] it is not this either. Beckett, instead, contemplates nothing in order to demonstrate that Being is on the same spectrum as nothing: nothing has the potential to become Being (as in the case of an idea, such as "Godot"); Being has the potential to become nothing (as in the cases of death and decay, two of Beckett's most omnipresent themes).

Ross, as I mentioned earlier, suggests that the Godot we do not see is more real than the actual Godot. Does Godot exist? Maybe. Maybe not. While there is truth in Ross' assertion, the nothingness in Beckett's work cannot be seen, but it (e.g., Godot) *exists* in the way that it has an effect upon reality. By exploring the *response* of the characters to nothingness (e.g., Godot), the audience member sees nothingness *in relief*. While it is true that the nothingness in Beckett's work never materializes, the continued actions/inactions of Beckett's characters in response to the nothingness shape Beckett's characters and the world they inhabit.

In this way, Beckett is clearly a philosophical writer. Beckett's interest in the father of modern philosophy, René Descartes, is well studied, and his interest in Ludwig Wittgenstein, considered the most important twentieth-century philosopher, is known, but not well-studied. However, just because Beckett was philosophical and read philosophers does not mean that he was a devotee to any particular philosophy. Beckett's writings were not tracts on Descartes' mind–body dualism, nor were they tracts on Wittgenstein's observations about language. (*And this is saying nothing about the two philosophers/ies most commonly associated with Beckett: Jean-Paul Sartre's existentialism and Albert Camus' philosophy of the absurd.*) Having read these philosophers, "interest in" does not mean Beckett *professed* these philosophies, but simultaneously it also does not mean that they (i.e., Beckett, Descartes, and Wittgenstein) were not pondering the same essential question: what is the relationship between mind and body, or thought and sensation? Beckett often seems to think the mind and body do not speak, in a sense, the same language. That is, Beckett seems to say that our sensations are incongruous with our language (minds) and our language is incongruous with our sensations (body). Given our limitations with being bound to language, we can neither communicate with each other, let alone with ourselves.

And this is why we see Beckett creating lingual fantasias about pain and immobility (sensations), and faltering memories and abstract notions of an offstage presence (thought). And these are the lasting images/words that remain with us in Beckett's oeuvre: Murphy tying himself to a rocking chair to escape his body and free his mind; Winnie buried up to her head and being able to conclude that "it is a happy day"; Nagg and Nell stuck in ashbins; the offstage game in *Act Without Words I* and the offstage prod that *prods* the characters out of their sacks in *Act Without Words II*; how Krapp's recorded tapes "protects the memory of the years gone by, but in so doing it exacerbates the feeling of irreparable loss of the present (59)"; "the movement [in The Trilogy – *Molloy*, *Malone Dies*, and *The Unnamable*] is towards incarnations more and more 'purified' of the characteristics of the external, recognisable world (88) . . . the material is chaotic, messy and disjointed – like the rambling, fragmented stories of [Beckett's] narrators" (89); and, "Famously, Watt is thwarted in his effort to name the pot that was not a pot. This moment indicates the elusiveness of the named object, its resistance to the efforts of language to pin it down" (84). And, of course, there is *Waiting for Godot*: Estragon struggling and in pain to take off his boot; Godot never coming; Estragon always forgetting that he and Vladimir are waiting for Godot; the expurgation when Lucky *thinks* after they remove his hat; and the final line of the play, "Let's go. (*They do not move.*)"

Importantly, Beckett's career does not have a sustained *thesis*, per se, but he does, though, at least seem to be continually preoccupied by the relationship between sensation and thought. If Beckett's subjects, situations, and experimentations with language change constantly throughout his career, then it would certainly be hard to pin down even Beckett, himself, as this-or-that type of writer – let alone attempt to label him with other writers as an "absurdist" (in any traditional sense of the label, as first espoused by Martin Esslin).

Chapter 5

Beckett's notable contemporaries

While Samuel Beckett may have been the most influential and studied writer of the group, Beckett was by no means the lone voice of the 1950s to 1970s. In fact, some of Jean Genet and Eugene Ionesco's plays preceded the theatrical debut of Beckett. While theatre was these four writers' dominant genre, both Genet and Pinter, like Beckett, also wrote fiction and poetry. The link among them is that these four major writers are all indebted in one way or another to Beckett. However, also common to these four, is that they each influenced a whole host of future writers.

Edward Albee

Edward Franklin Albee III was born in 1928 and was adopted as a baby by wealthy parents and grew up in the affluent town of Larchmont in Westchester County, New York. His adoptive father's wealth came from his father, Edward Franklin Albee II, who made his money by owning several vaudeville theatres. This is how Albee was first acquainted with the theatre. Knowing he was gay since he was in his early teens, and never having a good relationship with his adoptive parents, Albee bounced around from school to school, getting expelled at each one. After being expelled from Trinity College in Hartford, Connecticut, he moved to Greenwich Village in New York City and wrote *The Zoo Story* in 1958, which quickly brought him acclaim. Since that time Albee has continued to write plays over the past six decades and has been an ardent supporter of the works of emerging American playwrights.

Maybe more so than any other writer associated with absurdism, Edward Albee has a very complex relationship with the absurd. While Esslin includes Albee as an integral absurdist in his 1961 *The Theatre of the Absurd*, Esslin also notes how decidedly non-absurdist Albee's plays are. In addition, Albee has publically stated Beckett and Pinter as his influences and Albee is one of the few writers associated with the absurd to directly confront and comment upon the categorization of "absurd." In a 1962 article that appeared in *The*

New York Times, entitled "Which Theatre is the Absurd One?" Albee, despite much skepticism, does not *fully* run away from the absurdist label; instead, he suggests what the absurd theatre *does* do and what it *is*. Albee claims, semi-contra Esslin, that absurd drama is, in fact, more *realistic* than traditional theatre.

While there are clear lines of dramatic influence tracing back to Samuel Beckett and Harold Pinter, Albee is, at base, a decidedly *humanistic* playwright. Albee's plays are largely thoroughly human journeys of self-realization through reason, many times also contemplating ethical behavior in difficult (sometimes no-win) situations. The difference with Albee and many other humanistic writers is that it is many times the world itself, other characters, or the character's own situation that forces the character(s) into the process of self-realization. In the character's journey, the audience is simultaneously forced into their own journey of self-realization. Part of the journey for Albee and his characters is the exploration of language and how the *precision of language* is vital for understanding our reality. Even more so, in *Tiny Alice* (1964), after Julian, a lay brother in the Church who was in a mental institution for six years because of his complex relationship with faith, describes God through opposites, Butler questions, "Six years in the loony bin for semantics?" and Julian's response is, "It is not semantics!"[1] What Julian (and Albee) mean is that it is not *just* semantics (as in a question over word choice), but it (i.e., language) is our (sole) reality. Maybe more so than any other absurdist playwright (and at odds with Esslin's assertion that the playwrights of the absurd devaluate language), Albee places extreme importance and *value* on language and the necessity for clarity and precision in order to communicate effectively and deeply with other humans.

Given Albee's long career and long list of plays, I will limit my analysis of Albee's plays to his award-winning plays: *The Zoo Story*; *Who's Afraid of Virginia Woolf?*; *A Delicate Balance*; *Seascape*; *Three Tall Women*; and *The Goat, or Who Is Sylvia?* In Albee's first play, *The Zoo Story* (1958), which garnered Albee his first Drama Desk Award (*The Goat, or Who is Sylvia?* was his second), the audience finds an upper-middle class Peter on a park bench in Central Park and the transient, Jerry, butting into Peter's quiet afternoon. Over the course of the short play, through a series of personal stories and prying questions, Jerry harasses or disturbs Peter into a frenzy, invading Peter's private space, forcing into the open what Peter would like to remain private even (or especially) to Peter's own consciousness. Peter must question his own life, which seems at first to be a stable fortress of (particularly American) normalcy. With Jerry's "suicide" at the hands of Peter (who is holding a knife when suddenly Jerry runs into it), Jerry ensures that Peter cannot merely forget the afternoon or remember it as an aberration of an otherwise quiet and comfy life.

Jerry implanted the seeds of self-doubt that should lead Peter into a more self-aware state concerning himself and, especially, his place in humanity. As Central Park is the "zoo" (and there actually is a zoo in Central Park) – a menagerie of animals that find themselves fighting for the same park bench, for the same sense of quietude and peace – Peter must learn that to live in harmony with others (and therefore get the peace he wants himself), he must come to grips with the violence and the unfairness of the animal kingdom. When Jerry interrupts Peter's afternoon, Peter cannot ignore the hierarchy of the animal kingdom by sticking his nose in his book that transports him to an imaginary world. Peter must face the world's injustices as real and as fact. By the end, Peter is the "animal" that both he, himself, and others fear: the life-sucking animal – the parasite – that does not have to do anything to survive, feeds himself, not caring that those he feeds off will eventually die.

While *The Zoo Story* established Albee's humanistic themes, it is *Who's Afraid of Virginia Woolf?* (1962) that not only cemented Albee as a premier American playwright, with Albee capturing his first Tony Award for Best Play (*The Goat, or Who is Sylvia?* also won a Tony Award for Best Play), but really saw Albee find his dramatic voice. Albee mixes the humanistic themes and theatrical realism about absurd situations from *The Zoo Story* and *The Death of Bessie Smith* (1960) with experimenting with language, which he did with Beckett-like language filled with non-sequiturs in *The Sandbox* (1960) and *The American Dream* (1961), and Albee's newfound insight and preoccupation with the need for precision in language. The play focuses on George, an associate professor of history at a small liberal arts college, and his wife Martha, the daughter of the college's president. The night that the play takes place, George and Martha return from a faculty dinner party and Martha, unknown to George at the beginning of the play, has invited a new (and very young) faculty member, Nick, and his wife, Honey, over for drinks. George's love of history's "glorious variety and unpredictability," in *Who's Afraid of Virginia Woolf?*, counteracts the precision and predictability of Nick's field of biology: "It is 'the surprise, the multiplexity, the sea-changing rhythm of . . . history' that gives life its humanistic quality, and love – George and Martha's love – its un-easily identifiable, but complex richness."[2]

But while George's field of history might be valued by George for its "unpredictability," George, especially early in the play, is the most precise and exacting character when it comes to language. He is constantly correcting the other characters on their grammar and word usage. But as the play proceeds, George comes to embody the motto that "All truth being relative." George comes to realize that language, just like Albee's sense of theatre, is a living and breathing organism that can be *used*, and that make-believe and the power to play with language help create not just a new reality, but a more understandable one.[3] It takes games (i.e., all the "games" that George plays with Martha and the guests), make-believe (i.e., the delivery of the telegram), and verbal word play to create a reality/situation in which George and Martha (and Nick and Honey) can see reality in a more true light. By the end of the play, George and Martha find themselves alone, without a false, paradoxical "son"-figure (as opposed to a "Father"-figure) to guide and comfort them in their times of trouble. They, especially George, realize that they must be reliant, not on an *illusion* (of a made-up son to comfort them), but be reliant on themselves and their fellow human (i.e., each other).

The play is, as Albee contends about the absurd, "realistic theater," as the *fourth wall* is exposed to display a couple in the privacy of their home, to show "man's condition as it is" by showing us not the pretty exterior of the house, but to show the strangers, Nick and Honey (and us, the audience) the ugly side of humanity.[4] But, maybe even more importantly, ugliness is also in the eyes of the beholder, as Martha's declaration of love for George as the only man who ever made her happy can attest. Martha's tender list of paradoxes about her feelings for George (i.e., "George who is good to me, and whom I revile; who understands me, and whom I push off; who can make me laugh, and I choke it back in my throat . . . "[5] etc.) casts off a simplified notion of love, which, seen in its all-encompassing, altruistic, and unconditional form, is just as illusory as the false promises of salvation found in the Latin prayer George utters near the end of the play.

Albee revisits the notion of *fear* in his 1966 play, *A Delicate Balance*, for which he won his first Pulitzer Prize. In the play, Agnes and Tobias, a late-middle-aged couple, find themselves with a full house, as Claire – Agnes' "alcoholic" sister – Julia, their adult daughter whose fourth marriage is on the rocks, and their best friends – Harry and Edna – who are all of a sudden *terrified* in their own home, all wind up staying with Agnes and Tobias. However, just as Agnes refines the notion of her own sense of fear, Albee presents an even-more complex type of fear than the fear of anticipated loneliness that George, and especially, Martha have in *Who's Afraid of Virginia Woolf?*:

AGNES: What astonishes me most – aside from my theoretically healthy fear – no, not fear, how silly of me – healthy speculation that I might someday become an embarrassment to you . . . what I find most astonishing in this world, with all my years . . . is Claire.

TOBIAS (*Curious*): Claire? Why?
AGNES: That anyone – be they one's sister, or not – can be so... well, I don't
  want to use an unkind word,'cause we're cozy here, arcn't we?
TOBIAS (*Smiled warning*): Maybe.
AGNES: As the saying has it, the one thing sharper than a serpent's tooth is a
  sister's ingratitude.
TOBIAS: (*Getting up, moving a chair*) The saying does not have it that way.
AGNES: Should... [6]

Agnes realizes that "fear" is, in a sense, more accurately, the "speculation"
of something terrible. Specifically, Agnes, herself, speculates "[becoming] an
embarrassment," the very thing her sister, Claire, *should*, but does not fear.

Much of *A Delicate Balance* is about loyalty to others and to one's own
ideals (and, by extension, oneself), and the subsequent need for a psychological self-martyrdom in order to be loyal to something one detests – as is the
case with Agnes toward Claire, Julia towards her parents (and, maybe, everyone), and Tobias toward Harry and Edna. The play, however, is largely also
about the "fear," or rather, "speculation" about "nothing" in particular "to
be... frightened of."[7] In a sense, "speculation" – the act of basing truth on
insufficient evidence – ultimately results in the fear of not confronting oneself
and/or what one believes or holds true.

The resolution of the play comes when Harry and Edna decide to go home.
Edna realizes that so much of human action is based upon speculation, simply
because humans are too scared to confront, not just the truth about the world,
but more essentially, the truth about themselves:

EDNA: ... It's sad to come to the end of it, isn't it, nearly the end; so much more
  of it gone by as... than left, and still not know – still not have learned... the
  boundaries, what we may not do... not ask, for fear of looking in a mirror
  we *shouldn't* have come.
AGNES (*A bit by rote*): Now, Edna...
EDNA: For our own sake; our own... lack. It's sad to know you've gone through
  it all, or most of it, without... that the one body you've wrapped your arms
  around... the only skin you've ever known... is your own – and that it's
  dry... and not warm.[8]

Unlike the other characters, Claire has looked in the mirror and at herself.
And, thus, Claire is the perfect tragicomic heroine. She could be an utterly sad
and pathetic character, but she is not because she knows what she *is* and what
she *is not*. And this willingness to see herself and, ultimately, laugh at it with
self-deprecating humor leads her to some type of spiritual freedom that eludes
the other characters. Claire, in some ways, is the ultimate Sisyphean heroine,

who not only *accepts* the reality of her situation, but looks straight into her own eyes – as she, herself, is much of the cause of her own suffering, and she knows it – and *laughs in revolt.*

In the next two decades, Albee entered what critics call his "hermetic period" because, as Albee says of his own plays, they are both "dense" and made to expand the boundaries of theatre."[9] This increase in experimentation is similar to what Beckett does in his plays in the late 1960s and 1970s, where both Beckett (as explored in the last chapter) and Albee examine the limits and possibilities of theatre and language. After plays like *Box* (1968) and *Quotations from Chairman Mao Tse Tung* (1968), which depart from any traditional sense of Aristotelian plot – or any *plot* for that matter – and what constitutes *dialogue,* Albee's *Seascape* (1975), which also won a Pulitzer, is slightly more traditional in dramatic structure, though, of course, it is about a human couple and two lizards at the beach.

While the element of the fantastical and ridiculous emerges with the introduction of talking anthropomorphic lizards, Albee's *Seascape* is, at base, still about Albee's constant preoccupation with language, both in the necessity for precision and, in part due to, the overlap between language and the border between fiction and reality. A conversation between the humans, Nancy and Charlie – a conversation that sounds as if it could come right out of the pages of the book, *Men are from Mars, Women are from Venus* – maybe captures Albee's sense of language better than any other passage in his entire oeuvre:

NANCY: . . . You asked me about the petulance – why it comes on me, even
        rarely. Well, it's like the sting of the bee: something you say, or do; or don't
        say, or don't do. And it brings the petulance on me – not that I like it, but it's
        a healthy sign, shows I'm still nicely alive.
CHARLIE (*Not too friendly*): Like when? Like what?
NANCY: What brings it on, and when?
CHARLIE (*Impatient*): Yes!
NANCY: Well, so many things.
CHARLIE: Give me *one.*
NANCY: No; I'll give you several.
CHARLIE: All *right.*
NANCY: "You've had a good life." (*Pause*)
CHARLIE (*Curiously angry*): All right. Go on.
NANCY: Do you know what I'm *say*ing?
CHARLIE: You're throwing it up to me; you're telling me I've had a . . .
NANCY: No-no-no! I'm saying what you *said*, what you told *me.* You told me,
        you said to me, "You've had a good life." I wasn't talking about *you,* though
        you *have.* I was saying what you said to me.

CHARLIE (*Annoyed*): Well, you have! You *have* had!
NANCY (*She, too*): Yes! Have *had*! What *about* that!
CHARLIE: What about it!
NANCY: *Am* not *having*. (*Waits for reaction; gets none*) Am not *having*? Am not
     having a good life?
CHARLIE: Well, of *course*!
NANCY: Then why say had? Why put it that way?
CHARLIE: It's a way of speaking!
NANCY: No! It's a way of thinking! *I* know the language, and I know *you*. You're
     not careless with it, or didn't used to be. Why *not* go to those places in the
     desert and let our heads deflate, if it's all in the past? Why not just *do* that?
CHARLIE: It was a way of speaking.
NANCY: Dear God, we're *here*. We've served our time, Charlie, and there's
     nothing telling us to do *that*, or any conditional; not anymore. Well, there's
     the arthritis in my wrist, of course, and the eyes have known a better season,
     and there's always the cancer or a heart attack to think about if we're bored,
     but besides all these things . . . what is there?
CHARLIE (*Somewhat triste*): You're at it again.
NANCY: I am! Words are lies; they *can* be, and you *use* them, but I know what's
     in your gut. I *told* you, didn't I?[10]

Nancy (and Albee) realizes how words *can* be *used*, in both their *fictive* and
factual uses. And without understanding or at least trying to understand, the
relationship between language and the self (or another), it is impossible not
to be muddled in confusion and fiction (both *through* language and *within*
oneself). As Albee writes, "Seascape wonders whether we are an evolving
species or perhaps a devolving one."[11] It is quite possible that the answer to
that question might be whether or not we realize what Nancy realizes above.
And if not, then we are not much different than talking lizards.

   While Albee's 1991 play, *Three Tall Women*, which captured a Pulitzer Prize
(Albee's third, surpassed only by Eugene O'Neill for most Pulitzers in drama),
is a surreal psychological, maybe, nightmare, this play about A, B, and C (who
are all the same woman, but at three different ages) is a look into the mind of a
woman, literally and figuratively, confronting herself. As a humanistic journey
across time and across identities (at different times), there are both continuities
among A, B, and C, and there are, naturally, clear differences among the three
selves. Despite the splintering of the self into three (unnamed) parts (and
something of an homage to Beckett's *Krapp's Last Tape*), *Three Tall Women*
is, in a sense, Albee's simplest play. But it is also his most lucid expression of
humanism: one is always on a journey with one's self, and only one's self. And
the only way to make sense of this journey (i.e., life) is to confront oneself (or,
more appropriately, one's selves).

Three Tall Women cemented Albee's legacy as one of the greatest American playwrights. *The Goat, or Who Is Sylvia?* (2002) displayed that Albee still had more in him, as many expected the elder Albee to be way past his prime, and the play garnered Albee a Tony and a Drama Desk Award. The play is not for the prudish, but it is also not really about what it is about. *The Goat* is about Martin, a Pritzker-prize winning architect, who – despite all appearances (and realities) of having a wonderful family life – falls in love with a goat named Sylvia. In some ways, especially given the fact that Martin's teenage son is struggling with his new-found homosexual identity, this play (using bestiality as a parallel) is a thinly veiled allegory about homosexuality: it is a tragedy to have desires that one cannot fulfill in a socially acceptable manner. But when one starts to apply this logic to, say, a pedophile (and this is hinted at when Martin tells the story of a father who bounces his baby on his lap and gets an erection), there is something utterly tragic here; also, think about a psychopath who lusts for killing. Whose fault is it that a pedophile or a psychopath have those desires? It's no one's fault, especially one's own. But what if they act on their desires? Of course, they are held (and should be) responsible. But are we not to feel bad for them? In a sense, it *is* unfair that they can never have some of their most basic urges and desires satisfied. *The Goat* is perhaps Albee's most socially aware play: not in its most traditional guise like in the confrontation of social/economic classes as in *The Zoo Story*, but it is a deep investigation into human-and-society and human-and-self-in-society.

Like Albee's most iconic play, *Who's Afraid of Virginia Woolf?*, *The Goat*, however, is also a stunningly complex love story. Martin and his wife, Stevie, have the very banter that George and Martha could have (if not for the fear and sadness within them). Martin and Stevie are best friends, lovers, and each other's greatest inspiration. And despite Martin's affair with a goat, Martin deeply loves Stevie. And while parallels can be made to a bisexual-heterosexual couple – where the bisexual (may or may not) be fully satisfied with sex from only one sex/gender, but still utterly loves their heterosexual partner – Albee's play boils down to two fundamental questions: what is love? And is there any way to love (or be loyal) to more than one person?

The first question – what is love? – is raised when Martin tries to persuade the rest of the characters that Sylvia loves him (and it is not him raping an innocent, non-consensual being). And through this investigation, we start to wonder things like, does my dog or cat actually love me? If so, why? And, if not, do humans actually love, or, is love something made up to justify ourselves feeling good and getting what we want? This question is unanswered. The second question – is there any way to love (or be loyal) to more than one person? – has more of a concrete answer: no, or at least, probably not.

The question appears to be something like, is it ok to have two partners?, but it is really a much deeper question. It is almost as though this question is ripped from the Hebrew bible, and particularly, the story of Abraham and Isaac, and the New Testament, particularly the parable of the "prodigal son" (also known by scholars as "a certain man had two sons"). In both of these biblical stories, while it appears on the surface that Abraham and the father choose wisely, think, however, about the emotional scars left on Isaac (knowing that his father chose God over his own life) and on the elder brother (who always did the right things, and was never acknowledged for his devotion to his father and to his own good sense of morality and ethics). This raises a deeply problematic issue: as soon as one doles out love to one person (as love is a person-to-person bond), it appears to anyone else (and is partly true), that love is being withheld from others. And, thus, despite everything that Martin does do for Stevie, or his son, the moment that these two find out that Martin has given his love (even a part of his love) to the goat, it is as if all of Martin's love is dangled in front of Stevie and the son's face, and given instead to a goat. The sacrifice of the ram and the slaughtering of the kid (in the two biblical stories), and Stevie's slaughtering of the goat (in the play), all three of which do not actually resolve the problem, all reinforce the tragedy, or really, absurdity (in Camus' strictest sense of the idea) of the fact that human desire(s) is never met by the reality of the world. For all of the above questions that *The Goat* raises, it is in this play – perhaps more so than any other play or piece of literature discussed in this entire book – that Albee has created the single greatest expression of Camus' sense of absurdity.

In Albee's plays, then, it is easy to see the four common threads typical of writers of absurd literature. While Albee's take on these four threads is markedly different than those of Beckett or the other writers in this chapter, Albee clearly (1) experiments with language and contemplates the need for precision in language; (2) writes tragicomedies, as his plays, despite often being tragic (often because of lost love), are also hysterical in their incisive wit (often between two warring main characters, most notably George and Martha, and Martin and Stevie); (3) most noticeable in *The Zoo Story* and *The Goat*, Albee's plays (while conforming to some modern sense of the unities, except in plays like *Three Tall Women*, which deconstructs the unities) ultimately leaves so many of his plays with loose ends that are not tied up; and (4) Albee's characters and the audience, while not in nonsensical situations, find themselves in clearly unusual situations that produce feelings of discomfort (i.e., the situations are somewhat plausible, but ridiculous in that who would ever find themselves in such uncomfortable positions as Albee's characters are placed?).

But like Jean Genet, it is not as though Albee stuck to some of the absurd formula. Albee, particularly in the 1970s, was really experimenting with what theatre is and what it can do. And like Genet in *The Blacks*, Albee, even more frequently in this period, broke the "forth wall." Clearly, it would be wrong to assert that Albee's only influence is Beckett and the organic growth of absurd literature. Albee, writing in the US, was also (either directly or indirectly) influenced by the experimental theatre during the 1960s–70s, with attacks on realism, many times by breaking the "fourth wall."

Jean Genet

Jean Genet was born in 1910 to a French prostitute, who put him up for adoption at the age of one, after which he was raised in Alligny-en-Morvan in central France by a foster family. Despite a supposedly loving father and doing well in school, his childhood and the rest of his life were marked by attempts at running away and petty theft. Finally jailed without parole for homosexuality and released by pardon after a number of writers showed their support for him, Genet was politically active from the late 1960s onward. Having developed throat cancer, Genet was found dead in a Paris hotel room in 1986, apparently dying from falling and hitting his head on the ground.

One idea most typifies the plays and novels of Jean Genet: confusion reigns supreme. Whether it is the audience member/reader or the characters themselves, there is always some veil hiding the truth, causing confusion, because of some type of initial confusion. For Pinter, the audience/reader feels lost because the subtext is simply not there; for Genet, the layers of illusion must be stripped away before Genet's work can make sense. Thus, the absurdity and ridiculousness of the play is not necessarily the situation of the characters, as many of them are aware of what is happening, but that the characters cannot know what is going on when their actions seem so nonsensical. The lack of logical linearity in his dialogue, punctuated by equally non-linear plot lines, creates something of the sense of Lucky's monologue in Beckett's *Godot*: there are extremely intelligent lines and phrases that get lost in the episodic verbal outpouring. However, for Genet (whose playwriting preceded Beckett's playwriting) this similar effect occurs, rather, because we do not know the whole story, usually because the characters are hiding or not divulging the truth, sometimes just to us (i.e., the reader/audience) and sometimes to other characters. In short, and this is best represented in his play *The Blacks*, as long as confusion remains, as long, though, as someone does know the truth, then revolt and the ability to have control (where it does not seem possible) is still within reach.

While Genet is not necessarily seen as a political writer, and his own history of being jailed because he was gay is not generally at the forefront of his work, Genet's contemporary history of French colonial and post-colonial revolt cannot be ignored, especially since Genet's contemporary writers, Sartre and Camus, made such a public feud over whether or not France should continue its patriarchal role in relation to Algeria. As Genet seems to concur, revolt was only possible when those who were colonized (and this also works for slaves) continued to let the colonizers (masters) think they knew both how things stood and that they, the colonizers (masters), were in total control. While not really ever directly referring to this trope, in order to make things better and more equal, the archetypal black trickster (though taking many different guises) is needed in order to spread confusion in Genet's dystopic socio-economically uneven worlds, while having some master plan to improve things.

In Genet's three most notable plays, *The Maids* (1947), *The Balcony* (1958), and *The Blacks: A Clown Show* (1959), we see the similar uneven relationship play throughout: servant-master, commoner-autocrat, and colonized-colonizer, respectively. *The Maids* begins with what appears to be a wealthy Madame berating her, talking down to her, and being unreasonably demanding, seemingly for no other reason than to put the maid in her place. The Madame keeps implying/saying that her maid only loves her because she wants to inherit something. Thus, there is an uneasy, totally unequal relationship between Madame and her maid: Madame wants to believe her and truly loves her, and the maid must make the Madame believe that she does, in fact, truly love her. Madame must fool herself; the maid must fool Madame. But this uneven relationship becomes both confusing and more complex in the "I'll have my crown and I shall stroll about the apartment" maid's attempt at reassuring the Madame:

SOLANGE: I want to help you. I want to comfort you, but I know I disgust you. I'm repulsive to you. And I know it's because you disgust me. When slaves love one another, it's not love.
CLAIRE: And me, I'm sick of seeing my image thrown back at me by a mirror, like a bad smell. You're my bad smell. Well, I'm ready. Ready to bite. I'll have my crown and I shall stroll about the apartment.[12]

Somehow, now, they are both "slaves," "mirror" images of one another. It seems that they are both beholden and enslaved by the power dynamic created between the two.

Their own delusion, or audience confusion, pops when the doorbell rings: it is the *real* Madame, and they go back to both being maids. The two maids have been playing, pretending or role-playing, or *acting out* the actual relationship they both have with her boss, the Madame of the house. When the Madame does leave, the two maids go back to the roles they were playing before the Madame arrived.

Genet's version of the absurd imparts its strangeness because the audience is missing the whole story and therefore some lines seem out of place or just plain odd. But one thing that really separates Genet from almost every other absurdist is that all of the needed information does eventually come out. Plus, unlike Beckett and Pinter, who both – more so than any other absurdist – never even hint at providing a reliable back story and/or subtext, Genet's plays kind of resolve and become comprehensible once the truth behind the illusion is exposed. Genet's notion of strange and ridiculous, *his* absurd, is really a battle of appearance versus reality and the way that we become uncomfortable when those two are juxtaposed. That is, we are forced to decide about the reality we thought we knew and, subsequently, take up another/a new reality to make sense of what is in front of us.

In Genet's play *The Balcony*, much of the confusion arises because what is happening in the play – a revolution – is precisely the moment where power roles are in upheaval: reversed, changed, and/or subverted. And the mini-world of the play, the brothel in the same city that is undergoing a revolution, serves as a microcosm of the shifting roles in power dynamics that are going on in the larger city because of the revolution. In this play, everyone is in revolt. But, most importantly, that revolt takes many forms. Almost more so than any other piece of absurd literature, *The Balcony* is both the greatest homage and the greatest critique of Camus' *The Myth of Sisyphus*. Genet's revolution-within-a-revolution suggests that humans are built for revolt, by nature and by nurture. But the play also demonstrates how revolt can be rationalized both for good, or for evil. Revolt becomes a pretext for selfish or selfless behavior. The rebel (via Camus), but adapted by Genet, justifies/rationalizes the suffering to him or herself, either as inevitable (for the villain), or as probable, but avoidable (for the hero).

The Balcony both blurs and confuses the line between hero and villain, probing the ways revolt is necessary and unwarranted. It is in seeing how closely the hero and villain are to one another that the audience is left unsure of how to proceed in a world where the good and the bad are essentially one in the same, and the return to *status quo* becomes inevitable because of this (and the pre-revolutionary *status quo* returns at the end of the play).

It is with *The Blacks: A Clown Show* that Genet and all of his preoccupations are at their best. The play is a verbal bricolage of utter nonsense, beautiful poetic prose, and simple direct speech to the audience. Played, or meant to be played by black actors, some wearing white masks, the black characters/actors put on a "clown show" for the white autocrats. The black characters/actors say they must reenact the murder of a white woman so that the court of whites may pass judgment and punish the murderer. However, this "clown show" we come to find out is a simple ruse to distract the whites in order that the blacks can execute, offstage, a traitor to their own cause. In the Notes for the play, Genet says that the play must be performed for a white audience. The idea here is that the white (implied) colonizers must confront our own illusions about civilizing the black colonized. Given that it is so easy to miss the fact that the entire play-within-the-play exists only to mete out justice out of the eyes of the white autocrats, since it is only a passing remark that the trader is killed offstage, the whites in the audience are just as much being fooled as the colonizers. But, the white audience is equated and implicated as being no different than the white colonizers on stage.

The white masks both depersonalize the whites and make their action seem universal. But the "clown show" of civility is also the subject of ridicule, and the silly masks demonstrate the ridiculousness of trying to mask the real project behind the civilizing effort of colonization: that is, masking the power and land grabbing that led to plundering the natural resources of the country all in the name of offering a patriarchal helping hand of civilizing the "black savages." Through the "trial" of the black murderer, it is rather the white audience who is under trial; the white audience must because of what is implied, put themselves, and their passivity and complicity on "trial."

But while this is simultaneous, Genet's most generically "absurd" play, as his experimenting with various types of language; his non-Aristotelian fragmented and stopped and restarted plot lines; the "strangeness" of such a confusing narrative and dialogue; and the mix of humor both comic and dark, within a clearly tragic story (i.e., a murder)– it depends tremendously on one key feature: it breaks the "fourth wall," not only in the play to do so in the absurd canon, certainly one of the few (along with a few of Albee's plays and Jack Gelber's *The Connection*). That is, we can place this play just as easily under the influence of Bertolt Brecht and avant-garde experimental theatre as much as we can put it alongside the other absurd plays and other pieces of absurd literature. That is important to know because it demonstrates that while there are elements that clearly allow us to group absurd writers together, these are not a monolithic group. They, including Genet, share certain techniques and forms, but clearly they each have their own voices and influences, too.

While Genet's plays do not have an autobiographical air to them, his novels are quite a different story. The subject of his two most famous books,
The Thief's Journal (1949) and *Our Lady of the Flowers* (1943) is almost an
homage to the lifestyle Genet, himself, led. In and out of prison throughout
Europe his entire life for stealing and homosexuality, Genet captures a sense of
the eroticism of stealing and (what was then illegal) with homosexuality. Crime
is thrilling, beautiful, and erotic in these books as Genet/narrator writes in *The
Thief's Journal*, "there is a close relationship between flowers and convicts."[13]
The narrative explains, that they are, in a way, two sides of the same coin: "the
fragility and the delicacy of the former are of the same nature as the brutal
insensitivity of the latter."[14] The narrator is drawn to crime because it is made
up of such "chronic conditions" as "smells of sweat, sperm and blood."[15] The
fine line between good/beauty and evil/ugliness that is explored in *The Thief's
Journal* was explored first in *Our Lady of the Flowers* through paying homage
to the criminal within us. As Genet writes at the beginning of *Our Lady of
the Flowers* that, "it is an honor of their crimes that I am writing my book."[16]
The "their" refers to the pictures of criminals that the narrator hung on the
his prison walls. Thus, the story told throughout is the story of the narrator's fictional criminals. But these criminals are all versions of the narrator
himself.

Part of the novelty of *Our Lady of the Flowers* is this clearly fictional story
told in a seemingly real story, but yet, the fictional story aims to tell the truth
of the narrators in her life, maybe better and more truthfully than any straight
narrative history could. This story is something like modified cubism, where
artists (most notably in the early Picasso) exposed the inner parts in the shape
of a three-dimensional view, instead of just the surface. Here, Genet fractures
the narrator – each character, then, being rounded and fleshed out from their
nameless two-dimensional photographs – and the many inner parts of the
narrator can be captured separately, but more capably of seeing the narrator
as a whole: though the narrator claims that "this book aims to be only a small
fragment of my inner life."[17]

One thing to note, and one of the major reasons that I use the date 1950s to
1970s in this book, is that these two earlier books by Genet are not particularly
experimental with their language, and they are told in a relatively normal arc
typical of novels of that time, and thus, it is hard to see these books as absurd.
However, if we consider the preoccupations of the two books (particularly
the Cubist-like fragmentation of *Our Lady of the Flowers*), then we see how
the content later affects the form. Thus, by the time we get to especially *The
Balcony* and *The Blacks* in the late 1950s, the fragmentation of reality matches
the fragmentation of both language and narrative arc.

While there has been nothing written on Genet and the British philosopher, F. H. Bradley, and it is highly doubtful that Bradley influenced Genet, it is almost uncanny how Bradley's philosophy, biggest at the turn of the nineteenth century, anticipates Genet's work. In short, Bradley suggests that reality is splintered into many appearances, while all appearances can never be put back together to form/observe a coherent whole truth about an object, the best way to approach the truth of an object is to view as many of its splintered parts/appearances as possible. Whether it is the criminals that are fleshed out in *Our Lady of the Flowers* to represent a fragmented collage of the inner life of the narrator; the two maids acting out the power dynamic they both experience, by one being a maid and the other being a Madame; the microcosm that is pulled out separately from the streets of the revolution; or the play on top of the play in order to hide the truth; Genet's most notable works both explore reality by exposing us to splintered appearances, which when viewed alone are confusing and fragmentary, but once all the pieces are viewed together, some truth/reality emerges.

Eugene Ionesco

Born Eugen Ionescu in 1909 in Romania to an Orthodox Christian father and Protestant mother. Ionesco was raised primarily in France. After his parents divorced in 1925, he returned with them to Romania and eventually studied French literature at the University of Bucharest. He returned in 1938 to finish his doctoral thesis, after which he returned to Romania after the outbreak of WWII. In 1942 he returned to France, living first in Marseilles until he moved to Paris after the Liberation. Ionesco died in 1994 at the age of 84.

When I am casually asked, what is absurd literature, or I am teaching an introduction to absurd literature, I always begin by sharing the plot of Samuel Beckett's *Waiting for Godot*: two men wait and engage in idle discourse for the entire play for someone named Godot, who never comes. First, this is the very play by the very writer who gave this organic "movement," if you will, its wings. Second, it is considered one of the greatest plays ever written (though I would personally also include Albee's *Who's Afraid of Virginia Woolf?* in that list along with Sophocles' *Oedipus Rex*, Shakespeare's *Hamlet*, O'Neill's *Long Day's Journey into Night*, and perhaps because of its influence on the shape of twentieth-century drama, Pirandello's *Six Characters in Search of an Author*). Third, if you took every absurd piece of literature and somehow morphed them together into a single work, *Godot* would probably most resemble that amalgamate piece of absurd literature. And fourth, Beckett and his *Godot* is the most likely writer and play (along with *Virginia Woolf*) to have been read, or at least heard of, by university-educated general readers. However, especially if my interlocutor(s) has not heard of Beckett or *Godot*, and if he or she (or they) has not read a good ten-plus examples of absurd literature, my natural follow-up to explaining a typical example of a plot of absurd literature is Eugene Ionesco's *Rhinoceros*: on an utterly normal day, out of the blue, a single rhinoceros runs through a small provincial French town; eventually more and more rhinoceroses run through town, and one by one, the townsfolk turn into rhinos, with only one man, the town's semi-drunk, left to save humanity.

Actually, there are many times when I question why I normally choose this play to serve as an example of the absurd, when Ionesco's use of the *fantastical* is, for the most part, a huge departure from other absurd writers. But I fall prey to giving (at least in a learned fashion) the general reader a simplified account of these plays and play somewhat into the semi-correct and semi-incorrect public imagination of the absurd by referring to *Rhinoceros* as a prime example of this genre of literature. What I mean, as I discussed at length in Chapter 1, is that so often the general educated reader thinks that the absurd is more or less the avant-garde, and some of the most notable works of avant-garde literature in the twentieth century are works that run counter to realism. These most notable twentieth-century experiments against realism – Kafka's "The Metamorphosis," Pirandello's *Six Characters in Search of an Author*, any and all plays by Brecht that break the "fourth wall" – are *not* pieces of absurd literature, the first two are magical/fantastical, the third is simply jarring as it works against suspending our disbelief when we see a play or read or watch a movie, and makes us realize that what we are watching really is not real. So by using Ionesco's *Rhinoceros* to typify the absurd, I worry that I, myself, am perpetuating this myth (that *I* have tried so hard to demystify) that absurd equals avant-garde/avant-garde equals absurd.

However, I do feel justified in turning to *Rhinoceros*, ultimately because while a sense of ridiculousness is common throughout absurd literature, much of that sense is very subtle. And *Rhinoceros* is the outward expression/manifestation of the inner sense of ridiculousness and absurdity that is the hallmark feature of absurd literature. *Rhinoceros* has the same sense of universality of Beckett's works. Set in a semi-nondescript French provincial town, the audience is treated to a hilarious typical meeting at a café between a serious, earnest chap, Jean, and his coworker, Berenger, essentially a drunk. Most of the sense of the absurd in Ionesco's work, and especially in *Rhinoceros*, rises from the utter lack of general and self-awareness. It is as if, and when, the characters are unable to hear themselves think and speak for a single moment of reflection that the illogical and nonsensical nature of what has just been said is exposed. Take, for example, the conversation over work and duty that transpires between Jean and Berenger, Jean says that everyone has to work; then later, "The superior man that fulfills his duty."[18] But if everyone is, following logic, superior, then nobody is "superior." This is a preview of the character of the logician, and his vastly illogical syllogisms that yield even more illogical conclusions. It is one thing if the logician does not see his own errors in his logic, but it is entirely another issue when the townsfolk praise such faulty logic. The audience laughs because how can someone miss what is so obvious, but, then laughing at the characters, is to laugh at ourselves. Ionesco deeply implicates his audiences, but the guise of his general silliness makes the medicine easier to swallow: aggressiveness leads to defensiveness, while laughter allows what needs to be said to be said.

The both funny and sad (though hidden in laughter) part of the play is the very earnest discussion about whether the townsfolk saw one rhino twice, or two different rhinos. They are in deep, serious conversation, and for that, they should be admired. However, once the townsfolk come together as a group, it is as if they cloud each other's vision; nobody is able to see above the clouds. Meaning, nobody seems aware of either how dangerous and unusual it is that a rhino is stampeding through the town. There is safety in numbers, but that is precisely why this is such a dangerous situation, for the lack of individual concern is quieted by the safety of the group. And that is why, one by one, the plague of rhinoceritis becomes seemingly irreversible. And the only one left in the battle for the sake of humanity is ironically the one character in the beginning of the play that appeared to drink precisely to escape from the pain of humanity. Given that Ionesco's early play, *The Bald Soprano* (1950) is subtitled, "Anti-Play," maybe this is why, in part, that Berenger is something (as is commonly argued) of an anti-hero.

This brings us back to Ionesco's early play, *The Bald Soprano, Anti-Play*. As just the title suggests, Ionesco is trying to subvert the (implied) traditional play. The beginning amusingly attacks the very technique that absurd literature essentially did away with: exposition. Exposition, again, is the technique of relaying the back story and/or subtext so that the audience has a sense of context. In this way, the anti-play is less of a noun, as an opposite to (traditional) plays, but more of a verb, against a (traditional) play. Here, Ionesco is exposing how unrealistic theatrical realism actually is. The character Mr. and Mrs. Smith, must awkwardly and unnaturally talk about themselves, what is going on, and provide context for themselves and their actions.

But soon, maybe because the play is exposed as a play, the linearity of the Aristotelian arc dissolves. A couple, who are called Mr. and Mrs. Martin, realize they are husband and wife, even though another claims that this cannot be since neither is the person we think they are. Fire Chief visits our first couple, Mr. and Mrs. Smith and nonsensical stories are altered by the Fire Chief. By the end of the play, after language, itself, begins to disintegrate:

MR. SMITH: The pope elopes! The pope's got no horoscope. The horoscope's bespoke.

MRS. MARTIN: Bazaar, Balzac, bazooka!

MR. MARTIN: Bizarre, beaux-arts, brassieres!

MR. SMITH: A, e, i, o, u, a, e, i, o, u, a, e, I, o, u, i!

MRS. MARTIN: B, c, d, f, g, l, m, n, p, r, s,t, v, w, x, z!

MR. MARTIN: From sage to stooge, from stage to serge!

MRS. SMITH [*imitating a train*]: Choo, choo, choo, choo, choo, choo, choo, choo, choo, choo, choo![19]

The audience, maybe in anticipation of the future circularity of Beckett, though, realizes that the play has not come to some resolution, but just starts all over again with Mr. and Mrs. Martin. The end of the play is not natural; we are left with a new beginning and an untold end.

Ionesco's *The Chairs* is his most tragicomic play, only because the two characters on stage are very old. The basic plot of the play is an old couple who is hosting a party, but nobody, despite them thinking otherwise, comes or occupies the many chairs set up around the stage. We see the same ridiculousness of the lack of self- or just general awareness as the couple misses the fact that nobody is there. But it is also deeply sad, in part because they are old, and (1) either their faculties are gone, and/or (2) all their friends and acquaintances are dead, and nothing is left but empty chairs.

Once his career moves into the 1960s and 1970s, most notably with *The Killers* (1959), *Exit the King* (1963), and *Macbett* (1972), unlike with Beckett plays where the language gets more and more experimental, sometimes barely even resembling language and/or theatre, Ionesco's language is more natural (than in the 1950s), and he observes more of an Aristotelian arc (than in the 1950s) in his later plays, showing how little he was beholden to any formula or ideal that organically first grew among absurd writers in the 1950s.

Harold Pinter

Harold Pinter was born in Hackney in East London in 1930 to lower-middle class Jewish parents. After doing well at the Hackney Downs School where he played cricket and began to write poetry and acted in school plays, Pinter attended the Royal Academy of Dramatic Arts from 1948 until he dropped out from a nervous breakdown in 1949. During the war, he went to trial twice and was fined for his registration as a conscientious objector, after which he attended the Central School of Speech and Drama. Pinter began a twelve-year stage career as an actor, touring frequently, and this was where he met his wife, Vivian Merchant, herself a noted actress. After an affair, Pinter married the historian, Antonia Fraser, to whom he was married for thirty-three years, until his death in 2008. At first, Pinter was criticized for not taking a political stand in his writing, but became very politically active during the last twenty-five or so years of his life. Pinter won the Nobel Prize in Literature in 2005.

Much like Albee, Pinter cares deeply about human communication. While Albee demonstrates the constant tinkering with precise language that needs to be done in order for genuine communication and relationships to blossom, Pinter portrays more of the dystopic vision when/where communication is unsuccessful. For Pinter, language so often rests on what is not being said; Pinter's experiments with silence, pauses, and vapid questions dominate the pages of his writing. Thus, since language fails to communicate in the world of his writing, the result is that much positioning for power and attention is needed. While, over the course of his writing career, Pinter's vision becomes less abstract, more subtle, and less philosophical/more personal – that is, his writing moves more toward something of a family room tragicomedy versus his earlier absurd tragicomedies, which are more experimental in language, are set in more ridiculous (less plausible) situations, and given the lack of subtext, lack exposition and endings – Pinter's *oeuvre* constantly returns to the feeling of isolation that he explores in his earliest writings. In short, because human communication fails, or at least so often humans fail at communication, humans must jostle for attention/affection by seeking to be in a more powerful position. But these necessary attempts at gaining power also ruin humans' chances of receiving genuine attention and affection. And, thus, paradoxically, humans become entrapped and isolated by the very things they do in order to try to prevent isolation. This cycle highlights the ridiculous and absurd situations Pinter's characters find themselves in due to their inability to say what needs to be said.

Pinter began his writing career by dabbling in short stories before he found his general genre of choice, drama. Pinter's second short story, composed in 1955 (though published later), "The Examination" is a short story that seems as though it could have been written by Franz Kakfa. Two men are in a room, one interrogating/examining the other: it has the universal and timeless quality of Kafka, and imparts the feeling of the helplessness of being acted upon by the powerful quality of Kafka's *The Trial* or "In the Penal Colony." Being trapped, in a sense, in a single room is a metaphor that Pinter returns to over and over again, even though later in his career the metaphor is only subtly drawn. As Pinter has publically stated many times about Beckett's influence, this short story also feels like a Beckettian game, for example (though Pinter wrote his first), the game between the offstage presence and the man in the desert in Beckett's *Act without Words I*. Without anything spoken but a *posturing of silences*, in both Pinter's "The Examination" and Beckett's previously mentioned play, the roles reverse between the two participants, the one who first finds himself subject to the other ends up having control by the end.

Pinter literally puts on stage this feeling of being trapped and alone in a room shortly after in two one-act plays, *The Room* (1957) and *The Dumb Waiter* (1960). In his first play, *The Room*, Rose and (apparently her husband) Bert lease a room, where the entire action of the play takes place. Wondering whether or not someone has moved in to the basement apartment, Rose is greeted by a couple looking to lease her room. After a confusing conversation with the landlord, Rose is told that her father wants her to return home. She meets an old black man, Riley, who appears to be her father telling her to come home. At the end of the play, Bert beats up Riley, and Rose says she can no longer see. Here much of the confusion rests with the language due to the fact that there is no subtext, as the backstory leaves out the necessary details to put the puzzle pieces together. The story, and thus how it is told, feels random because we are missing so much of the connecting information. But what is known is all at a metaphorical level. Rose's room, her home, is threatened by the prospects of her being forced out, and the confrontation with her possible father –there seems to be a troubled past – destroys her sense of (fore)sight.

Whereas *The Room* focuses on the weak and an intrusion that leaves Rose literally and metaphorically less connected with the world (i.e., through losing her sense of sight), *The Dumb Waiter* appears to be about two hit men, or men who are carrying out some job like hit men. Both waiting in a room for instructions from some unknown person, Ben and Gus are subject to the whims of this mysterious person in power. Waiting for directions for the job, they start receiving messages for food requests through the dumb waiter in the room. Throughout the play, Gus constantly leaves the main part of the room to use the restroom. So while he leaves, he is never really gone. But when Gus does finally leave the room to get a glass of water, he comes back all beaten up. While clearly Pinteresque in style, this play is perhaps Pinter's greatest homage to Beckett and *Godot*. Ben and Gus are *waiting*, literally and figuratively, throughout the time of the play for instructions from some offstage person; their actions and thoughts are dependent upon this unknown entity. And Gus' trips to the restroom are reminiscent of the times when Vladimir leaves the stage to relieve himself. And, like Vladimir and Estragon, these two – Ben and Gus – have a semi-dependent relationship on the other. Whereas for Beckett, the world is an open expanse and there is simply nowhere to go because there is nothing to do (and Godot is appropriately set on a country road in seemingly the middle of nowhere), for Pinter, the world is like being trapped in a room because we are unsure of the whole story surrounding us – who controls us, what do we control, and what do we know or not know – and, thus, we are subject to the whims of those more powerful than us (or, maybe, those who *know* more than we do).

In further examining the idea of knowledge or lack thereof, Pinter also returns to the *examination*, or the interrogation, found in "The Examination," in his first full-length, but still his most famous play, *The Birthday Party* (1958). The play is well known for what has come to be known as the "interrogation scene" where Goldberg and McCann metaphorically beat Stanley into a grunting pulp by asking him a menacing series of rapid-fire questions, but as I have argued elsewhere, the play is full of interrogating. Maybe least obvious of these interrogations is the beginning of the play when Meg is questioning her husband Petey about every mundane aspect of his breakfast:

MEG: Is that you, Petey?
    Pause.
    Petey, is that you?
    Pause.
    Petey?
PETEY: What?
MEG: Is that you?
PETEY: Yes, it's me.
MEG: What? (*Her face appears at the hatch.*) Are you back?
PETEY: Yes.
MEG: I've got your cornflakes ready. (*She disappears and reappears.*) Here's your cornflakes....
    Are they nice?
PETEY: Very nice.
MEG: I thought they'd be nice (*She sits at the table.*) You got your paper?
PETEY: Yes.[20]

This type of dialogue (which continues for a couple more pages) is off-putting for theatregoers precisely because of how essentially meaningless the conversation is. Why dramatize the routine of breakfast? Drama is supposed to condense action and conflict, not literally drag on about inaction and "idle talk" (to go back to *Godot*), right? Pinter, however, wants the audience to see how much more needs to be said. Meg and Petey need to talk, but because they do not talk, paradoxically, Meg talks about things that do not need to be discussed. Meg appropriately keeps asking Petey questions, but they are really not questions, or not questions that require anything other than yes or no responses, and thus only facts are being communicated: nothing personal, nothing subjective, nothing with any emotion tied to it in order to actually connect with another human being. Thus, and which came first is indecipherable and does not even matter at this point, Meg's questions are beyond numerous and meaningless because she is just trying to find something, even a word out of Petey, and Petey has nothing left to say because he has repeatedly seemed to say it all and, at this point, is trying merely to quiet Meg's nagging and meaningless questions. And this is why Stanley, their boarder, is the object of Meg's attention. Having no communication with her husband, in an unhealthy manner, Meg has developed a bizarre mother/lover relationship with and dotes upon Stanley, who, himself cannot or will not communicate any truth about himself and his past. While the play appears to focus on Stanley, Stanley is the outward expression and demonstrates the consequences of Meg and Petey's lack of communication.[21]

The Birthday Party shows that there is potential for harm by not saying or risking anything. So often, Pinter seems to point out, our days are filled with meaningless conversations, conversations that have become routine, that require nothing of the self to be shared. And while sharing oneself can be difficult, can place one in a vulnerable state, and it seems much safer to not open up, Pinter wants the audience to know that there is (a metaphorical) danger lurking in playing it safe. Whether one becomes out of practice or loses one's will to have a meaningful exchange of subjective thoughts and feelings, one falls prey to menace of interrogation and eventually becomes deadened like Stanley at the end of the play.

With Pinter's *The Caretaker* (1960), we see another play with many of the same themes and techniques in his above plays and short story. However, while *The Caretaker* and the above three plays are Pinter's most notable early plays, it is his two versions of *The Dwarfs* (both as a radio play and a novel) that kind of mark a point of departure for Pinter. Of all of his works, what is it about *this* story that needs to be told via a radio play, which was also later adapted for the stage, and via a novel? Here, Pinter does, perhaps, give his most clearly stated expression of what is at stake in "rooms" in the play, *The Dwarfs*:

- The rooms we live in open and shut . . .
- They change shape at their own will, he said. I would have no quarrel, I wouldn't grumble, you see, if these rooms would remain the same, would keep to some consistency. But they don't. And I can't see the boundaries, the limits, which I've been led to believe are natural. That's the trouble. I'm

all for the natural behaviour of rooms, doors, staircases, the lot. But I can't rely on them. When, for example, I look through a train window, at night and see the yellow lights, very clearly, I see what they are, and I see that they're still. But they're only still because I'm moving. I know that they do move along with me, and when we go round a bend, they bump off. But I know that they are still, just the same they are, after all, stuck on polls which are rooted in the earth. So they must be relatively still, in their own right, insofar the earth itself still, which of course isn't, but that's another matter. The point is, in a nutshell, that I can only appreciate such facts when I'm moving. When I am still, nothing around me follows a natural course of conduct. I'm not saying I'm any criterion myself. I wouldn't say that. After all, but when I'm on that train I'm not really moving at all. That's obvious. I'm in the corner seat. I'm still. I am, perhaps, being, but I do not move. Neither do the yellow lights. The train moves, granted, what's a train got to do with it?[22]

In Pinter's early "rooms" – most especially in *The Birthday Party* and *The Dumb Waiter* – the link to the outside world comes from a newspaper. The train, and the movement it affords, is everything to do with it, and the only way to observe stability is to be in the process of moving without having to exert any motion oneself. In short, the early "rooms" are stuffy and dead, the only sign of life whirling about comes from a newspaper. In *The Dwarfs*, however, one must be out in life, moving out of the room, in order to understand (what happens in) the room. Movement, simply, allows for perspective.

The novel and play follow the lives of four young Londoners, as they are the dwarfs:

> The dwarfs are back on the job, Len said. They're keeping an eye on proceedings. They clock in very early, scenting the event. They are like kite in a city disguise; they only work in cities. However, they are certainly skilled labourers and their trade is not without risk. They wait for a smoke signal and unpack their kit. They are on the spot with no time wasted and circle the danger area. There, they take up positions, which they are able to change at a moment's notice, if necessary. But they don't stop work until the job in hand is ended, one way or another.[23]

But why are they the dwarfs? Here, the answer goes back to the "room" and the entire question of perspective. While dwarfism can take various forms, the common notion of dwarf is a human with a small-proportioned body and normal-sized head. Given their use and that the play is set in post-WWII Britain, two main metaphors emerge: (1) the youth after WWII are young and naïve, innocent and childlike, given that they did not experience the horrors of the Holocaust and WWII, not having to face a tough life, they have not fully matured, but grow up in an age marked by peace and new opportunities, they have big heads, inflated with ideas and dreams, too inflated given the limitations of the not-yet-matured selves. And (2) they are level-headed, having grown up with the cautionary tales of WWII and the Holocaust, and this caution has instilled a desire to be still, not take chances, and the lack of this movement stunts their growth, atrophies their muscles, and they stay in place, moving and observing what goes on in rooms, but not sure how to live (in rooms), themselves.

The paradoxical thing about Pinter's career is that the more that Pinter (early in his career) focused solely on characters in just one room, the less it resembled a family room drama (the classic late-nineteenth and twentieth-century dramas where the action and story play out largely in the family and/or living room and/or kitchen). However, as his writing career progressed, and his rooms and locations became more numerous, the more that Pinter adapted the family room drama as a genre within absurd tragicomedy. *The Homecoming* (1965) is somewhat of the unofficial start of this move that lasts generally the rest of his career, while *Betrayal* (1978) is his most clear expression of adapting the family room drama within absurd tragicomedy.

In the entire corpus of absurd literature, along with Albee's *Who's Afraid of Virginia Woolf?* (1962), Pinter's *The Homecoming* (1965) perhaps most resemble one of the twentieth century's greatest (classic) tragedies: Eugene O'Neill's *Long Day's Journey into Night* (1940/1956). In *The Homecoming*, Pinter seems to suggest that if the home is dysfunctional, then its inhabitants can never escape its dysfunction, going back is necessary, despite difficulties, in order to move forward. While "strange" because of often-inexplicable behavior, this is a real family room drama, a deep psychological portrait of how the inner workings of a family continue to affect their world outside of the original family familial unit; about how each part affects the functioning (or dis-functioning) of the whole and the whole affects the (dys)functioning of each part; how we are never actually able to fully leave our home/family, returning to the dynamics established by the familial unit, especially when things are tough and we revert back to what we learned and knew first. In short, no matter how much we move, how far away we have gone, there is no escaping where you come from because it is always a part of you.

In his late play, *Betrayal*, we almost see the exact same message: in order to find out how we arrived at the/our current situation, we must move backwards. If we do not move to the point of origination, we will not be able to understand where we are in relationship to where we want to be and where we want to be going. The love affair is told backwards when betrayal gives the sense of movement in order to see the current situation in perspective.

Here we and maybe Pinter, himself have moved past the family, or simply accepted it, for our partners/spouses and friends are the family we choose and thus are partly responsible in terms of how their actions and our actions with them affect us. Pinter has moved far away from the "strangeness" in his early decontextualized plays, into plays where he searches for (and finds) the contexts that can explain the current situation. The late Pinter finds these very subtexts that were unknowable/unrecoverable in his early play: *this* is the *movement* of Pinter's search in his *oeuvre*.

Chapter 6

The European and American wave of absurdism

It is probably most productive to start this chapter in much the same way as the last chapter: while Samuel Beckett may have been the most influential and studied writer of the group, Beckett was by no means the lone voice of the absurd. In general, the writers associated with the absurd in this chapter follow on the heels of Beckett (Chapter 4) and Beckett's notable contemporaries (Chapter 5). The writers in this chapter are generally writing at a slightly later date, usually in the mid-1960s, and come from a much larger geographic area (i.e., the "Western" world that sits on both sides of the Atlantic, instead of just the two West European nations that sit on either side of the English Channel – the United Kingdom and France.) Besides, for the sake of brevity and space limitation, this section and the discussion of each of the writers is shorter for the primary reason that the majority of these writers are known for only a select few of their works, especially those that most influenced/were influenced by absurd literature. Plus, while all these writers were major writers in their own *time and place*, none of them has attained quite the international stature or the overwhelming critical acclaim of Beckett, Albee, Genet, Ionesco, and Pinter.

Arthur Adamov

Arthur Adamov, a son of wealthy Armenian parents, was born in 1908 in Russia. Given that he was brought up with his first language as French, he moved to Paris in 1924. There he became a part of the Surrealist Movement and start to write plays after WWII. Adamov died in Paris in 1970 after an overdose of barbiturates. While Adamov also wrote fiction and worked as well as a translator, he is best known as a playwright, most noted for his plays *Ping Pong* and *Professor Taranne* (and the uproar caused by his politically charged play, *Paolo Paoli*). Martin Esslin characterized Adamov as one of the four principal absurdists (along with Beckett, Ionesco, and Genet). Despite this categorization, Adamov is discussed in much less detail in this chapter because he and his work simply neither gained the critical acclaim, notoriety, nor influence that Beckett, Albee, Pinter, Genet, and Ionesco's work generated.

Adamov stressed that theatre was an art form free of message or identity constructed by allegory, and that his work could not be interpreted by mere word or action individually; only through theatric performance could his purpose be properly conveyed.[1] His protagonists were very often opposing manifestations of his own conscience, with dialogue stalled by a complete inability to communicate; they are "prisoners to a language of cliches", unable to consent to or even understand clear purpose.[2] This is no more clear than in his play *Ping Pong*. The two main characters, Arthur (a thinly veiled version of himself) and Victor (a thinly veiled alter-ego), are obsessed with pinball machines. Arthur is a "*nervous young man*" and Victor "*looks like a poor student*."[3] The two are prone to bickering (reminiscent of Didi and Gogo in *Godot*), and are like the left and right flippers on the pinball machine, and are "bound to jam" when both flippers are grabbed at once.[4] The play follows the two through their university days until they are elderly and watches as their obsession grows, particularly Arthur's constant tinkering with the pinball machine itself to improve and perfect the pinball machine. The pinball machine gets more and more complex, almost taking on a life of its own and taking over their lives.

Much like other absurd works, the title in the play itself is centered around an ambiguous metaphor, as Esslin observes, "The pinball machine has all the fascinating ambiguity of the symbol. It may stand for capitalism and big business, but it may equally well stand for any religious or political ideology that secretes its own organization and apparatus of power, that demands devotion and loyalty from its adherents."[5] This ambiguous symbolism or use of ambiguous metaphors also describes the two title characters of *Professor Taranne* and *Paolo Paoli*, who clearly stand for many things, but what exactly it is/they are is always beyond the grasp of the details found in the plays, typical of a parable in other absurd works of literature.

While Adamov was influenced by Surrealists as many other absurdists were, his works clearly display the metaphoric ambiguity that is so typical of absurd literature, and fall into the general category of tragicomedy for their mixture of wit and seriousness, he was also very clearly his own writer, as heavily influenced by Bertolt Brecht as any other writer. In *Paolo Paoli*, his Notes give instructions for quotations to be projected onto a screen that comments on the events being portrayed and for "tunes and songs" to be played for the audience while they read these quotations. These techniques are a page from Brecht's *Essays on Theatre*. Also Adamov's language is more didactically awkward than experimental, typical of Brecht's dialogue.

Fernando Arrabal

Fernando Arrabal Terán was born in Spain in 1932. In 1936, at the beginning of the Spanish Civil War, his father, a painter, remained loyal to the Republic, and was sentenced to death for mutiny. His father's sentence was changed to 30 years' imprisonment. He apparently faked mental illness to be transferred to a lower security mental hospital, which he escaped from soon after, and was never seen again. The same year, Arrabal was awarded a national prize for gifted children and studied at Las Escuelas Pías de San Antón (where Victor Hugo also studied). Awarded a three-month scholarship to study in Paris, where he contracted tuberculosis, Arrabal stayed on in a type of self-exile, as he considered himself both the expatriot and an exile. His literary output was extraordinary, penning over 100 plays, a number of novels, and 800-some books of poetry and art. Besides counting Andy Warhol and Tristan Tzara as friends, and being a member of André Breton's group of Surrealists for three years, Arrabal also had a year-long correspondence with Samuel Beckett.

While much of the discussion surrounding Fernando Arrabal considers his use of the grotesque and the re-imagining of his own troubled past,[6] Arrabal, while being included in Martin Esslin's 1969 expanded second edition of *The Theatre of the Absurd*, chose to define his own theatre as "theatre of panic," naming it after the Greek god Pan, the Greek god associated with the pasture, sexuality, and theatrical criticism. Perhaps best known for his short play, *Guernica*, the play that dramaticizes the famous painting of the same name, his "theatre of panic" and this play are typified by the character of the *homme panique*, the man Arrabal created whose refusal to take risks and the hero forces himself into a world beyond his control.

The *homme panique* in *Guernica* is Fanchou, whose wife Lira is buried in rubble after bombs fall from the sky. Fanchou does little during the whole play but talk, even after he says, "it's my turn to refuse to talk."[7] Meanwhile, a journalist and writer are commenting on their situation and what a good story that is for a novel, misinterpreting the people as heroic, instead of being paralyzed by panic. The play clearly breaks the standard Aristotelian arc with the coming and going of the journalist and writer. But it is Fanchou and the *homme panique* that really capture the Kafkaesque. Fanchou has become so paralyzed and unable to take any action that his conversations with Lira – as we hear her voice under the stones in pain, and asking for help – sound heartless, even though he is trying to show love with his words. For example, early in the play she is buried in the rumble and more stones fall on her. Already realizing his limitations, Lira tells him, "I can't rely on you," to which he responds, "oh yes you can. I've got a surprise for you: our present."[8] After which he blows up a balloon and ties it to a string, tied to a stone, which he proceeds to throw on top of the pile of rubble under which Lira is buried. This is the disconnect that is dramatized in this play and reminiscent of Kafka's characters.

Stemming from panic, this disconnect creates an illogical dialogue. However, this illogical dialogue does not stem, necessarily, from experimenting with language (though as a poet, too, Arrabal clearly experiments with language all the time). Instead, Arrabal exposes the lack of logic of one who fears, and how violence of Franco-led Spain, throughout Franco's brutal regime, leads an entire nation into a state of panic: with nobody being able to be the hero that is so sorely needed to combat the very violence that paralyzed everyone with panic in the first place. Arrabal's commentaries on this paradox are appropriate in the paradoxical genre of tragicomedy, where one does not know whether to laugh or cry.

Amiri Baraka

Amiri Baraka (born Everett LeRoi Jones) was born in Newark, New Jersey in 1934, and his father worked as a postal supervisor and a lift operator and his mother was a social worker. Winning a scholarship to Rutgers University in 1951, Baraka transferred to Howard University in 1952, studying philosophy and religion, though he never received his degree. He joined the US Air Force in 1954, but after he reached the rank of sergeant, an anonymous tip uncovered, his Soviet writings, which eventually led to a dishonorable discharge from the Air Force. After this, he moved to Greenwich Village in New York City and quickly became immersed in jazz and avant-garde Beats, Black Mountain poets, and New York School poets. After marrying in 1958, he and his wife founded Totem Press, which published works by Jack Kerouac and Allen Ginsberg. Until his breakout play, *Dutchman*, which won an Obie in 1964, Baraka had written essays on race and a book of poetry. In 1965, after the assassination of Malcolm X, he moved to Harlem and became critical of the civil rights movement for their pacifist and integrationist leanings. The 1965 poem, "Black Art," calls for violence and the need to have a black world. This poem, in part, was the manifesto of the Black Arts literary movement. Since that time Baraka had a rocky relationship with the Black Arts movement, and penned a number of anti-Semitic poems and articles in the late 1960s and early 1970s. In the mid-1970s, he began to distance himself from Black nationalism, becoming a

Marxist and supporter of liberation movements in Third World countries. In 1980, he renounced his earlier anti-Semitic writing. From then, Baraka worked at various universities and collaborated on some pop cultural projects. He died in 2014 in Newark.

Along with his poetry, especially the poem, "Black Art," Baraka is best known for *Dutchman*. Baraka's work has been discussed mainly as intense cultural and racial criticism using methods of deconstructing language and philosophy to appropriately address cemented social and cultural norms.[9] One of Baraka's most polarizing works, the one-act play *Dutchman*, is considered by George Piggford to be a "call to revolutionary action," in which he diagnoses the race problem in America, "and prescribes his cure: race revolution and murder."[10] As is typical of Baraka's work, the play is rather shocking. A seductive woman, Lulu, comes on to a young black man, Clay, on a subway train. The dialogue is quick and, as Lulu eats an apple, reminiscent of the sharpness of the serpent's tongue. Lulu basically plays mental games with Clay the entire time, sometimes acknowledging his sexual attention and sometimes scorning it. It is when Lulu talks about race, saying that Clay is black and passive, that Clay becomes violent. Eventually, Lulu convinces him to follow her suggestion – kill all the whites – at which point he quickly rescinds this desire. Clay goes to leave the train, but Lulu stabs him, after which she tells all of the passengers to throw his body off the train and get off at the next stop. Once this is done, she approaches another young black man. This demonstrates that there is a cyclical arc to the play, much like in *Godot*.

The metaphors in this play are multiple, while there is context around what is happening during the time of the play, the fact that Lulu has no-to-little context makes allegorical readings difficult. Clearly we see Lulu like Eve; Clay is malleable in his black identity and masculinity; and the title suggests the famous ghost ship, doomed to sail forever, the Flying Dutchman. Without knowing Lulu's back story and actual desires, the play lacks full closure and raises new questions. The highly metaphoric and parabolic nature, in part because of the name of the title characters, in part because of the lack of back story and subtext, certainly gives the feeling of being an absurd play. But it is really the situation, being accosted by someone on a subway train, who may be crazy, that is both normal (it happens at times if you live in a city) and unusual (in that the conversation was more than a few sentences). Clay gets caught in the trap, and whichever way he tries to mold (like "Clay") to the situation, Lulu is able to mold better and faster to put him in another, equally uncomfortable situation. This utter inability to get out of the situation produces a feeling of the Kafkaesque (like K. in *The Trial*).

Friedrich Dürrenmatt

Friedrich Dürrenmatt was born in Konolfingen, Switzerland in 1921. His father was a Protestant pastor and his grandfather was a conservative politician. Attending the University of Zurich in 1941 to study philosophy and German language and literature, Dürrenmatt moved after one semester to the University of Bern (Bern is where the family had been living since 1935) where he dropped out in 1943 to pursue a writing career. His first play, *It Is Written*, was produced in 1947 to great controversy, as its very subject – a cynic and a religious fanatic battle while their town is under siege – is quite provocative. His early plays are more in the vein of Brecht's epic theatre, exploring – especially in *Romulus the Great* – historical movements and presenting a dialectical view on it. It was with his 1956 play, *The Visit*, his most heralded work, that we see Dürrenmatt influenced by and influencing absurd literature. Becoming a painter later in life, Dürrenmatt died in 1990 of heart failure.

Subtitled *A Tragi-comedy, The Visit* was Dürrenmatt's take on the at-the-time burgeoning genre of "tragicomedy." The play is almost Beckett's *Waiting for Godot* in reverse. In Beckett's also self-billed "tragicomedy," two tramps wait the entire play for Godot, who will, presumably, solve all of their problems. Of course, Godot never comes. In *The Visit*, the down-and-out town almost immediately gets a visit from an old native of the town, who is now an elderly millionaire. Excited by the very prospect of her millions, the town starts to boom. Only once enmeshed in the new plans does the town realize that this money is conditional on a murder of an old lover for personal revenge. In *The Visit*, there is no wait for the Savior; simply, the Savior disappoints. While in *Godot*, the disappointment of the Savior never coming is evident, the fact that Didi and Gogo have waited for 50 years suggests that they maybe do not need their Savior.

The play is hilarious and utterly dark in the fact that the town, on Alfred Ill's request, votes unanimously to kill him, and once he is dead, the town concludes that he died of joy. Dürrenmatt is the one absurdist that replaces the Brechtian with the Kafkaesque. The situation is clearly "strange," requiring unique actions as is typical of the Kafkaesque and much of absurd literature. But the context is utterly clear, the language is awkwardly didactic, an inscription is written during the scene, and – more than anything – this is a play clearly about social/political/economic justice, with the unique situation that it makes the audience ask the question, what would I have done in this situation? (Brecht's *modus operandi*). William Gillis claims 'justice' to be a near-obsessive idea of Dürrenmatt's; its attainment is, for mankind, "something he must leave to heaven," while Edward Diller denotes a related central theme in Dürrenmatt's work: inevitable revelation of finite humanness through a "grotesque" real-ization of inexplicable paradox.[11] It can then almost be suggested that the very sense of what makes something absurd (while not quite experimental in language, and following something of an Aristotelian arc) is the genre of tragicomedy mixed with a very unusual situation.

Dürrenmatt's play is the (maybe only) real link between Brecht and the absurd, or maybe, rather, it is simply a sign of a writer who when he began to write was writing while Brecht was celebrated, and then as he matured as a writer continued to write as organic avant-garde theatre was emerging in Europe. Given that Dürrenmatt spoke German and reached his 20s (and started writing) in the early 1940s, when Brecht's influence was great, this may well explain the influences in *The Visit*. This is in contrast to most of the other writers in this book who came into their young and impressionable 20s during the early 1950s (though Beckett and Genet were writing in their 30s and living in France by the early 1940s, which also explains why they were not influenced by Brecht).

Jack Gelber

Jack Gelber was born in Chicago to Jewish parents of Romanian and Russian descent. Working as a sheet metal worker (his father's trade), he financed his education at the University of Illinois, graduating in 1933 with a degree in journalism. After a four-year stint spent in San Francisco, where he met his wife, he moved to New York City in 1957 when he started writing *The Connection*. Two years later the play was produced by The Living Theatre (founded in 1947), which brought both Gelber and The Living Theatre to great prominence, with *The Connection* winning an Obie award and propelling The Living Theatre to the upper-echelon of American theatre companies. While Gelber continued to write (his second play, *The Apple*, was also produced by The Living Theatre), Gelber more or less disappeared from the limelight and into academia. Gelber died in New York in 2003 of blood cancer. Mel Gussow quoted Edward Albee in his obituary of Gelber in *The New York Times*: "I was so affected [as a young man] and energized by *The Connection*. It was exciting, dangerous, instructive and terrifying – all things theatre should be." While Gelber may have been a one-hit wonder, as evidenced by greatly affecting probably the most important and influential American playwright of the second half of the twentieth century, *The Connection* was quite a home run, a controversial sensation, to say the least.

The Connection is a play-within-a-play, as Jim Dunn who is the "producer" and Jaybird who is the "writer," are trying to put on a production about jazz musicians and narcotics using "real" addicts. These "addicts" are waiting for their "connection" (i.e., the drug dealer). Eventually Cowboy brings the heroin and one of the characters overdoses, after the fact that the actors have already convinced the audience members that these really are addicts.

Jack Gelber's *The Connection* is his primary contribution to the absurd theatre, and scholars debate its meaning; whether it be social commentary, criticism of the drug war, or if the play even exhibits absurd characteristics.[12] It is hard to really classify *The Connection* as absurd literature, except for its influence on Albee and, maybe key, the extreme feeling of the Kafkaesque it produces for the audience, those same audience members, who (especially considering this was 1959 and performance art was some way off) come to the theatre and expect to sit back and observe the story, but instead get thrust into thinking what am I being asked to do here in the audience? Can I get up to help? Is that allowed? Is this really real? Should I call out, is there a doctor? Should I find a phone and call a doctor? This is really the first play, not by subject matter, which really personally put the audience members in a very uncomfortable situation that certainly (the audience would think) required an extraordinary response.

Václav Havel

Václav Havel was born in Prague, Czechoslovakia, in 1936 into a well-known family with ties to Czechoslovakian cultural and political events in the 1920s–40s. Because of politics, Havel was not accepted to study humanities at a university. Instead, he studied economics at the University of Prague, dropping out after two years. After a few years of military service, he got a job as a stagehand and enrolled via correspondence for a degree in dramatic arts at the Academy of Performing Arts in Prague. After some vaudeville work, Havel's first full-length play, *The Garden Party*, was presented in a theatre of the absurd series at the theatre on Balustrade. This play and his second, *The Memorandum* (which was also performed by The Public Theatre in New York in 1968 and won an Obie award), brought him international acclaim. After 1968, when his plays were banned, he became a political dissident and activist. While he is known as a premier playwright, he became much more widely known and influential for his second career: politician. Despite not being interested in politics, he was voted in as the president of Czechoslovakia in 1989. He also became the Czech Republic's first president in 1993, which he held until 2003. Havel died in 2011.

While the discussion surrounding Václav Havel concerns his early roots in the Theatre of the Absurd and how the ideas that fueled his work prefaced his rise in the European political arena,[13] the subject of ridicule in *The Garden Party* and *The Memorandum* is the absurdity of bureaucracy. In *The Garden Party*, Hugo crashes a garden party of the liquidation office and his clear thinking eventually gets him the ridiculous job of constructing a central commission for inauguration and liquidation from the two offices that he helped create (the liquidation office and the inauguration office). As similarly seen in *The Memorandum*, where an artificial language, Ptydepe, is created to avoid redundancy and an error-ridden office, with words up to 319 letters (because each word needs to be as different from other words as possible), but were replaced with another language, Chorukor, which has as much similarity in words as possible – Havel experiments with language through a mock-legalese, mock-bureaucratic dialogue.

For example, in *The Garden Party*, the director of the liquidation office is trying to clarify what is being liquidated by what is being inaugurated:

> And will it then be inaugurated by a liquidationally trained inaugurator trained by an inaugurationally trained liquidation officer, or by an inaugurationaly trained liquidation officer trained by a liquidationally trained inaugurator.[14]

Or, in *The Memorandum*, we get the ridiculous exchange between the teacher of the second artificial language, Chorukor, and an employee:

LEAR: ... Monday becomes in Chorukor 'ilopagar', Tuesday 'ilopager', Wednesday 'ilopagur', Thursday 'ilopagir', Friday 'ilopageur', Saturday 'ilopagoor'. Now, what do you think Sunday is? Well?
(*Only* THUMB *raises his hand.*)
THUMB: (*Gets up*) Ilopagor. (*Sits down*)
LEAR: Correct, Mr. Thumb. You get an A. It is easy, isn't it?[15]

These two examples demonstrate the absurdity and lack of logic given the confluence of bureaucracy, language, and (lack of) logic. It is as if Havel suggests that bureaucracy breeds a lack of logic tied to its equally ridiculous language; if logic is skewed, so is the language, and visa versa. And the plots, thus, follow the (lack of) logic of bureaucracy, resulting in lunacy and redundancy.

Adrienne Kennedy

Adrienne Kennedy (née Adrienne Lita Hawkins) was born in 1931 in Pittsburgh, Pennsylvania. Her mother was a teacher and her father was a social worker. Growing up in an integrated neighborhood in Cleveland, Ohio,

Kennedy did not face much prejudice as an African-American until she went to The Ohio State University. There she met her husband, Joseph Kennedy. An important leading figure in the Black Arts Movement, she also was a founding member of the Women's Theatre Council in 1971. In addition to her eighteen plays (two of which won Obie Awards), she wrote autobiographies, a novella, and a short story. She currently lectures at universities in the United States on the east and west coasts.

Adrienne Kennedy's one-act play, *Funnyhouse of a Negro* (1962), while not her only well-known play – as she is also well known for her other early one-act play, *The Owl Answers* (1963), which displays a similar surreal, dreamlike quality where characters are unstable entities – helps us really understand both the absurd (in general) and the absurd's nuanced and varied expressions. Discussion of Adrienne Kennedy is largely based on her methods of addressing ambiguous identity with her main protagonists becoming intimately close with the audience, exemplified most often by her 1964 play *Funnyhouse of a Negro*.[16]

The arc of Kennedy's *Funnyhouse of a Negro* is reminiscent of other absurd plays, in that it does not follow any type of Aristotelian arc, and is – in the most traditional sense – a play without any specific conflict, resulting in an arc much reminiscent of Beckett's *Waiting for Godot*: a flat line. However, part of the difficulty in saying this is the fact that the play is dreamlike and takes place mostly in the head of the protagonist, Sarah. Dreams generally do not have an Aristotelian narrative arc but mimic much more of a senseless line that simply moves forward (generally) in time. Also, in this play, the audience does not understand the subtext, not because the exposition is totally absent, but because the audience hears multiple and contrasting backstories (reminiscent of and mimicking dreams).

We also must view this play alongside and in contrast to Langston Hughes' play, *Mulatto* (1935). Hughes took the figure of the "tragic mulatto" out of the hands of (generally racist) white writers of the previous century. Hughes' play is a melodrama set in the Jim Crow south, where Robert (his father, a white landowner, and mother, a black servant) is battling his mixed race identity in light of the racist South. Robert wants to be seen for his white side, but as in the well-known melodrama, Dion Boucicault's *The Octoroon* (1859), Robert's drop of Black blood marks him as Black in his Southern environment. Robert's *rebellion* against the whites in his town is an *external* rebellion, and leads him to take his own life instead of giving the whites the pleasure of lynching him. Robert's story is a Greek tragedy: Robert is clearly heroic and it is his pride – his *hubris* – that leads to his tragic fate.

In Kennedy's *Funnyhouse*, the "tragic mulatto" is recast. The tragedy comes from no fault of Sarah's own, having been born into her, in essence, *absurd situation*: neither black nor white. Sarah's rebellion, unlike Robert's external one, is in her head and is an *internal* rebellion against and with her two selves: Sarah's interior world is more chaotic than, if we believe the ending of the play, her exterior one. The tragic and horrific elements of the play mix with, not exactly the comic, but the carnivalesque. The language in Kennedy's *Funnyhouse* mirrors the randomness and lack of linearity of both a funnyhouse and a dream: spoken lines are repeated but morph just slightly; the characters are unstable in their identities; and truth seems justified, but only in the moment, until the next moment comes.

Arthur Kopit

Arthur Lee Kopit was born in New York City in 1937. He grew up in Lawrence, New York, and attended Harvard University. A two-time Pulitzer Prize finalist and three-time Tony award nominee, much of the conversation about Arthur Kopit concerns his criticism of Western mythology in *Indians* and the imprisonment of inevitabilities, which ties him to the theatrical absurd.[17] However, his most notable contribution to absurd literature came from his 1962 play, *Oh Dad, Poor Dad, Mama's Hung You in the Closet and I'm Feelin' So Sad*, which garnered him the Vernon Rice Award (now called the Drama Desk Award). Kopit has also taught at City College of New York, Wesleyan University, and Yale University.

Oh Dad, Poor Dad is about a pushy and obnoxious mother who takes her son to the Caribbean, and also takes the body/coffin of her deceased husband with her. Kopit calls the play a "Tragifarce." And it is this double mix of an underlying seriousness and its element of farcical comedy that is in line with other absurd works. The general awkwardness of the conversations and having to deal with the corpse of the dead father/husband certainly creates unique situations for many characters in the play. Maybe most notable of all these "strange" moments is when a woman (Rosalie) tries to seduce the son (Jonathan) on his mother's bed. As she is undressing him (and Jonathan is trying to refuse her), the closet door swings open and the corpse of the father falls on Rosalie. Her response is: "LISTEN TO ME, JONATHAN! STOP LOOKING AT HIM AND LOOK AT ME!"[18] This is the ultimate tragifarcical moment. Of course, the whole situation is bordering on proposterous, but the underlying psychological dynamics of the familial unit are palpable too: the overbearing mother controls both the son and the husband even in his death, and the son cannot (and does not know how to) be with another woman. And Rosalie's response is so inhuman that she reacts to the dead corpse of the father of the man she is trying to have sex with falling on her like it is a pesky bug distracting Jonathan. But it is this depth of insight, in the moment of utter chaos and pure comedic ridiculousness, that exposes Jonathan's own tragedy (owing to the dynamics of a very unhealthy family unit).

Sławomir Mrożek

Sławomir Mrożek was born in 1930 in Borzęcin, Poland. During WWII, his family lived in Krakow. A year after finishing high school in 1949, he began writing about politics. After marrying in 1959, Mrożek and his wife first traveled to and then defected to Italy in 1963. His first full-length play, *Tango* (1965), was to be his most successful play and catapulted him to the top of Poland's foremost dramatists. Mrożek continued to both write and move from country to country: France, USA, Germany, and Mexico. He returned to Poland in 1996, then lived there until 2008, when, after a stroke in 2002, he emigrated back to France, living in Nice until his death in 2013.

While the overwhelming narrative surrounding the work of Mrożek concerns the reception of his work by Eastern European culture and Western culture, and his tendency toward realism lends itself to realistic interpretation, with the common use of Freudian theory,[19] like Vaclav Havel, much of Mrożek's work, including *Tango*, is a product of the totalitarian context of an Eastern European state. And like Ionesco's *Rhinoceros*, Mrożek is clearly attacking the totalitarian and/or post-totalitarian mentality, but like *Rhinoceros*, the play is too open-ended and ambiguous to simply label it a political tract against totalitarianism. *Tango* is about a family staging their own Bohemian rebellion in the microcosm of their house. Given that this type of rebellion produces something of a type of anarchy owing to getting rid of all standards and rules, the servant basically runs the household, eventually cuckolding the father of the house, who no longer even cares to object. The absurdity of the play comes from a mix of improbable and probable, and the illogical and logical situation and nature of the family.

Mirroring something like a power vacuum, the family does espouse logical ideals, but the ideals of rebellion against traditional forms of hierarchy, domination, and traditional standards, when taken to the extreme, produce the lack of logic typical of the laws of entropy, the movement toward increasing randomness. The resulting situation of the household is utterly improbable at face value, as one who walked into their house would think he or she has walked into a Kakfa story or a tragicomic dystopia. But given their (il)logical ideals, the result of this micro-experiment actually follows its probable course into randomness and apathy. The combination of the characters missing so much of the obviousness of the errors of their (il)logical thinking and the humorous frivolity of it all produces quite the tragicomedy.

Tadeusz Różewicz

Tadeusz Różewicz was born in 1921 in Radomsko, Poland, a few years after Poland regained its independence. He published his first poems in 1938, and served in the underground Home Army during WWII. After the war, he finished high school and went to Jagiellonian University of Krakow before moving to Gliwice, his residence for thirty years, and where he wrote his most notable work, the play *The Card Index* in 1960, following which he made a name for himself as an acclaimed poet, publishing fifteen volumes of poetry. He moved to Wrocław in 1968, living there the rest of his life, and wrote many other plays and poems. He died in 2014.

The Card Index is a long one-act play but does not have much of a plot other than people passing through and stopping to talk to the main character, referred to as the "Hero," down the street that seems to pass through the Hero's room. With each new passerby, the Hero's name and his own story and history changes. In short, the narrative lacks any traditional arc and is episodic and somewhat random, much like the narrative arc of *Godot*. In an explanation of Różewicz's dramatic works, scholars focus mainly on his deconstruction of traditional storytelling, language, and dramaturgical style, which tie him to the theatrical absurd.[20] Other scholars put more emphasis on the postwar environment.[21] While clearly this absurd tragicomic arc is noticeable, and is part of what is reminiscent of the Kafkaesque, what is even more noteworthy is that Różewicz anticipates the central tenet of postmodernism: that is, that there is really no such thing as one fact or one truth; that multiple truths exist. This is evident in that the hero really does seem to be talking in earnest with each passerby, and while it may also seem like our Hero is simply indecisive at first glance, on closer inspection it is revealed that the wishy-washy way in which he answers the questions are due, rather, to the fact that there is no single answer. The last lines of *The Card Index* probably best illustrate Różewicz and future postmodernists' point about the multiplicity of truth:

JOURNALIST: I see . . . Do you believe in salvation?
HERO: Yes . . . no . . . that is . . . up to a certain point . . . funny question.
JOURNALIST: If I'm not mistaken, you are an ordinary person?
HERO: Yes.

JOURNALIST: Do you know that you hold the fate of the world in your hands?

HERO: Up to a point.

JOURNALIST: What do you intend to do to maintain peace in the world?

HERO: I don't know.

JOURNALIST: Do you realize that in the event of nuclear work their humanity will perish?

HERO (*almost gaily*): Naturally, naturally.

JOURNALIST: And what are you doing to prevent the explosion?

HERO (*laughs*): Nothing.

JOURNALIST: But surely, you love humanity?

HERO: Naturally.

JOURNALIST: But why?

HERO: I don't know yet. It's difficult to say, it's only five in the morning. Perhaps if you drop in around midday I might know.

JOURNALIST (*puts his notebook away*): I haven't learned much here.

HERO: You've come too late.

JOURNALIST: Goodbye.

HERO is silent.[22]

Here, the ambiguity of plot, metaphor, and meeting are philosophically derived by Różewicz, versus the aesthetics, linguistics, and narratives of ambiguity (that is more common in absurd literature).

Sam Shepard

Sam Shepard Rogers VII was born in 1943 in Illinois. His father was in the Air Force but retired to be a farmer. Shepard grew up in Duarte, California on a farm and studied agriculture at San Antonio Junior College. When his father began to drink and family life became intolerable for him, he left college and joined a touring company of actors, the Bishops Company Repertory Players. He was soon appointed playwright-in-residence at the Magic Theatre in San Francisco. Moving to New York in 1963, he waited on tables at one of the most famous jazz clubs in New York, the Village Gate, to earn money while he wrote plays. Some of his one-act plays were produced off Broadway the following year at such experimental theatres like La Mama and the Open Theatre. Shepard is extremely prolific, and like Jack Kerouac, he almost never revises his work.

Shepard started getting real critical acclaim by the 1965–66 season. He won three Obie Awards for his plays *Chicago, Icarus's Mother,* and *Red Cross.* Despite continued success and critical acclaim for his play *Mad Dog Blues,* which was produced in 1971, Shepard moved to England where he lived until 1974. While there, he wrote several plays that were successful both in New York and in London, most notably *The Tooth of Crime*. His next big success came in 1979, when he won the Pulitzer Prize for *Buried Child*. Also, in 1985 he won the New York Drama Critics' Circle Award for *A Lie of the Mind*. In 1986, at the relatively young age of 43, he was elected to the American Academy of Arts and Letters. He has won an astonishing ten Obie Awards in his career. On a side note, Shepard is an actor, too. He appeared in such major motion pictures as *The Right Stuff, Fool for Love, Country* and *Crimes of the Heart*. *The Tooth of Crime* was first performed at the Open Space in London on July 17, 1972. The play was directed by fellow ex-patriot Charles Marowitz, who, twenty years earlier left for London in protest against the Korean War. It is *The Tooth of Crime* that established him as a major playwright, but it, especially given its later date (considering the absurd started to peter out in the 1970s), is *The Tooth of Crime* that might very well be the best and most highly crystalized capstone of this organic movement (and because of this, I will spend some time discussing this play).

   The Tooth of Crime is somewhat Aristotelian in arc and is divided into two acts. This division marks the absence and presence of Crow. There are no scenes. Act One opens with the song "The Way Things Are." This is an act to set the stage and let us know the way things are for Hoss and his posse. We find out that he was once very successful and that he is in the decline. We also find out that he has been "marked." So, the first act establishes what is at stake for Hoss and anticipates the coming of the killer, Crow. Whereas the first act anticipates his coming, the second act features the interaction between Hoss and Crow. With Crow conflict comes to a head and our two main characters are left to butt heads, and we know that the stronger of the two will be left standing. Again, the stage is set in Act One, and the action of Act Two brings us to a deadly climax, with a short dénouement, or unraveling, following it.

   The staging lets us know immediately that we are not going to witness "milk-pail realism":

> SCENE: A bare stage except for an evil-looking black chair with silver studs and a very high back, something like an Egyptian Pharaoh's throne but simple, centre stage. In the dark, heavy lurking Rock and Roll starts low and builds as the lights come up. The band should be hidden. The sound should be like "Heroin" by the Velvet Underground. When the lights are up full, HOSS enters in black rocker gear with silver studs and black kid gloves. He holds a microphone. He should look like a mean Rip Torn but a little younger.

Shepard, for that matter, writes about a *fantasy* world, a world of rock 'n' roll and killers for hire, a world that few are privileged to see, and a world that even fewer can understand. But we will get to that later. One might argue that the bare stage only reinforces the menacing presence of the "evil-looking black chair." One might also argue that this is a world devoid of everything else but the ominous. Both might, in fact, be right. But I want to argue that Shepard creates a chair with a surrounding bare stage to decontextualize it, in essence, creating a world in which objects have little or no meaning other than the meaning that humans attach to it with language. This gets at the very heart of the play (and maybe a lot of absurd literature).

Let me explain. By the staging, we have no context for the black chair. Where is this black chair found? Are we seeing the throne room of a palace? Or a living room? The chair is just waiting to be contextualized. Because we don't know the context of the chair, it is hard to read it. What can a chair like this mean when there is nothing surrounding it? This simple, but revealing stage direction foreshadows the world of the play: it has no context: the very mark of much of absurd literature. This play features rock 'n' roll and killers, but we don't have the context to figure out which world we are witnessing. We understand that there are "hits" in this play, but we are left only with a word that has two meanings: musical hits and hits that hitmen do. So, because this play lacks any context, denying us the possibility of knowing whether we are in the world of musicians or the world of hitmen, we are left only with words that humans can interpret in more than one way.

Even though the chair lacks context, we can still examine the chair on its own. The chair looks like it is meant to be sat on by someone who exhibits the same qualities of the chair. The chair has two contradictions: it is black and shiny and like a Pharaoh's throne, but simple. It is a chair that is powerful, a bit dangerous, but is also no nonsense. Its very high back means that it is meant to loom large. We soon see the mirror image of this chair. Hoss wears "black rocker gear with silver studs with black kid gloves." Hoss looms large.

The songs in the play are written by Shepard. This is especially telling in the first line of "The Way Things Are." Hoss sings, "You may think every picture you see is a true history of the way things used to be or the way things are." We must think back to Poststructuralism to understand that there are multiple truths. Hoss sings here about a picture, which supposedly offers empirical evidence of the situation. As the old saying goes, "A camera does not lie." But Hoss sings that this is not the case, that you do not see the true history. A camera may lie here, or at least not demonstrate the whole history. We know that this is the case for both the past and the present, so we must be wary of what Hoss and his friends say about both his past successes and his present situation. The last line of the song affects how we are to view the play: "So here's another fantasy about the way things seem to be to me." Here is that word that I alluded to earlier: fantasy. It is difficult to say whether or not this is a fantasy world, a dream, or a reality that feels like fantasy. More on that later. But we have to take away from it the fact that appearance might not represent straightforward reality. The "here's," or here is, lets us know that the fantasy will proceed Hoss's remark. The song, then, becomes almost a prologue to the play, marking the themes of the play and letting us know that we are here to see a play. What follows this remark is "a fantasy about the way things seem to be to me." Instead of singing "the way things are" and orating a definitive version of reality, Hoss pulls back and offers "the way things seem to be," not how they really are. But most importantly here, the line ends with "to me," "the way things seem to be to me." No longer does Hoss sing about the objective truth. "The way things seem to be to me" lets us know that this is a subjective appearance that we are witnessing. At the beginning of *The Glass Menagerie*, Tom lets us know that we are witnessing his subjective memories. Is this play something like *The Glass Menagerie*? Is it a problem that Hoss dies in the end? Is this, then, in fact, Hoss's fantasy of his own end? For after all, he ends his life with a "genius mark."

We hear that they will be playing a game, though we also quickly hear a pair of contradictions. Hoss proclaims "I want that fuckin' gold record." Then when Star-Man leaves, he says, "I'm too old fashioned. That's it. Gotta kick out the scruples. Go against the code. That's what they used to do. The big ones. Dylan. Jagger. Townsend. All them cats broke the codes. Time can't change that. BECKY: But they were playing pussy, Hoss. They weren't killers . . . You're a killer, man. You're in the big time." Whereas Dylan, Jagger, and Townsend were playing pussy, according to Becky, Hoss is a killer. So what is this game? Is it a game? Is Hoss a musician? Is he a killer? What are hits?

Hoss continues to say he is going to go against the code. Becky tells him that he can get thrown into the slammer for that. Thus there are real consequences for breaking the rules, and apparently this is a ruling body. Hoss doesn't seem to care:

BECKY: Why do you wanna throw everything away. You were always suicidal
    like that. Right from the start.
HOSS: It's part of my nature.
BECKY: That's what we saved you from, your nature. Maybe you forgot that.
    When we first landed you, you were a complete beast of nature. A sideways
    killer. Then we molded and shaped you and sharpened you down to
    perfection because we saw in you a true genius killer. A killer to end them all.
    A killer's killer.

We learn a lot about Hoss from this exchange. Hoss is reckless. He doesn't take time to think of what he has earned and how quickly he can lose it from rash actions. In this respect he is suicidal. His actions are severely self-destructive; it has always been that way. Becky and the gang saw this self-destructive nature in Hoss and they needed to calm it down before it overtook him and he hurt himself in some way. They took on this challenge because they saw talent, "a true genius killer" in him. Hoss disagrees with this point: "Sure I'm good. I might even be great but I ain't no genius. Genius is something outside the game. The game can't contain a true genius. It's too small." If we think about the fact that geniuses think outside the box, we start to comprehend what Hoss is saying. Einstein could not follow Newtonian physics, so he created his own theory, the theory of general relativity. Shakespeare did not follow the form of other sonnets, so he created his own form, the Shakespearean sonnet. Geniuses don't follow the rules; they create new ones. Hoss may be extremely talented and may have a self-destructive streak, but he would not go against the code. He is incensed every time he mentions someone going against the code. Thus Hoss's character, and his flaws are finally developed. Up until this point, from the opening stage direction onward, Shepard has done two things. First, he has given us the context, albeit a decontextualized context. And second, he has developed the character of Hoss. From this point until the end of Act One, Shepard sets up the conflict. Act Two is the staging of the conflict.

Galactic Jack arrives on the scene with his charts. He is a disc jockey and his charts seem to hint to musical hits. Galactic Jack brings news that Hoss is a "shooting star." But pretty soon he says, "You is the coldest on the circuit." Galactic Jack is clearly part of Hoss's entourage. Or rather, he is clearly telling Hoss what he wants to hear. Speaking of the Gypsies, Jack says, "These boys are losin' to the cruisin' baby." Hoss is a bit more realistic, or maybe pessimistic about the situation: "They've got time on their side. Can't you see that. The youth's goin' to 'em. The kids are flocking to Gypsy Kills. It's a market opening up, Jack. I got feeling. I know they're on their way in and we're going out. We're getting old, Jack." There is something in Hoss's voice that tells us that he wants to be more like them. "But they got balls. They're on their own . . . I'm inside and they're out. They could unseat us all." These comments anticipate Hoss's later yearning to be like the Gypsies. Martin Tucker in his book entitled *Sam Shepard* describes Hoss. He says,

> Hoss knows he is flirting with his own mortality by allowing such a decadence of the rock spirit. He knows that, having been on top and away from the spur of peer competition, he has forgotten how mean his compatriots can, on further push, be. He yearns to be like the Gypsies,

who feel no guilt for their lack of human sympathy; he yearns to become again that cool and mean man he once thought he was. Yet Shepard indicates that Hoss was always different from his rock others, always a man with feelings that the other stars in the rock world lack.

When Jack leaves, Becky gives Hoss some bad news: "we just got word that Eyes sussed somebody's marked you. HOSS: What! Marked me? Who? BECKY: One a' the Gypsies." Hoss's fears are realized. A second ago he said "What if they turned the game against us. What if they started marking us." Now they did mark him. Hoss, who appeared to have always played by the rules, by the codes, realizes that he can no longer be successful by following it: "Nobody's playin' by the rules no more. We been suckers to the code for too long now. Now we move outside." But Hoss does not take this so easily. He is torn up inside by the game he now has to play. He says, "Without a code it's just a crime. Not art involved. No technique, finesse. No sense of mastery. The touch is gone." For Hoss there is beauty in following the code, in following rules. The Gypsies do not apprentice and do not learn technique. This is the downside to playing outside of the rules. The beauty is gone.

In Crow, we see a character with some of the same attributes as Hoss. As for Hoss, style is important, and Crow seems to exhibit some of the killer and self-destructive attributes that Hoss has. The swastika means that Crow either dishes out or desires others to dish out pain and death to Jews. The patch over his eye means that he jumps into things that are destructive to him. Like Stanley Kowalski exudes sexuality, Crow exudes a violent arrogance, and we witness this by the fact that he twirls a silver chain in his hands, that he violently chomps on his gum, and that he comes into another's house and proceeds to sit in their special chair. This also shows contempt for Hoss. Given the fact that Crow behaves the same way when Hoss is absent or present gives us an idea that Crow is full of self-confidence.

After they exchange a few words and Hoss goes to get some red wine, the stage directions read, "Crow tries to copy Hoss's walk. He goes back and forth across the stage practicing different styles until he gets the exact one. It's important that he gets inside the feeling of Hoss's walk and not just the outer form." Crow is sizing up Hoss, trying to get a feel for who he is by literally trying to walk in his shoes. This foreshadows their upcoming battle and method of fighting. After Hoss comes back, Hoss tells Crow about how he expected Crow's arrival: "I was onto a Gypsy pattern early yesterday. Even conjured going that way myself. CROW: Cold, Leathers. Very icy. Back seat nights. Tuck and roll pillow time. You got fur on the skin in this trunk. HOSS: Yeah, yeah. I'm just getting bored I guess. I want out. CROW: I pattern a conflict to that line. The animal says no. The blood won't go the route. Re-do me the right or wrong? HOSS:

Right I guess. Can't you back the language up, man. I'm too old to follow the flash." We understand a lot about Hoss and Crow from this quick interchange.

(1) Hoss's desire to go Gypsy is confirmed here.
(2) Hoss is sick of the life he is living: he is bored and wants out.
(3) Crow is smart. He understands Hoss perfectly. Hoss is an animal by heart, and as much as he wants out, his killer animal instinct wants in.
(4) Crow is up on current language, which highlights how much Hoss is old and in the past.

After a little more jabbering, a little more of feeling each other out, Crow says, "The Game hammered the outside." Hoss responds, "And how you hammer us with fucking indifference! This is incredible. It's just like I thought. The Outside is the Inside now." Hoss's worst fears are realized. The game has gone Gypsy. Where the game used to be played by the rules, where the game was contained and all of the players played inside the bounds of the game, now the players, the Gypsies, no longer follow the rules of the game. Immediately after this Hoss asks, "How did you get to fucking Neptune in a '58 Impala?" Hoss means how did you manage to get to the outside, outside of earth-bound rules, by driving such a standard car as a '58 Impala. Crow responds, "How did you get to earth in a Maserati?" For the first time, Crow slipped out of his persona. His language was sort of normal. Hoss catches him on this: "There! Why'd you slip just then? Why'd you suddenly talk like a person." Hoss is extremely empowered by this. What seemed to be an intrinsic coolness, is actually just a façade that Crow created. Hoss tells Crow to get the fuck out of his chair. The stage directions read, "Crow slides out of the chair and starts walking around, twirling his chain and chomping his gum. Hoss sits down. He sips his wine. Slowly through the dialogue Crow starts to get into Hoss's walk until he's doing it perfectly." Crow seizes the opportunity, when he is down, to show Hoss that he knows something about him, too. With this exchange, the bout is on: "Yeah, so this is how you play the game. A style match."

They decide that knives are not appropriate for this fight. They are just battling with language and style. This is a battle of deconstruction. If anyone has seen Zoolander and thinks about the walk-off, you'll undertand what Hoss and Crow are doing. In Zoolander, Zoolander and Hansel battle on the runway with the challenge, take the other person's walk and make it your own by improving on it, thus throwing the other person off and throwing off their style. The battle for Hoss and Crow is about inhabiting style so well that it throws off your opponent. They must feed off the language and the style of the other to try to throw the person off their game. They must, in effect, deconstruct the other person, rendering them normal, without style. The battle begins.

I am not really going to spend time going through the battle, partly because of time, but also because the battle does not teach us much about their characters except the couple of things I am going to tell you. First, it is very important to Hoss that there is a referee. We know that the code is central to Hoss's character. So the presence of a ref would probably help Hoss out more than Crow. And second, Hoss disputes some of Crow's points saying that they are not clean. Remember, Crow is a Gypsy; he doesn't play by the rules.

When the ref calls a T.K.O., Hoss shoots him. This is a symbolic act. It appears that for Hoss's whole life, the code and rules were an essential part of his being. By killing the ref, the enforcer of rules, Hoss has killed a central part of himself. Remember, Hoss was described as suicidal and is definitely self-destructive. If the code is dead to Hoss, what else is left for him but to be like the Gypsies? And since he has always played by the rules, he must learn the way of the Gypsies. So when Hoss asks Crow to teach him, Hoss is searching for a new identity to replace the identity that he shot dead. All Hoss has left is his land, and when Crow asks for that, Hoss is left in a state of despair. Hoss would have nothing left, but without the code and without knowing the ways of the Gypsies, Hoss has no way to defend his land. So he has no choice but to give up his land and learn from Crow. But Hoss struggles to learn from Crow because even though he killed the code himself, that was his defining characteristic. He can't learn from the Gypsy because he really isn't one. Hoss's suicide is a result of his understanding his hopeless situation. Without the code, he is nothing. And with the code, he realizes that he is not good enough, that you can't just follow the rules, but you must adapt to the situation. That's why Hoss calls Crow "a master adapter. A visionary adapter." Crow is not bound to the rules but makes the rules work for him. In Hoss's suicide, Hoss can go out the way he chooses, in the style that suits him best. He is not backed into an action, but he chooses this action for himself. He is empowered in his suicide.

As I alluded to earlier, this play is a fantasy. It is a fantasy of the power of language, the power of language to create a possible world, to create possible identities. But as is typical of absurd literature, this fantasy is not so clear cut. This fantasy is simultaneously a utopia and a dystopia, and simultaneously comic and tragic. With language, anything is possible, a bare stage except for a chair can create a fantastic world of rocker or hitmen, it spawns gloriously magnetic personalities that can influence others by reeling off a couple of sentences. With language, Crow is a master adapter, in control of every situation. The mastery of language brings with it mastery of every situation. But for those not quite so skilled, the world falls apart. Identity becomes dangerously tied to rules that provide only so much support. Without full mastery, language creates an ambiguous world where characters pay for their lack of skill with their life. The scary thing about this is that *humans are reliant on language* and the context that language so importantly and necessarily creates for us to understand our reality, and thus humans can never escape either the glory that language engenders or the horror of language's inadequacy: in some ways, this is the greatest and most clear pronouncement of where absurdity derives from in all of absurd literature.

N.F. Simpson

N. F. (Norman Frederick) Simpson was born in London in 1919. After serving in WWII, Simpson graduated from the University of London with a degree in English literature. He then taught adult education for nearly twenty years. His first play, *A Resounding Tinkle*, was noted in the newspaper, *The Observer*. He is best known for his third play, *One Way Pendulum* (1959), but continued to write until 2010, one year before his death.

Most of the conversation surrounding N. F. Simpson concerns the validity of his ties to absurdism and casts doubt about whether his work is meant for anything other than a quick laugh.[23] And I wholeheartedly tend to agree with this assessment by other scholars. Just as Simpson himself said in the late BBC radio interview that he never heard of Eugene Ionesco (a playwright to whom he was frequently compared, though this claim is highly doubtful and probably just another Simpson joke) and was closer to writers like Lewis Carroll and P. G. Wodehouse.[24] Especially the lunacy of Carroll's overall nonsense and zany, quirky characters (e.g., the Mad Hatter) is most reminiscent of the characters in *One Way Pendulum*: the father reconstructs an Old Bailey court replica in their living room; the mother pays a woman to come help eat the family's leftovers; and the son is trying to train 500 machines to sing Handel's Hallelujah chorus. This play, as well as his others, are comedies, with essentially no attempt at portraying the tragic elements that are also present in absurd literature's genre of tragicomedy.

Tom Stoppard

Sir Tom Stoppard was born Tomáš Straussler, in 1937 in Zlín, Czechoslovakia, to non-observant Jewish parents. His family fled to Singapore the day that the Nazis invaded Czechoslovakia. Sent with his brother and his mother to Australia before Japan occupied Singapore, his father, a doctor, died when Stoppard was four. They emigrated once more; the three went to Darjeeling, India, and there he attended an American school, where his name was changed to Tom. His mother married Kenneth Stoppard, a major in the Army, in 1945 where Stoppard got his surname, and the family moved to England in 1946. Leaving school at the age of 17, Stoppard went to work as a journalist, eventually writing about theatre. Starting to write radio plays in 1953, his first play was staged in 1960. But it was with his 1966 play, *Rosencrantz and Guildenstern Are Dead*, which won a Tony Award, that Stoppard rose to the upper echelon in the theatre world. Stoppard has continued to write for the theatre, but with forays into radio, television, and movies. Besides his most famous play, *Rosencrantz and Guildenstern*, Stoppard is also well known for his more recent plays, the comedy, *Travesties* (1974), *Arcadia* (1993), much about chaos theory, and his epic trilogy, *The Coast of Utopia*. Stoppard was knighted in 1997.

Rosencrantz and Guildenstern Are Dead is a spin-off of Shakespeare's *Hamlet*, where Stoppard's play follows the two servants who are supposed to bring Hamlet to his death but instead are executed (because of Hamlet's cleverness) in his place. Stoppard's play focuses on these two, with the other characters and happenings in the play being the minor characters and events. Besides the fact that Stoppard was clearly influenced by other absurd writers – as even in the 1980s the translated works by Mrożek and Havel – and the fact that while the play is hysterically comedic, the tragic element that hangs over the entire play is that the audience already knows that Rosencrantz and Guildenstern are going to die. The only reason that this play, in particular, is seen as absurd is that (1) the banter between the two is reminiscent of Didi and Gogo, often making it hard to distinguish personality differences, and (2) while not "experimental," per se, Stoppard loves to play around with language, with the famous opening dialogue about the probability of flipping a coin heads or tails is the most notable of his career. Roberta Barker is one of many who interprets Stoppard's theatre as political and social commentary.[25] Tom Stoppard's work, though, is largely concerned with chaos theory, the unpredictability of the human element, and its effect on the current human condition in relation to the cyclical nature of the universe.[26] Acknowledging that he is/was a language nerd, Stoppard, maybe more so than any other playwright in this book, really makes language into an enthralling and fun game of wits. For much more on this play and Stoppard's other work, see William W. Demastes' *The Cambridge Introduction to Tom Stoppard*.

Chapter 7

Post-absurdism?

Is there such a thing as post-absurdism? While clearly absurdism is not the dominant "genre" of the theatre (or fiction) anymore (as it was for a while in the 1950s and 1960s, especially), would it be more accurate to say that the arts have (1) moved past the absurd? or (2) incorporated the absurd? There is an argument to be made for both of these assertions.

The influence of the absurdist "movement"

As I quoted Enoch Brater at the end of the Introduction, his words are worth repeating: the absurd "is *all* around." In part, because the influence of the absurd is so great, it is very difficult to truly or accurately measure it. And while some lines of influence are still very direct, as many contemporary writers look to Beckett, Pinter, and Albee as their major and/or primary influences, the absurd's web of influence is seemingly immeasurable (and if we add Kafka, Dadaism, Surrealism, and Joyce to this list, as they influenced Beckett, Pinter, and Albee in one way or another, the web of influence absolutely does become immeasurable). Yes, it is easy to see how tightly wound a web is near its center, but the further one moves away from a web, the gaps between the web's strands widen, and the outside of a web is almost invisible to the naked eye. And such is the influence of the absurd and the height of its expression in the 1950s, 1960s, and 1970s.

It can be suggested, then, that *this* literary avant-garde, which was *experimental* at its inception, in some ways made *experimenting with form, language, and content* – even made *avant-garde* writing – acceptable and more approachable to general readers and theatregoers. And whether we argue that absurd literature had modernist and/or postmodernist leanings, it is quite clear that before the absurd, the leading literature of the day was modernist, and postmodern literature, which generally does experiment with form, language, and content, began to flourish right after the incorporation/assimilation/and so

115

on of absurd literature into mainstream literary techniques. Especially with Beckett's novels, and particularly his Trilogy, we see the transition from the modernist tome in Joyce's *Ulysses* to the grumblings of postmodern (especially) fiction.

The common techniques and themes found in postmodern literature – fragmentation; paradox; trumpeting the multiplicity of truths over a single truth; irony; black humor; wordplay; a mix of high and low culture; and unreliable narrators – begin to emerge in absurd literature. *From* Beckett's fragmentary prose and narration full of wordplay (which became more extreme as he moved from *Murphy* to *Watt* to the "Trilogy") *to* Pinter's "conceptual incompleteness" (which negates the possibility of a single truth/narrative, allowing for the simultaneous presence of multiple truths) *to* Albee's park bench (which symbolically and literally thrusts the worlds of high and low culture into one space) *to* Ionesco's tragicomic worldview (full of irony and black humor), the overall paradoxical nature of absurd literature appears to have laid the foundation for the emergence of postmodern literature. In short, especially since many do consider Beckett the first postmodern writer – by simply acknowledging the previously stated fact that before the 1950s, modernism was the dominant strain of literary expression, and after the 1970s, postmodernism was/is the dominant strain of literary expression – it both logically and circumstantially follows that the literary *absurd* was *a* (if not, maybe, *the*) bridge between literary *modernism* and *postmodernism.*

Dramatic and theatrical conventions following the absurdist "movement"

Looking particularly at dramatic and theatrical conventions following absurd theatre in the 1950s through 1970s might yield something more concrete. At base, and I will leave it stated simply, *twenty-first century audiences are now thoroughly used to "absurd" (or just simply, "experimental") dialogue, settings/situations, and non-Aristotelian arcs.* But there are other extremely important contributions that absurd theatre made, and these contributions have gone largely, or almost totally, unnoticed.

One of the untold innovations of the theatrical absurd is how the audience responds to the events on stage. In general, tragedy and comedy arouse (most generally) sadness/pity and laughter, respectively. While these previously mentioned emotions may be shared by the characters and the audience, many times the audience responds to the characters' *situation*, thus being once-removed from the emotions felt by the characters. That is, the audience might mourn or enjoy the situation of the characters but does not feel the same emotions as the characters, especially for the same reason. For example, in Eugene O'Neill's one-act "Sea Plays," the audience feels sad that the characters are in a hopeless situation and the characters feel trapped by the sea. But the audience does not feel "trapped," themselves. Or when Yank dies in the "Sea Play," *Bound East for Cardiff* (1916), after a fall, the audience is not sad because Yank is going to die, as though the audience was losing its friend. In the play, Driscoll is sad because he is losing Yank, his best friend, but the audience is sad at the situation, or sad for Driscoll's loss. Or the audience feels a sense of loss when Walter Lee Younger, in Lorraine Hansberry's *A Raisin in the Sun* (1959), loses much of the inheritance and jeopardizes the family's future, but the audience, unlike the Youngers, is not feeling as though his or her own future is in jeopardy. In the recent Tony Award-winning smash hit, *One Man, Two Guvnors* (based upon Carlo Goldoni's eighteenth-century *Commedia, The Servant and Two Masters*), the audience is hysterical at the absolutely exasperating situations the main character, Francis Henshall, finds himself in after agreeing to work for two bosses ("guvnors"). When the audience sees Francis try to serve dinner to his two "guvnors" in two neighboring dining rooms without mixing up their orders and keeping his double-employment a secret, the audience laughs hysterically at the same circumstances that Francis, though, finds utterly exasperating.

But especially in the absurd's most quintessential, recognizable, and well-studied plays, the audience feels the same feelings as the characters, for the audience undergoes the same, or at least very similar, experience as the characters on stage. The audience experiences the same ups and downs of waiting and hoping for Godot to arrive; the menace and feeling voiceless during the interrogation scenes[1] in *The Birthday Party*; the audience feels supremely uncomfortable and has the same great sense of unease as do Nick and Honey in *Who's Afraid of Virginia Woolf?* as we enter the private home, at a private hour, and are forced to listen to the normally private quarrel of the two venomous feuding spouses, George and Martha. Likewise the audience makes light of the comic triviality of Rhinoceritis (when, just like the characters, the audience realizes – during Berenger's final stand – that the audience should have recognized the tragedy and horror of the worsening situation and realized that they, the audience, are not much better than the characters who similarly made light of the situation, but become, at last, empowered to fight with Berenger for humanity).

Because the audience many times *subjectively* experiences the same emotions as the characters on stage, the audience find themselves more a part of the onstage world that does not make sense (than in, say, the *objective emotional* responses of "traditional" theatre). Thus, the response to the contradictions presented onstage in an absurd play cannot be merely an *objective intellectual* response (what Bertolt Brecht favored in his Epic Theatre over the *objective emotional* response of "traditional" theatre), where, however, the impulse to make sense of the situation can easily be ignored, but because it is a *subjective emotional* response, the audience feels personally part of the world that does not make sense and must resolve their own emotions; however, in order to resolve those emotions, it is necessary to have a subsequent *subjective intellectual* response.

To further develop J. L. Styan's prescient and insightful arguments in his book, *The Dark Comedy* – which suggests that much of twentieth-century drama has eschewed the traditional genres of tragedy and comedy, creating not tragicomedy in the traditional Aristotelian sense, but a comic tragedy that he thinks is best described as "dark comedy" – maybe the greatest contribution that the absurd made on the theatre is that "tragicomedy" has become the default "genre" in the theatre. For over two millennia, plays were either "tragedies" or "comedies." And any "mixing" of the two before the twentieth century generally caused quite a controversy. And while we can say that *Godot*'s contribution was that it got rid of the beginning and the end of a play, maybe we can also say that Beckett wrote the first truly "mixed" play, so mixed between tragedy and comedy that the world could not fathom how expressions of despair and joy could be uttered within minutes, if not seconds, of each other.

And while *absurd tragicomedy* – the specific brand of tragicomedy found in absurd literature – might no longer dominate the stage, theatrical realism is now essentially tragicomedy and tragicomedy is now essentially theatrical realism. If we consider a list of the most well-studied and taught (in Western university classrooms), English-language plays since the 1980s (the decade following the end of the height of the theatrical absurd), we see how many of them are tragicomedies (**in bold**): *Translations*; ***Crimes of the Heart***; ***Master Harold and the Boys***; *'night Mother*; ***Glengarry Glen Ross***; ***Fences***; *M Butterfly*; ***The Heidi Chronicles***; ***The Piano Lesson***; ***Angels in America***; ***Buried Child***; ***The Goat, or Who is Sylvia?***; ***Topdog/Underdog***; and ***August: Osage County***.

In a recent production of Eugene O'Neill's *Long Day's Journey into Night* at the Guthrie Theater in Minneapolis, the play, normally put on as a serious tragedy, was not just humorous, but very funny (inducing laughter). While the above plays owe a great deal to O'Neill's family-room tragedies, this production was only possible because of the steady diet of tragicomedy fed to audiences over the past thirty-odd years.[2] In short, the norms of witnessing a tragicomedy/tragicomic worldview appears to have become so commonplace that even some plays that were not originally understood as tragicomedies can be read or seen tragicomically.

(Later) female absurdists

Adrienne Kennedy was writing in the early 1960s and was a part of Edward Albee's New York City theatre workshop (i.e., The Playwrights Unit). Particularly by this first-degree connection and clearly part of this not-self-proclaimed movement of the absurd, female playwrights were largely absent from the theatrical absurd of the 1950s and 1960s. There are many possible hypotheses as to why this was the case: no matter what, in the 1950s and 1960s male playwrights still dominated the stage; slightly later, women were beginning the fight for equal rights and respect, and feminist concerns were the primary topic of many plays by female writers; and also there seems to be something particularly "male" about the philosophical nature of sometimes/somewhat universal-absurd situations (i.e., these absurd plays seem to induce linear objective thinking about grandly stated ideas versus plays that portray much more personal situations that tend to invoke emotional responses). However, for whatever reason that audiences did not encounter many female absurd voices in the 1950s and 1960s, that does not mean that the absurd is primarily a "male" phenomenon: simply, it took a little while for the absurd to find its own expression in female voices and visions of the absurd in the 1970s and 1980s. And while the female absurd might not manifest itself in plays of the exact same tone, arc, or cadence, that does not by any means preclude them from being considered as an absurd writer, as in these three female playwrights (and many more could be added to the list).

Beth Henley

Beth Henley is an American playwright best known for her 1980 Pulitzer Prize-winning play, *Crimes of the Heart* (which also won the New York Drama Critics Circle Award for Best American Play and was nominated for a Tony Award for Best Play). While Henley's realistic writing style, especially in *Crimes of the Heart*, is somewhat antithetical to the experimentation with non-realistic language generally found in absurd literature, Henley – maybe more so than any other female writer of absurd literature – really captures the absurd *situation* for women. Henley's absurd situations are not some philosophical or universalized situation: Henley is writing about localized female bodies in everyday domestic situations that are quite ridiculous and absurd.[3] Henley thematically dramatizes, in a humorous manner, the tragic plight of the *second sex*: taking up so many issues found in Simone de Beauvoir's 1949 classic of the same name that became the seminal text for second-wave feminism that lasted, especially in the United States, well into the 1980s. But while many of the earlier male absurdists only hint at a solution to the presented-absurd situation (forcing the audience/reader to figure it out, themselves), Henley does suggest a solution: sisterhood.

Crimes of the Heart is a play in a real town in the South in the United States, taking place five years after a real hurricane that centers around Babe, a young woman stuck in a loveless marriage who shoots her husband because she "didn't like his looks."[4] But along with Babe, her two sisters, Meg and Lenny, (while maybe in less ridiculous circumstances) find themselves in typical absurd situations: Meg is gorgeous and just starting to age past her prime, struggling to become an actress in Los Angeles and Lenny has a bad ovary and cannot have children. It takes a ridiculous act like shooting her husband because Babe claims she "didn't like his looks" to expose how absurd everyday situations are for many women. (This is not unlike the instant-classic, Marsha Norman's *'night Mother*, which preceded Henley's play by three years, however, Norman's play is mostly straight tragedy.) Again, while in the narrative arc of theatrical realism, along with realistic language, Henley creates both humor and sorrow, a somewhat tragicomic view, encased in the absurd. But as mentioned before, Henley provides sisterhood as a model to combat the absurd situations that females find themselves in, and with this solution, *Crimes of the Heart* has a happy, uplifting, and hopeful ending.

Maria Irene Fornes

Maria Irene Fornes, a Cuban-born American playwright, writing at her height in the early 1980s, comes off of the cultural and literary feminist wave of the 1970s. Her plays examine, especially in *Mud, The Conduct of Life*, and *Sarita*, strong women placed in difficult, many times no-win, absurd situations. Writing frequently in many scenes, her plays rebel against the Aristotelian narrative arc. Instead of two flat lines that comprise Act I and Act II of *Waiting for Godot*, her scenes, one after another, tend to have a rising action, but neither climax nor resolve; much like *Godot*, the audience is left hanging, but with Fornes' more on the edge of their seats. Fornes experiments with language, not in a way that feels like experimental language, but is clearly not attempts at language that is neither supposed to mirror real speech nor is flowery. Fornes does work with *non sequiturs*, but the brevity and curtness of much of her dialogue is almost as jarring.

The end of *Mud* really epitomizes, to me, the central debate/tragedy/ advice/outcry of Fornes' work. *Mud* is about a young woman, Mae, subservient to and torn between two men. She is bound to one by a sense of obligation, bound to the other by a promise of a better life (which she learns, later, he cannot give). The ever-present iron in the center of the kitchen table (placed in the center of the room) is a literal and metaphorical reminder of her domesticity, both to place in the home and her place in relation to the two men in her life. Finally, a series of realizations leads Mae to harden her resolve and act for her sake:

> I'm leaving, Lloyd. I'm going somewhere else. I'm leaving you and Henry. Both of you are no good. I got rotten luck. I work too hard and the two of you keep sucking my blood. I'm going to look for a better place to be ... Just a place where the two of you are not sucking my blood. I'm going to find myself a job. And a room to live in. Far away from you. Where I don't have my blood sucked.[5]

Mae's absurd situation, and her only solution for a better life, reminds the audience of the absurd situation discussed in Virginia Woolf's *A Room of One's Own*. Mae must find "a room to live in" and with "a job," a source of her own income so she is not reliant on a husband and the responsibilities of a family that generally accompany marriage, in order to thrive. Mae's death at the end both accomplishes her desire to leave her current life, but it comes at a tragic cost.

Cut into short scenes that also rise in tension (like *Mud* and *The Conduct of Life*), Sarita, the young title character of *Sarita*, whom we follow over the years, also finds herself bound to two men. There are two things, though, notable, about this play in comparison to *Mud* and *The Conduct of Life* (which is about a woman who is married to a soldier who constantly rapes a young girl whom he holds against her will), which both have tragic endings: (1) at the end of the play, Sarita's future appears hopeful, and (2) there are many songs in this play. And maybe it is these very songs that Fornes uses to disrupt the traditional Aristotelian narrative arc that actually helps the audience understand the play. These simple songs all come at big dramatic moments in the play after something major has happened to a character. But these songs also do not add any previously unknown information. So since the words themselves can almost be ignored, the songs essentially set the mood for a moment of contemplation and reflection. Unlike Bertolt Brecht – who used songs in his plays to break the narrative arc so that the audience would emotionally distance themselves from the characters and their stories in order to think more about social and political change – Fornes' use of songs in *Sarita* seems to provide a pause to let the audience sink deeper into a personal and emotional moment of individual change. Much like Henley's *Crimes of the Heart*, Fornes does not paint a portrait of a universally absurd situation and have the audience contemplate a philosophical response; she places very real female characters in very real (and visceral) absurd situations and has the audience ride an emotional journey sometimes so disturbing (especially in a play as graphic and horrific as *The Conduct of Life*) that the audience's only response must be an intellectual one in order to process what the audience just saw (i.e., what just happened to these female characters).

Caryl Churchill

Caryl Churchill is a British playwright whose works have spanned an astonishing seven decades. She is thought of as one of the most important female playwrights in the second half of the twentieth century, and her plays are hugely influential. Much like Fornes, Churchill's most notable play comes out of the wave of feminism in the 1960s and 1970s. Much like Beckett, Churchill is a great experimenter with language. And her language is definitely Beckettian in flavor. Not only is her language full of Beckettian *non sequiturs*, but also *non sequiturs* fill her narrative arcs, plots, and the resultant actions, most particularly in her most famous 1979 play, *Cloud 9* (so well-studied that I will neither summarize nor analyze it here other than offering the following brushstrokes). Beckett's use of the *non sequitur* in some ways mirrors the general condition of absurdity – both in the disconnect between the reality of the world and our desires and in a general sense of ridiculousness. However, in Churchill's plays, particularly *Cloud 9*, the language and its lack of linearity – with language's essentially unstable meanings – mirror (much less generally and more directly) the instability of character and, most particularly, gender and/or sexuality. This can be seen in evaluation, especially the sex and the sexuality, of the characters that appear, first in Act I, as largely oppressed characters in the nineteenth century imperial and colonial British Empire and, later, in Act II, in their contemporary, much less-delineated but more-liberated identities. Like Henley's *Crimes of the Heart*, Churchill provides a type of solution to the absurd situation she presents in *Cloud 9*: that is, there would be much more personal – and, by extension, societal – contentment if identities were not drawn by draconian formulations where sex determines sexuality and identity.

The multicultural absurd?

One of the criticisms of the "Theatre of the Absurd" is that it was an exclusively white male endeavor. This may be true to a point, but it is not quite an accurate reflection of what was going on when and who these writers were. First, while the most studied and influential absurdists in the 1950s and 1960s were white males, it was not *quite* the case that they – Beckett, Pinter, Ionesco, Genet, and Albee – constituted the *archetypal white male*: Beckett was Irish, raised Protestant (versus the dominant religion in Ireland, Catholicism), and lived as an adult in Paris; Pinter was Jewish; Ionesco was Romanian and lived in Paris; Genet was gay; and Albee is gay and was adopted into a white, American family of wealth. That is in no way to say they were still not *white males*, but they certainly had some reasons to feel like they were not a part of the *white-male hegemony*. And while these five writers in particular were all white and were all males, we cannot forget about Amiri Baraka (an African-American male) and Adrienne Kennedy (an African-American female), both of whom were writing in the United States in the 1960s. Scholars generally consider them to have been outliers writing after the fact, but if we consider the fact that the literary absurd did not even make it to the United States until 1958, Baraka and Kennedy were writing right during the height of absurd literature in the United States.

Especially in the early history of theatre (and literature, too) in the United States, "multicultural" was synonymous with African-American literature. Without the same long theatrical lineage as whites (usually males), early plays by African-Americans, such as Langston Hughes' *Mulatto*, were a bit behind the theatrical moment. Hughes' play was a hit because of its exploration of contemporary issues, but the play itself was a melodrama, the dominant form of drama for most of the nineteenth century. It was not until Lorainne Hansberry's *A Raisin in the Sun* that African-American drama had enough of a history and, with this play, a truly great play, to build upon. But once Hansberry helped African-American dramatists catch up, in a sense, to where American drama was, immediately after we see playwrights like Baraka and Kennedy on the "cutting edge" (avant-garde). Amiri Baraka and his involvement in the Black Arts Movement had a huge influence on all types of African-American writers. And much like the rest of, especially, the history of US multicultural drama, African-American drama (and literature as a whole) opened up the doors and paved a path to the flood of multicultural voices in the 1980s, not only in the United States, but around the world.

While it may be hard to definitively make this statement, it could be suggested that Baraka's own *satiric* take on absurd literature (e.g., while Baraka's famous play, *Dutchmen*, is very satir-ical, Baraka literally satirizes Genet's *The Blacks: A Clown Show* with his own short Menippean satire, *Great Goodness of Life: A Coon Show*) influenced and was prime instigator of African-American satiric novels that really emerged and came to prominence in the 1970s to 1990s. Some of the most typical elements of African-American satire are the frequent use of *reductio ad absurdum* and the presence of chaos.[6]

The satire in African-American novels, while generally written in straightforward prose (but not always in a straightforward narrative structure, as postmodern pastiche and fragmentation are clearly present in many later African-American satiric novels), incorporates the reduction to absurdity, the chaos, and a type of universality present in much of absurd theatre from the 1950s to 1970s in order to (specifically in African-American satire) critique the logic of racism (among other things). These elements are all found in Baraka's works, and given his monumental stature and influence in the arts in the African-American community, it seems like a plausible suggestion that African-American satiric novels emerged out of Baraka's own version of the literary absurd.

Absurdism's legacy outside of the theatre: Fiction and poetry after the wake of the 1970s

What really set absurd literature apart from other avant-garde literary "movements" before (or even, maybe, after) is that avant-garde literary movements – think of avant-garde movements such as expressionism, futurism, Dadaism, and constructivism – while flourishing for a short while, were always on the outside of the mainstream (in theatre and literature) and eventually withered into oblivion. But as stated before, absurd literature, particularly the theatrical absurd, became the mainstream theatre of the day (for a relatively short while, a decade or so). But, largely, like the statement made earlier that twenty-first-century audiences are now thoroughly used to absurd elements found in contemporary plays, readers of late-twentieth and twenty-first century fiction and poetry are much more used to experimentation with language, content, and form. By the late 1970s and early 1980s, fiction frequently features non-realistic and/or experimental language, much more questionable and/or not clearly-defined narrators, experimentation with form (such as, for example, the use of lists and footnotes/endnotes), and absurd/ridiculous situations. By the same time, if not earlier, poets have been experimenting with language (and a renewed sense of the sound of language), experimenting with/removing the voice of the poem, and continually playing with the poem's form.

Apart from genre and "movements," as a whole, absurd literature is also made up of the works of *individual* writers, and these writers were by no means a homogeneous group. The web of influence, for example, emanating just from Samuel Beckett, spans the globe. Besides such theatrical giants as Edward Albee, Eugene Ionesco, Harold Pinter, and Tom Stoppard, the famed novelists John Banville, William S. Burroughs, and J. M. Coetzee, a foremost literary critic and theorist, Jacques Derrida, and noted poets, Paul Muldoon and Edna O'Brien, have all publicly (either directly or indirectly) stated Beckett as an influence of their work. But when we move away just from Beckett, we see even more vagary in the lines of influence. For example, maybe most notable among the other absurd writers, Amiri Baraka's influence, as mentioned earlier, on the Black Arts Movement was monumental to an entire generation or two of African-American novelists and poets.

Absurdism in pop culture

Pop Culture takes its cues from so many sources that it is hard to assess precisely the influence absurd literature has had on it. But as in how readers (and audience members) of twenty-first century literature are used to many absurd elements that featured prominently in the works of Beckett and absurd plays of the 1950s to 1970s, it is hard to imagine the success, for example, of commercials like the ones from the American insurance company, Geico, if the absurd has not seeped into the very fabric of late-twentieth and twenty-first-century popular culture. And while most absurd elements found in popular culture are probably very indirect, here are some examples of much more or very direct references to absurd literature.

Sesame Street's Monsterpiece Theater, *"Waiting for Elmo"*

Maybe the most direct reference to the literary absurd in popular culture, in the March 15, 1996 episode of the classic children's television show, *Sesame Street*, the play *Waiting for Elmo*, airs on *Sesame Street's* semi-regular sketch, "Monsterpiece Theater" (a parody/homage to PBS's *Masterpiece Theatre*, America's longest-running weekly primetime drama series). The host of "Monsterpiece Theater," Alistair Cookie (i.e., Cookie Monster) pronounces that the play, *Waiting for Elmo*, is, "so modern and so brilliant that it makes absolutely no sense to anybody, including Alistair. Okay, maybe you can figure it out." Set in front of a bleak and empty backdrop and next to a tree with no leaves on it, two *Sesame Street* characters are "waiting, waiting, waiting" for Elmo to come meet them at the tree.

Seinfeld's "The Chinese Restaurant"

One of television's most successful and influential sitcoms, *Seinfeld* – commonly referred to and known as "a show about nothing" – got into the absurd act with its (both popularly and academically) much-discussed May 23, 1991 episode, "The Chinese Restaurant," written by Larry David and Jerry Seinfeld. Taking place entirely in real time, *Seinfeld*'s main characters – Jerry, Elaine, George, and Kramer – come in and wait to be seated at a Chinese restaurant. Spending their time in idle, meaningless discourse (which, itself, is a hallmark of *Seinfeld*), for one reason or another, other people are constantly being seated before them. Nothing happens the entire episode except waiting and talking until in the show's final minute when they leave the restaurant having never been seated, and a few seconds later, which are the closing seconds of the show, their name is called to be seated.

Waiting for Guffman

Waiting for Guffman is a 1997 mockumentary co-written and directed by Christopher Guest, whose 1984 mockumentary, *This is Spinal Tap*, made the mockumentary (i.e., mock-documentary) film genre famous. Featuring some of Guest's regular members of his ensemble cast (for example, Catherine O'Hara, Eugene Levy, and Guest himself), *Waiting for Guffman*, obviously taking its name from *Waiting for Godot*, follows the townsfolk of the fictional town of Blaine, Missouri, who are putting on a community theatre performance of a musical documenting Blaine's history in honor of the town's 150th anniversary. The zany director, who had a past in "off-off-off-off" Broadway theatre, uses his connections to invite a Broadway producer to review their musical. The *hope* is that a good review from this producer will land the musical on Broadway. During the whole film, the townsfolk hope for this producer to come. During the show's premier in Blaine, the cast of the musical gets excited because they think that the producer is in the audience. However, he turns out to be simply a relative of a resident of Blaine. After the show, the director reads a telegram stating that the Broadway producer's airplane was grounded by snow in New York City and that he will not make it to Blaine: that is, Blaine's "Godot" never comes.

Curb Your Enthusiasm

Larry David, the co-creator of *Seinfeld*, is the creator and star of *Curb Your Enthusiasm*, which airs on HBO (allowing David more artistic freedom than he had with *Seinfeld* on network television). *Curb Your Enthusiasm* follows typical days in the life of "Larry David," a fictional, comedic alter-ego of the real-life Larry David (for example, in the show, "Larry David" is still the co-creator of *Seinfeld*). Much like how *Seinfeld* is "a show about nothing," *Curb Your Enthusiasm*, too, displays many of the traits of being *about* "nothing": in some ways, *Seinfeld* has much more ridiculous plots (and *Seinfeld*'s elements of ridiculous situations makes the show quite absurd), while *Curb Your Enthusiasm* is *about* "nothing" in that the action concerns so much of the meaningless day-to-day routines and situations that one finds oneself regularly in. One thing that differentiates *Curb Your Enthusiasm* from *Seinfeld* is that while the characters in *Seinfeld* are really just despicable people (versus, say, *I Love Lucy*, who are endearing like so many other characters from sitcoms before *Seinfeld*), the absurd situations that Larry David finds himself in are much more absurd in the vein of Camus' brand of absurdity, where Larry's desires are constantly not being met by the realities of the world. In *Curb Your Enthusiasm*, Larry so often tries to do the right thing, and when he does try to do the right thing, it always turns out to backfire and work against him. And, partly because of this, Larry, alternatively, often has to be selfish, deceitful, and conniving, precisely because his attempts at doing the right thing are so often thwarted by the realities of the world. In short, since Larry lives in outrageously absurd situations, despite his attempts at being a good person, he is often forced, in order to try to get what he wants (and sometimes deserves), to be much more like one of the characters found in *Seinfeld*. *Curb Your Enthusiasm*, then, is kind of a contemporary comedic take on Bertolt Brecht's *The Good Person of Szechwan*, where the main character of that play, a kindly business woman, who is too kind, not making enough money to survive, is essentially forced to create a fake relative who is mean and shrewd in order to make enough money to survive.

Chapter 8

Absurd criticism

The scholarship surrounding the major writers traditionally affiliated with the theatrical absurd (e.g., Beckett, Ionesco, Genet, Pinter, and Albee) has generally worked under, or alongside, the rubric of absurdism. These playwrights' not-self-proclaimed affiliation with the "absurd" came about, and, in part, in response to, with Martin Esslin's 1961 book, *The Theatre of the Absurd*, following his article by the same name in 1960. Using Camus' philosophy of the absurd, Esslin argues that the plays of the Theatre of the Absurd investigate the "metaphysical anguish" of the human condition and the purported purposelessness of life.[1] Yet Esslin was not the first scholar to characterize the poster child of absurdism, Beckett, and his work as "absurd."[2] In what appears to be the very first academic article on Beckett, Edith Kern, in 1954, described *Waiting for Godot* as portraying, "the absurdly comical situation" of "man's place in the universe."[3] The philosophical world of Beckett, as argued by Kern, stands in stark contrast to that imagined by Esslin. Esslin's Beckett imagines the world without a God and – in many ways stemming from this – ultimately, without purpose. Kern's Beckett sees human tenderness as that which not only gives humans meaning, strength, and the will to go on, but as something that which, itself, replaces the God-like redeemer: "Beckett's characters in [*Waiting for Godot*] glorify rather the all-surpassing power of human tenderness which alone makes bearable man's long and ultimately futile wait for a redeemer and which, in fact, turns out itself to be the redeemer of man in his forlornness."[4]

Esslin states that "By 1942 Albert Camus was calmly putting the question why, since life had lost all meaning, should man not seek escape in suicide?"[5] This leads Esslin (and the field) to a very bleak reading of Beckett's work. However, Camus' entire book, *The Myth of Sisyphus*, was explicitly about why one should *not* commit suicide because we can make meaning for ourselves only through our act of defiance against our absurd situation. David Carroll explains that for Camus, "suicide represents a flight from the Absurd ... Absurd reasoning, as a thinking of difference, separation and divorce, strives to maintain these tensions and make them the reason to live ... "[6] Camus was *not* an existentialist (as argued forcefully by Marc Blanchard).[7] Camus idealized the human and believed in a basically essentialist, good human nature, and Camus used reason, something antithetical to existentialist, not experience, to make meaning out of our lives. As I argued many times elsewhere, Camus revolted against nihilistic existentialism, especially Sartre. Peter Royle characterizes the differing philosophies of Sartre and Camus in this wonderfully pithy and fully correct assessment: Sartre is an "existential phenomenologist in the grand European philosophical tradition," and Camus is a "disabused heir of the Enlightenment."[8] Kern's insights into Beckett's work, however, were pretty much lost once Esslin's book shaped the field of the Theatre of the Absurd and scholarship surrounding the above-named "absurdists."

Esslin

Martin Esslin spent the final 40-plus years of his career contemplating the absurd, particularly in the theatre. In addition to his three editions of his classic, *The Theatre of the Absurd* (1961, 1969, and 2004), Esslin wrote numerous pages over the years, seemingly trying to come to grips with his initial success: to me, it seems as though Esslin found himself in the pull of wanting to say more, maybe even contradict his earlier statements and categorizations about the absurd, and being bound to his legacy associated with writing *The Theatre of the Absurd*. While, as time went on, his readings lightened up and focused more on laughter than the "metaphysical anguish" that characterized much of his initial work on the subject, Esslin's own criticism seemed to fall prey to his own legacy associated with the legacy *of The Theatre of the Absurd*. As each edition of *The Theatre of the Absurd* came out, simultaneously more and more playwrights were categorized as absurd, while at the same time, maybe hearing the criticism and understanding the limitations of categorizing himself, Esslin eased up a bit on the bleak view of life often associated with the category of the absurd.

Esslin's contemporaries

Ruby Cohen, the first scholar to write a dissertation on Samuel Beckett, in some ways took the torch from Esslin, with her earlier books reading Beckett in relation to the absurd. But Cohen, whose much-respected, decades-long career was not the only voice about the absurd. Besides Esslin's first edition in 1961 and second edition in 1969 of *The Theatre of the Absurd* that bookended the 1960s, Leonard Cabell Pronko wrote *Avant-Garde: The Experimental Theater in France* (1962), Arnold P. Hinchcliffe wrote *The Absurd* (1969), and George Wellwarth wrote *The Theater of Protest and Paradox: Developments in the Avant-Garde Drama* (1971). These books, while by no means challenging Esslin's seminal book, did attempt to place the theatrical absurd in the tradition of the avant-garde. This scholarly move to place the absurd in the avant-garde tradition makes a lot of sense in the context of the then-present rise and study of experimental theatre with the founding of groups like Bread and Puppet Theater, La MaMa, and The Open Theater, as a well as notable performances at The Living Theatre.

The lull in absurd criticism

While the reasons are unknown why the "absurd," as a subject unto itself, became essentially non-existent in the 1970s, there are four (and probably more) viable explanations, especially if taken in conjunction[9]: (1) the rise of deconstructionism and "theory" had literature and theatre departments de-categorizing and theorizing texts in relation to the theories of the day; (2) the battle between scholars of dramatic literature and scholars of theatrical performance started to be waged with the rise of "professionalism" in departments; (3) it is possible that since so much had been written on the subject of the absurd in the preceding decade, scholars just simply ran out of steam and desire; and (4) with the rise of "professionalism," scholars also began to specialize in more and more niche topics, as the simultaneous rise of the "expert" emerged in academia; therefore, those who had been focusing on the absurd, started to focus on instead just one, or maybe two, of the writers associated with absurd literature.

The resurgence of absurd criticism in the new millennium

Though Esslin's hold on the field remains strong even today (five decades later), there is an unstated – and possibly un-self-aware – shift back to Kern's original understanding of Beckett's work. In recent books, especially about Beckett, the playwright generates by far the most scholarship, and this scholarship takes the lead and trickles out to the other writers associated with the, especially theatrical, absurd. In 2006, academia celebrated Samuel Beckett's 100th birthday. The outpouring of scholarship was monumental. Greeted with a special issue in *Modern Drama* and well over a dozen books solely about Beckett's work within the two years after his centenary, Beckett scholarship remains a vibrant force in literature departments. Milestone birthdays such as this offer a unique opportunity to look back *and* forward to contextualize what Beckett meant and continues to mean to the academy, to writers, readers, directors, actors, theatergoers, students, and so on.

Books such as Linda Ben-Zvi and Angela Moorjani's edited collection, *Beckett at 100: Revolving it All* (New York: Oxford University Press, 2008); S. E. Gontarski and Anthony Ulhmann's collection, *Beckett After Beckett* (Gainesville: University Press of Florida, 2006); Brigitte Le Juez's *Beckett Before Beckett* (London: Souvenir, 2008); Ronan McDonald's *The Cambridge Introduction to Samuel Beckett* (Cambridge University Press, 2006); and Christopher Murry's collection, *Samuel Beckett: 100 Years: Centenary Essays* (Dublin: New Island, 2006) demonstrate both the continued pull of Esslin's original reading and also provide some of the attempts that are being made to break free of it. These five books, which are all meant to in some ways serve as a critical assessment of Beckett's work demonstrate the uneven progression of Beckett scholarship, but also show how variegated the topics explored can be and how Beckett's work supports such variety. In the wide range of criticism found today in the field of Beckett, which in a sense provides an excellent snapshot of the field of absurd criticism as a whole, scholarship can be still be located, I think, within the broad spectrum created by Esslin and Kern's early opposing assessments of Beckett's work, from a bleak, dark world to a world where human tenderness gives life meaning.

While the 1980s and 1990s saw a brief burst of books about the absurd,[10] as maybe scholars were most likely over the exhaustion of the outpouring of absurd criticism in especially the 1960s and had some important things to say, now with a bit of hindsight, absurd criticism exploded once more in the first decade of the twentieth century: besides celebrating Beckett's 100th birthday, Edward Albee rediscovered his former glory, especially with the modern, *The Goat: Or Who is Sylvia?: Notes Towards a Definition of Tragedy*, and Harold Pinter was awarded the Nobel Prize in Literature. Alongside scholarship on the absurd firmly rooted in the United States and Western Europe, a dramatic rise in scholarship on the absurd from every corner of the world began (maybe to more years of access to translations and maybe also due to the ease of retrieving scholarship through the internet, making the scholarly communities, or at least access to them, more accessible). And this flourishing of articles on the absurd,[11] is also reflected by the publication of two major books: Neil Cornwell's *The Absurd in Literature* (2006), an extremely comprehensive survey of absurd literature and my own *Reassessing the Theatre of the Absurd* (2011), the first book, as I mentioned earlier, to pose an outright challenge to Esslin's *The Theatre of the Absurd*.

Cornwell's book is important in that it is the first book to examine in detail the literary absurd not just through its most-recognizable and most highly-crystalized form in the theatre, but through fiction as well as poetry. Cornwell's book also places the absurd in a long lineage of literature dating back to the Greeks. My book has one main goal: to show how some of the most quintessential plays of the absurd can be read as hopeful and suggesting how life can be made meaningful, and thus by suggesting the opposite reading of Esslin's readings that the two readings would cancel each other out, thereby freeing the plays from the absurd label. In order to aid in reaching this primary goal, (1) I argue that Esslin both misread Camus as an existentialist and mistranslated Ionesco's definition of the "absurd," which has unofficially remained the definition of the "absurd," and (2) I suggest an "alternative" term (not a term to replace, but to sit alongside), "parabolic drama," reflecting solely structural elements that I observe are common to these plays. Since, especially, the publication of *Reassessing the Theatre of the Absurd*, the study of the absurd has been re-invigorated as well as the freedom to challenge the *status quo* of absurd criticism, as evidenced by two titles of recent doctoral dissertations – "Re-envisioning the Theatre of the Absurd: The Lacanian Spectator and the Work of Fernando Arrabal, Arthur Adamov and Eugene Ionesco" (2011); "Waiting for Virgilio: Reassessing Cuba's Teatro del Absurdo" (2013) – as well as the defense of at least five other doctoral dissertations on various topics on the absurd around the world just between the years 2011 and 2013.[12] This increase in scholarly output surrounding absurd writers and their literature demonstrates solid evidence that the study of the absurd is alive and well, and that absurd literature will remain an important object of study well into the twenty-first century.

Notes

Chapter 1. Introduction: Overview of the absurd

1. Walter Kaufmann, *Existentialism: From Dostoevsky to Sartre* (New York: Plume, 1975), 11.
2. Ibid.
3. Christopher Innes, "The Canon: The Theatre of the Absurd. By Martin Esslin," *Times Higher Education* 18 June 2009.
4. Michael Y. Bennett, *Reassessing the Theatre of the Absurd: Camus, Beckett, Ionesco, Genet, and Pinter* (New York: Palgrave Macmillan, 2011), 7–8.
5. Martin Esslin, *The Theatre of the Absurd* (New York: Anchor Books, 1961), xviii.
6. Esslin xviii–xix.
7. Esslin xix.
8. Esslin xix.
9. Esslin xix. Esslin's quoting of Ionesco has more or less defined the "absurd" for both the public and many academics. However, a look at the original French source reveals that Ionesco's "definition" has the basically opposite meaning of "absurd" to Esslin's translation of it. See Michael Y. Bennett, *Reassessing the Theatre of the Absurd: Camus, Beckett, Ionesco, Genet, and Pinter* (New York: Palgrave Macmillan, 2011), 9–10.
10. Esslin xix–xx.
11. Esslin xx.
12. Esslin xxi.
13. Esslin xvii–xviii.
14. "Label," *Oxford English Dictionary*, 2nd edn., 1989.
15. "Convention," *Oxford English Dictionary*, 2nd edn., 1989.
16. Charles Juliet, *Conversations with Samuel Beckett and Bram van Velde* (Dalkey Archive Press, 1996): 148–9.
17. Edward Albee, *Conversations with Edward Albee*, Ed. Philip C. Kolin (Jackson: University Press of Mississippi, 1988), 132.
18. "Ridiculous," *Oxford English Dictionary* 2nd edn., 1989.
19. Marvin Carlson, *Theories of the Theatre: A Historical and Critical Survey, from the Greeks to the Present* (Ithaca: Cornell University Press, 1984), 23.
20. Carlson 31.
21. Carlson 45–6.

22. Carlson 53–4.
23. Carlson 46–55. In Spain, a similar quarrel sprung up between Spain's two greatest literary talents: Miguel de Cervantes (1547–1616) and Lope de Vega (1562–1635). In short, Cervantes sided with the classical rules (*arte*) and Lope de Vega sided with Spanish custom (*uso*). Cervantes defended the ancient precepts of theatre, while Lope de Vega went so far as to qualify the traditional positions by the demands of the audience, and thus, he suggested that tragedy and comedy, much like the conversation surrounding the "tragicomic pastoral" in Italy, may be mixed (Carlson 61–2).
24. See Neil Cornwell, *The Absurd in Literature* (Manchester University Press, 2006), 33–64.
25. "Eugene Ionesco, The Art of Theater No. 6," Interviewed by Shusha Guppy, *The Paris Review* 93 (Fall 1984).
26. For a thoroughly comprehensive, first-rate book on the history of the theatrical avant-garde, which discusses Alfred Jarry, expressionism, Futurism, Dadaism, and constructivism all at great length, see Günter Berghaus, *Theatre, Performance, and the Historical Avant-Garde* (New York: Palgrave Macmillan, 2005).
27. Ramona Fotiade, *Conceptions of the Absurd: From Surrealism to the Existential Thought of Chestov and Fondane* (Oxford: Legenda, 2001), 3.
28. Fotiade 4.
29. Fotiade 4.
30. See Marc Blanchard, "Before Ethics: Camus's *Pudeur*" *MLN* 112.4 (1997): 666–82; David Carroll, "Rethinking the Absurd: *Le Mythe de Sisyphe*," *The Cambridge Companion to Camus*, ed. Edward J. Hughes (Cambridge University Press, 2007), 53–66; Jacques Ehrmann, "Camus and the Existential Adventure" *Yale French Studies* 25 (1960): 93–7; Jeffrey Gordon, "The Triumph of Sisyphus" *Philosophy and Literature* 32.1 (2008): 183–90; H. Gaston Hall, "Aspects of the Absurd" *Yale French Studies* 25 (1960): 26–32; Philip Hallie, "Camus and the Literature of Revolt" *College English* 16.1 (Oct. 1954): 25–32, 83; Lawrence D. Kritzman, "Camus' Curious Humanism or the Intellectual in Exile" *MLN* 112.4 (Sept. 1997): 550–75; Sir Herbert Read, "Foreward," *The Rebel: An Essay on Man in Revolt*, by Albert Camus (New York: Vintage Books, 1956), 3–11; Avi Sagi, *Albert Camus and the Philosophy of the Absurd*, Trans. Batya Stein (Amsterdam: Rodopi, 2002); Emmanuelle Anne Vanborre, ed., *The Originality and Complexity of Albert Camus's Writings* (New York: Palgrave Macmillan, 2012).
31. For more on Camus and Sartre's relationship and quarrel, see Ronald Aronson, *Camus and Sartre: The Story of a Friendship and the Quarrel That Ended It* (University of Chicago Press, 2004); Michael Y. Bennett, *Words, Space, and the Audience: The Theatrical Tension between Empiricism and Rationalism* (New York: Palgrave Macmillan, 2012), 84–9; Germaine Brée, *Camus and Sartre: Crisis and Commitment* (New York: Delacorte Press, 1972); Leo Pollmann, *Sartre and Camus: Literature of Existence*, trans. Helen and Gregor Sebba (New York: Frederik Ungar Publishing Co., 1970); Peter Royle, *The Sartre-Camus Controversy: A Literary and Philosophical Critique* (University of Ottawa Press, 1982); and David A. Sprintzen and Adrian van der Hoven, eds. and trans., *Sartre and Camus: A Historic Confrontation* (Amherst, New York: Humanity Books, 2004).

32. For more on Beckett and Joyce's relationship, see James Knowlson, *Damned to Fame: The Life of Samuel Beckett* (New York: Grove Press, 1996). There are, of course, other biographies of Beckett that can be consulted, as well.

33. "Strange," *Oxford English Dictionary*, 2nd edn., 1989.

34. In *Reassessing the Theatre of the Absurd*, I suggested that these theatrical non-Aristotelian plot lines take the form of the *parable*, with the plays termed as being examples of "parabolic drama"(Bennett, *Reassessing the Theatre of the Absurd*).

35. See, particularly, the section on "Tragedy and Tragicomedy" by J. L. Styan, *The Dark Comedy: The Development of Modern Comic Tragedy*, 2nd edn. (Cambridge University Press, 1968), 31–8.

36. Enoch Brater, "After the Absurd: Rethinking Realism and a Few Other Isms," *Around the Absurd: Essays on Modern and Postmodern Drama*, eds. Ruby Cohn and Enoch Brater (Ann Arbor: University of Michigan Press, 1990), 295–300.

37. Brater, 300.

Chapter 2. Setting the stage

1. Eugene Ostashevsky, "Editor's Introduction," *OBERIU: An Anthology of Russian Absurdism* (Evanston: Northwestern University Press, 2006), xv.

2. Alfred Jarry, *Exploits and Opinions of Dr. Faustroll, Pataphysician*, trans. Simon Watson Taylor (Boston, MA: Exact Change, 1996), 21.

3. Alfred Jarry, *Ubu Roi*, trans. Beverly Keith and G. Legman (Mineoloa: Dover Publications, Inc., 2003), 1–2.

4. Richard Schechner, "Puzzling Pinter," *The Tulane Drama Review* 11.2 (Winter 1966): 176.

5. Franz Kafka, "In the Penal Colony," *Metamorphosis and Other Stories*, trans. and ed. Malcolm Pasley (London: Penguin Books, 2000), 131.

6. Anna Ford, *Pinter, Plays & Politics*, BBC television interview, 1988.

7. Ostashevsky, xiv.

8. Ibid., xv.

9. Ibid.

10. Ibid., xxii.

11. Daniil Kharms, "The Saber," *OBERIU: An Anthology of Russian Absurdism*, ed. Eugene Ostashevsky (Evanston: Northwestern University Press, 2006), 87.

12. Adrian Morfee, *Antonin Artaud's Writing Bodies* (Oxford University Press, 2005), 18–19. A recent book is worth mentioning here as it examines the contradictions of Antonin Artaud, himself: Kimberly Jannarone, *Artaud and His Doubles* (Ann Arbor: University of Michigan Press, 2010).

13. Antonin Artaud, *The Theater and its Double*, trans. Mary Caroline Richards (New York: Grove Press, 1958), 12.

14. Ibid.

15. Ibid.

16. Gene A. Plunka, "Antonin Artaud: The Suffering Shaman of Modern Theater," *Antonin Artaud and Modern Theater*, ed. Gene A. Plunka (London: Associated University Press, 1994), 23.

17. Ibid.

Chapter 3. The emergence of a "movement": The historical and intellectual contexts

1. Tony Judt, *Postwar: A History of Europe Since 1945* (New York: Penguin Books, 2005), 89.

2. "These goods, when sold in each country, would generate so-called 'counterpart funds' in the local currency which could be used according to bilateral agreements reached between Washington and each national government. Some countries used these funds to purchase more imports; others, like Italy, transferred them into their national reserves in anticipation of future foreign exchange needs" (Judt 93).

3. Judt 94.

4. Judt 325. The new, now younger, Europe – as post-war births in Europe were significantly up, such as in France where 869,000 babies were born in 1949 compared to 612,000 in 1939[4] – was ready, and in need, of greater consumer consumption. Washing machines, refrigerators, toys, and clothes were being made in larger and larger quantities, while the high demand for these items brought prices down. But, as Judt suggests, "The greatest single measure of European prosperity was the revolution wrought by the family car" (331).

5. Alan S. Milward, *The Reconstruction of Western Europe 1945–51* (Berkeley: University of California Press, 1984), 470.

6. Milward 470.

7. Milward 477.

8. Judt 282.

9. Judt 284. However, French political concerns were not just focused on their colonies. France was concerned with positioning itself well within Europe. Stemming originally from the Brussels Conference of December 1950 and from a 1951 French proposal to create a European army (which would simultaneously, "restrict German influence while appeasing American demands for the enrollment of German troops in western defense" [Hitchcock 153]), the European Defense Community (EDC) Treaty was signed on May 27, 1952. Needing parliamentary ratification from the signing nations, the formation of the EDC became a national issue for politicians and the press. The left-leaning presses – *Combat* (Camus' old newspaper), *l'Express*, and *France-Observer* – opposed European rearmament and confrontation with the Soviets, while the center–left *Le Monde* worried that the EDC would strengthen Germany and possibly pull France into liberating eastern Germany (Hitchcock 172). (France's parliament eventually rejected ratification of the EDC in 1954.)

10. Judt 286.

11. Ross 22.

12. Ross 76. As such, a 1951 investigation/survey in the relatively new *Elle* magazine, entitled "La Francaise, est-elle propre?" ["Is the French Woman Clean?"] caused quite an uproar. Ross draws out the subtle implications of this article: "Perhaps certain people (Germans) had left a polluting stain on France, perhaps certain French (collaborators) had to be purged and eliminated, perhaps certain French women (brothel owners and prostitutes) were tainted, perhaps literary language was hopelessly metaphorical and in need of a good scrubbing, but to question the personal hygiene of *la Francaise* – the French woman? . . . This – as Frantz Fanon said around the same time à propos of France's own campaign to colonize Algeria according to the well-known formula "Let's win over the women and the rest will follow" – is to target the innermost structure of the society itself" (76–7).

13. Ross 78.

14. Tony Judt suggests that French intellectuals, in particular, did not know how to deal with the outburst of repression in Central and Eastern Europe from 1947–54. Many French intellectuals personally had connections to those on trial, and that fact, combined with the fact that totalitarianism was spreading so close to Western Europe, meant that what was happening in the Soviet bloc was a prominent matter in France (*Past Imperfect: French Intellectuals, 1944–1954* [Berkeley: University of California Press, 1992] 103–15).

15. Judt *Postwar* 213.

16. Lottmann writes, "The last years of Stalin, years of arbitrary accusations and arrests, placed increased strains on Communist credibility. French Party members and fellow travelers were required to accept not only the purges of veteran Communists once praised for their courage and loyalty, but to write and to make speeches justifying the purges, to visit the countries where they were taking place, just as French collaborationists had been brought to Germany during the war" (269–70).

17. Judt *Postwar* 210.

18. Judt *Postwar* 211.

19. Pauline Gregg, *A Social and Economic History of Britain 1760–1965*, 5th edn. Rev. (London: George G. Harrap & Co. Ltd., 1965), 575.

20. Gregg 549.

21. Milward 471.

22. James T. Patterson, *Grand Expectations: The United States, 1945–1974* (New York: Oxford University Press, 1996), 407–8.

23. Ibid. 410.

24. Ibid. 418. The fear of placing nuclear warheads atop missiles like Sputnik was legitimate, especially since the United States had difficulty predicting the behavior of Khrushchev (John Lewis Gaddis, *The Cold War: A New History* [New York: Penguin Books, 2005], 68). Khrushchev stood in stark contrast to Eisenhower:

> The supremely self-confident Eisenhower was always in command of himself, his administration, and certainly the military forces of the United States. Khrushchev, in contrast, was excess personified: he could be boisterously clownish, belligerently cloying, aggressively insecure. (Gaddis 69)

25. Ibid. 450–1. For a tremendously in-depth examination of American economics during that general period, see Michael French, *US Economic History Since 1945* (Manchester University Press, 1997).
26. Patterson 451.
27. Ibid. 451.
28. Ibid. 452.
29. Ibid. 443–4.
30. Ibid. 444.
31. The year 1960 saw the birth of the "sit-in" when four African–American freshmen at North Carolina A&T College in Greensboro, NC, sat at the counter asking to be served at the local Woolworth department store until the store closed a half an hour early (Paterson 430). The sit-in movement grew, and it was fueled by unsung local activists, many of whom came to be leaders in the Civil Rights movement years later (Paterson 431). For Mary L. Dudziak, the Cold War and the Civil Rights movement were closely intertwined. The diplomatic impact of race during the Cold War was notable given that the United States had to ensure that democracy was appealing to other peoples and nations. Mary L. Dudziak, *Cold War Civil Rights: Race and the Image of American Democracy* (Princeton University Press, 2000), 6. With a similar argument but different details, Thomas Borstelmann writes a sweeping history about race relations and the Cold War. See Thomas Borstelmann, *The Cold War and the Color Line: American Race Relations in the Global Arena* (Cambridge: Harvard University Press, 2001), 85–171. Coming out of the era of "McCarthyism," civil rights groups had to carefully balance, "making it clear that their reform efforts were meant to fill out the contours of American democracy, and not to challenge or undermine it," so as not to be thought of as "subversive" like others who criticized American society; thus, there was no room for a broad critique of racial oppression within the strictures of Cold War politics (Dudziak 11). Despite the obstacles to the expansion of the Civil Rights movement, the United States needed reform "in order to make credible the government's argument about race and democracy" (Dudziak 14).
32. Though existentialism had the popular appeal and the intellectual dominance in France, Kelly argues that existentialism was contested from the very beginning, most especially from the Catholic right-wing movements (176).
33. David Drake, *Intellectuals and Politics in Post-War France* (London: Palgrave, 2002) 3–4.
34. For an in-depth account of Sartre and *Les Temps modernes*, see, Anna Boschetti, *The Intellectual Enterprise: Sartre and Les Temps Modernes*, trans. Richard C. McCleary (Evanston: Northwestern University Press, 1988).
35. Drake 24.
36. Drake 23.
37. Drake 27.
38. Drake 30.
39. Lottmann notes the danger of Camus' approach to the Communists: "Socialists had to choose between the Communist doctrine that ends justify means – i.e., that murder can be a legitimate act – and the rejection of Marxism except as a critical tool . . . In refusing

to choose between Communism and capitalism, in trying to 'save bodies,' Camus became (or so charged Emmanuel d'Astier de la Vigerie) an unwitting accomplice of capitalism" (260–1).

40. Drake 84. Germaine Brée offers a different point of view of the quarrel and the significance of *The Rebel*: "Although the controversies that fused around *The Rebel* reveal much concerning the politico-literary tangles of the time, they missed the fact that Camus had intuitively glimpsed the French political situation returning to relative normalcy . . . A new situation was emerging which did not fit the catastrophist patterns of social change through a proletarian revolution" (Germaine Brée, *Camus and Sartre: Crisis and Commitment* [New York: Delacorte Press, 1972] 6–7).

41. Drake 82.

42. For possibly the most concise and understandable overview of the works of Sartre and Camus, as this book covers all of the major texts of each philosopher in chronological order in simple jargon-free language, see Leo Pollmann, *Sartre and Camus: Literature of Existence*, Trans. Helen and Gregor Sebba (New York: Frederik Ungar Publishing Co., 1970). For another excellent book that examines the difference between the two philosophers – this one goes deeper into the philosophical implications of each philosophy – see Peter Royle, *The Sartre-Camus Controversy: A Literary and Philosophical Critique* (Ottawa: University of Ottawa Press, 1982). For more on Camus' philosophy, see the very readable, *The Cambridge Companion to Camus*, ed. Edward J. Hughes (Cambridge University Press, 2007). For more on Sartre's philosophy, see the sometimes unreadable but extremely complex and in-depth, *The Cambridge Companion to Sartre*, ed. Christina Howells (Cambridge University Press, 1992).

43. Royle describes the two philosophers' sense of the absurd: "Whereas for Camus the absurd is the relation between man and the universe for Sartre, insofar as one can properly use the term at all, it is absolute Being itself that is absurd; or perhaps we should say that for him the absurd is a relation between two relations, the subjective and objective relations of man to the world; which is another way of saying that we invent meanings instead of discovering them" (48).

44. Albert Camus, *The Rebel: An Essay on Man in Revolt* (New York: Vintage Books, 1956) 15.

45. Camus 6.

46. Royle 49.

47. Jean-Paul Sartre, "Existentialism Is a Humanism," *Existentialism: From Dostoevsky to Sartre*, ed. Walter Kaufman (New York: Plume Book, 1975) 349.

48. Camus 11.

49. Camus 22.

50. Camus 22.

51. Pollmann 116.

52. Ronald Aronson, *Camus and Sartre: The Story of a Friendship and the Quarrel that Ended It* (The University of Chicago Press, 2004) 115. Whereas Camus was fiercely against Stalinism, Judt explains how Sartre and others like him responded to Stalin: "Unable to join the Communists and unwilling to part company from them, a significant number

of prominent French Intellectuals devoted themselves not to condemning or defending the works of Stalin but to explaining them" (*Past Imperfect* 119)

53. Francis Jeanson, "Albert Camus, of The Soul in Revolt," *Sartre and Camus: A Historic Confrontation*, Eds. and Trans. David A. Sprintzen and Adrian van der Hoven (Amherst, New York: Humanity Books, 2004) 95–6.

54. Jeanson 101.

55. Albert Camus, "A Letter to the Editor of *Les Temps modernes*," *Sartre and Camus: A Historic Confrontation*, Eds. and Trans. David A. Sprintzen and Adrian van der Hoven (Amherst, New York: Humanity Books, 2004) 111–12.

56. Jean-Paul Sartre, "Reply to Albert Camus," *Sartre and Camus: A Historic Confrontation*, Eds. and Trans. David A. Sprintzen and Adrian van der Hoven (Amherst, New York: Humanity Books, 2004) 155.

57. Sartre 155.

58. Sartre 158.

59. Sartre 158.

60. Aronson 2.

61. There are a few books that specifically explore this relationship and both the convergent and divergent philosophies of Husserl and Frege. See Claire Ortiz Hill, *Word and Object in Husserl, Frege, and Russell: The Roots of Twentieth-Century Philosophy* (Athens: Ohio University Press, 1991); Claire Ortiz Hill and Guillermo E. Rosado Haddock, *Husserl or Frege?: Meaning, Objectivity, and Mathematics* (Chicago: Open Court, 2000); and J. N. Mohanty, *Husserl and Frege* (Bloomington: Indiana University Press, 1982).

62. Gottlob Frege, "Über Sinn und Bedeutung," *Zeitschrift für Philosophie und philosophische Kritik*, 100: 25–50; Gottlob Frege, "On Sense and Reference," Trans. M. Black, *Translations from the Philosophical Writings of Gottlob Frege*, eds. P. Geach and M. Black, 2nd edn. (Oxford: Blackwell, 1960), 56–78.

63. Bertrand Russell, "On Denoting," *Mind* 14.56 (October 1905): 479–93.

Chapter 4. Samuel Beckett

1. Linda Ben-Zvi, "Introduction," *Beckett at 100: Revolving it All*, eds. Linda Ben-Zvi and Angela Moorjani (Oxford University Press, 2008), 7–11.

2. Ruby Cohn, "Foreword," in Samuel Beckett, *Disjecta: Miscellaneous Writings and a Dramatic Fragment*, Ed. Ruby Cohn (New York: Grove Press, 1984), 8.

3. In *Reassessing the Theatre of the Absurd*, I suggested that these theatrical non-Aristotelian plot lines take the form of the *parable*, with the plays termed as being examples of "parabolic drama"(Bennett, *Reassessing the Theatre of the Absurd*).

4. Michael Y. Bennett, *Reassessing the Theatre of the Absurd: Camus, Beckett, Ionesco, Genet, and Pinter* (New York: Palgrave Macmillan, 2011), 27–28 & 142.

5. Michael Y. Bennett, *Words, Space, and the Audience: The Theatrical Tension between Empiricism and Rationalism* (New York: Palgrave Macmillan, 2012), 101.

6. Bennett, *Words, Space, and the Audience* 91.
7. Bennett, *Reassessing* 50–1.
8. Ibid. 31.
9. "[In Beckett's] letter written in 1937, we notice that what Beckett criticizes in language is its materiality. As we have seen, he writes, "Is there any reason why that terrible materiality of the word surface should not be capable of being dissolved, like for example the sound surface, torn by enormous pauses, of Beethoven's seventh Symphony . . . ?" (172). The "terrible materiality" of language here means the fact that language can never be completely free from describing material things in the phenomenal world and expressing their meanings. It also means that language in its nature conceals the (non-)existence of what cannot be represented, when he says that language is "a veil that must be torn apart in order to get at the things (or the Nothingness) behind it" or "a mask." We could say that throughout his career as an artist of language, Beckett continues to fight with the "terrible materiality" of language." (Michiko Tsushima, "On the Boundaries between Materiality and Immateriality: *Words and Music* and *Cascando*," Samuel Beckett Working Group, *IFTR 2011 Conference*, Osaka, Japan.)
10. Samuel Beckett, *Murphy* (New York: Grove Press, 1957), 26.
11. Samuel Beckett, "Molloy," *Three Novels: Molloy, Malone Dies, The Unnamable* (New York: Grove Press, 1958), 7.
12. Samuel Beckett, "Malone Dies," *Three Novels: Molloy, Malone Dies, The Unnamable* (New York: Grove Press, 1958), 179.
13. Samuel Beckett, "The Unnamable," *Three Novels: Molloy, Malone Dies, The Unnamable* (New York: Grove Press, 1958).
14. Samuel Beckett, *Watt* (New York: Grove Press, 1953), 81.
15. See Michael Y. Bennett, "'The Essential Doesn't Change': Essence Precedes Experience and Cartesian Rationalism in Samuel Beckett's *Waiting for Godot*." *Notes on Contemporary Literature* 42.1 (January 2012): 5–7; Michael Y. Bennett, "The Cartesian Beckett: The Mind-Body Split in *Murphy* and *Happy Days*." *ANQ: A Quarterly Journal of Short Articles, Notes, and Reviews* 25.2 (May 2012): 118–22.
16. Ciaran Ross, *Beckett's Art of Absence: Rethinking the Void* (Houndsmills: Palgrave Macmillan, 2011), 1.
17. Ibid.
18. Ibid. 58.
19. Ibid. 60.
20. I am taking this idea from the line, "The world a flux of movements partaking of living time, that of effort, creation, liberation, the painting, the painter" (*Disjecta* 138).
21. Samuel Beckett, *Disjecta: Miscellaneous Writings and a Dramatic Fragment*, ed. Ruby Cohn (New York: Grove Press, 1984), 139.
22. Ibid. 138.
23. "Gain," *Oxford English Dictionary*, 2nd edn., 1989.

24. See my article on Heidegger and Godot: Michael Y. Bennett, "Sartre's 'The Wall' and Beckett's *Waiting for Godot*: Existential and Non-Existential Nothingness." *Notes on Contemporary Literature* 39.5 (November 2009): 2–3.

Chapter 5. Beckett's notable contemporaries

1. Edward Albee, "Tiny Alice," *The Collected Plays of Edward Albee: 1958–1965* (New York: Overlook Duckworth, 2007), 452.
2. Michael Y. Bennett, *Words, Space, and the Audience: The Theatrical Tension between Empiricism and Rationalism* (New York: Palgrave Macmillan, 2012), 105.
3. Bennett 113–14; 122.
4. Bennett 113.
5. Edward Albee, "Who's Afraid of Virginia Woolf?" *The Collected Plays of Edward Albee: 1958–1965* (New York: Overlook Duckworth, 2007), 190–1.
6. Edward Albee, "A Delicate Balance," *The Collected Plays of Edward Albee: 1966–1977* (New York: Overlook Duckworth, 2008), 20–1.
7. Ibid. 46.
8. Ibid. 118.
9. Edward Albee, "Introduction," *The Collected Plays of Edward Albee: 1966–1977* (New York: Overlook Duckworth, 2008), 8.
10. Edward Albee, "Seascape," *The Collected Plays of Edward Albee: 1966–1977* (New York: Overlook Duckworth, 2008), 388–90.
11. Albee, "Introduction," 9.
12. Jean Genet, "The Maids," *The Maids and Deathwatch.* Trans. Bernard Frechtman (New York: Grove Press, 1961), 61.
13. Jean Genet, *The Thief's Journal.* Trans. Bernard Frechtman (Harmondsworth: Penguin, 1971), 5.
14. Ibid.
15. Ibid.
16. Jean Genet, *Our Lady of the Flowers.* Trans. Bernard Frechtman (Toronto: Bantam Books, 1964), 51.
17. Ibid. 56.
18. Eugene Ionesco, *Rhinoceros* (New York: Grove Press, 1960), 7. See Michael Y. Bennett, *Reassessing the Theatre of the Absurd: Camus, Beckett, Pinter, Genet, and Ionesco* (New York: Palgrave Macmillan, 2011).
19. Eugene Ionesco, "The Bald Soprano," *Four Plays.* Trans. Donald M. Allen (New York: Grove Press, 1958), 41.
20. Harold Pinter, "The Birthday Party," *Complete Works: One* (New York: Grove Press, 1976), 9.
21. See Michael Y. Bennett, "The Pinteresque Oedipal Household," *Reassessing the Theatre of the Absurd: Camus, Beckett, Pinter, Genet, and Ionesco* (New York: Palgrave Macmillan, 2011), 53–69.

22. Harold Pinter, *The Dwarfs: A Novel* (New York: Grove Press, 1990), 11–12.

23. Ibid. 53.

Chapter 6. The European and American wave of absurdism

Because the writers featured in this chapter are much less studied than those that appear in Chapters 4 and 5, and therefore it is much harder to find scholarship on the writers in this chapter (e.g., it is much easier to locate scholarship on Beckett, who has two academic journals devoted to him; Pinter has a journal, as does Edward Albee), the endnotes in this chapter are more extensive in their detail, directing the reader of this book to helpful and exact sources.

1. Fischler, Alexander. "The Absurd Professor in the Theater of the Absurd." *Modern Drama.* 21 (1978): 137–152.

2. For more on Adamov's artistic evolution, see: (Dietemann, Margaret. "Departure from the Absurd: Adamov's Last Plays." *Yale French Studies,* no. 46 (1971): 48–59).

3. Arthur Adamov, *Ping Pong* (London: John Calder, 1962), 33.

4. Ibid. 34.

5. Martin Esslin, *The Theatre of the Absurd* (New York: Anchor Books, 1961), 68.

6. Francis Donahue describes Arrabal as an "organic playwright"; Donahue cites Arrabal's troubled childhood as the main source of inspiration for his art; he uses an array of potentially controversial techniques to illustrate and exorcize his inner demons, such as sadism, masochism, cannibalism, or necrophilia (Donahue, Francis. "Arrabal: Organic Playwright." *Midwest Quarterly: A Journal of Contemporary Thought.* 25 (1984): 187–200. For more on the 'grotesque' techniques frequently employed by Arrabal, see Podol, Peter L. "The Grotesque Mode in Contemporary Spanish Theater and Film." *Modern Language Studies* 15.4 (1985): 194–207.

7. Fernando Arrabal, *Guernica and Other Plays,* 16.

8. Ibid. 14.

9. For a description of Baraka's paradoxical methods complemented by brutal, controversial language, see Jedrzekjo, Pawel; Baraka, Amiri. "Still a Revolutionary." *New Theatre Quarterly* 26.4 (2010): 340–50. Stephen Schryer describes Baraka's belief that European text is an "imprisoning system from which the artist must break free". For this and more on Baraka's role as a black cultural nationalist, see: Schryer, Stephen. "A Culture of Violence and Foodsmells: Amiri Baraka's The System of Dante's Hell and the War on Poverty." *Arizona Quarterly: A Journal of American Literature, Culture, and Theory* 66.1 (2010): 145–64.

10. For more on the psychoanalytic interpretation of the Black American mind in *Dutchman,* see Piggford, George. "Looking into Black Skulls: Amiri Baraka's Dutchman and the Psychology of Race." *Modern Drama* 40.1 (1997): 74–85. For an opposing perspective citing *Dutchman* as a play not advocating violent revolution, but as an attack on binary logic, see Kumar, Nita N. "The Logic of Retribution: Amiri Baraka's Dutchman." *African American Review* 37.2 (2003): 271–9.

11. See Gillis, William. "Durrenmatt and the Detectives." *The German Quarterly.* Vol. 35,1 (1962): 71–4, and Diller, Edward "Aesthetics and the Grotesque: Friedrich Dur renmatt." *Wisconsin Studies in Contemporary Literature* 7.3 (1966): 328–35. For more on Durrenmatt's concept of history as a construct beyond human control, see Diller, Edward. "Friedrich Durrenmatt's Theological Concept of History." *The German Quarterly* 40.3 (1967): 363–71.

12. Louis Kampf describes Gelber's *The Connection* succinctly as a "naturalistic documentary put inside the frame of an artificial experimental situation." For more on *The Connection* as a challenge to the audience in a modernist sense, see Kampf, Louis. "The Permanence of Modernism." *College English* 28.1 (1966): 1–15. Paul Hurley argues that due to its nature as social commentary, it is, in a way, conventional: see Hurley, Paul J. "France and America: Versions of the Absurd." *College English* 26.8 (1965): 634–40. Conversely, Mike Sell argues that, owing to the play's disjointedness, it is not possible to "establish a stable framework of values in which to consider the use of heroin," and that viewers cannot be certain they are seeing a "social-problem play." For more on *The Connection*'s relation to the "drug war," see Sell, Mike. "Jazz, Drama, and Drug War: The Living Theatre's Production of The Connection." *On-Stage Studies* 20 (1997): 28–47.

13. For an explanation of Havel's employment of language and absurdism in his earliest works, prefacing his ascendance into the Czechoslovakian social and political hierarchy, see Trensky, Paul I. "Vaclav Havel and the Language of the Absurd." *The Slavic and East European Journal* 13.1 (1969): 42–65. In *Politics and Pornography: Czech Performance in the International Arena,* Alan Sikes provides a more optimistic description of Havel's Absurdism through interpretation of *The Increased Difficulty of Concentration;* Sikes explains that Havel's Absurdist outlook is not "purely cynical", but stressing the "question of meaning by manifesting its absence." See Sikes, Alan W. "Politics and Pornography: Czech Performance in the International Arena." *Theatre Journal* 62.3 (2010): 373–387. For thorough discussion on Havel's status as a political dissident explored through his essay *The Power of the Powerless* and his play *The Leaving,* respectively, see Doxtader, Erik W. "Characters in the Middle of Public Life: Consensus, Dissent, and Ethos." *Philosophy and Rhetoric* 33.4 (2000): 336–369 and Meerzon, Yana. "Dancing on the X-rays: On the Theatre of Memory, Counter-Memory, and Postmemory in the Post-1989 East-European Context." *Modern Drama* 54.4 (2011): 479–510.

14. Václav Havel, *The Garden Party and Other Plays* (New York: Grove Press, 1993), 36.

15. Ibid. 126.

16. Werner Sollors perceives Kennedy's work as self-reflection which attempts to sort out a complex heritage and its contradictions. For more, see Sollors, Werner. "Owls and Rats in the American Funnyhouse: Adrienne Kennedy's Drama." *American Literature* 63.3 (1991): 507–32. For more on Kennedy's persona as a playwright and its effect on her protagonists in this self-reflective mode, see Barnett, Claudia. "An Evasion of Ontology': Being Adrienne Kennedy." *The Drama Review: A Journal of Performance Studies* 49.3 (2005): 157–86. Others, such as Jenny Spencer, see this organic method as a way to provoke viewers to share the experience with Kennedy's characters, not

merely understand them; She states "actively engaging with Kennedy's indeterminate, contradictory, and recursive writing is something readers and viewers necessarily share, right alongside the characters in her plays", and that "Kennedy effectively challenges the binaries and hierarchies of viewing." See Spencer, Jenny S. "Emancipated Spectatorship in Adrienne Kennedy's Plays." *Modern Drama* 55.1 (2012): 19–39. For a similar perspective concerning Kennedy's use of excessive emotion to connect creator to viewer, see Sichert, Margit. "The Staging of Excessive Emotions; Adrienne Kennedy's Funnyhouse of a Negro." *The Yearbook of Research in English and American Literature* 16 (2000): 229–51.

17. For more on Kopit's view of Western mythos, see O'Neill, Michael C. "History as Dramatic Present: Arthur L. Kopit's 'Indians'." *Theatre Journal* 34.4 (1982): 493–504 and Adler, Thomas P. "Public Faces, Private Graces: Apocalypse Postponed in Arthur Kopit's End of the World." *Studies in the Literary Imagination* 21.2 (1998): 107–18. Richard Brayshaw and Suzanne Burgoyne Dieckman see this mythology as an imprisoning entity, a common theme amongst Kopit's characters. See Brayshaw, Richard and Burgoyne Dieckman, Suzanne. "Wings, Watchers, and Windows: Imprisonment in the Plays of Arthur Kopit." *Theatre Journal* 35.2 (1983): 195–211. Kopit's ties to the Absurd are noted by James Hurt and Bernd Engler through critique of the plays *Wings* and *The Hero*, respectively. See Hurt, James. "Arthur Kopit's Wings and the Languages of the Theater." *American Drama* 8.1 (1998): 75–94 and Engler, Bernd. "Antidrama – Metadrama – Artistic Program? Arthur Kopit's The Hero in Context." *Connotations: A Journal for Critical Debate* 3.3 (1994): 279–90. However, Paul Hurley notes that Kopit's proclivity for direct symbolism separates him from the classic absurdist: see Hurley, Paul J. "France and America: Versions of the Absurd." *College English*. Vol. 26.8 (1965): 634–40.

18. Arthur Kopit, *Oh Dad, Poor Dad, Mama's Hung You in the Closet and I'm Feelin' So Sad,* 120.

19. Because of Mrozek's direct metaphorical depictions of realism, his characters are often viewed in a Freudian sense, such as the Oedipal theory in *Tango*. See O'Connor, John. "Dancing with Freud: Slawomir Mrozek's Tango." *Studies in the Literary Imagination* 34.2 (2001): 1–11. Marketa Goetz Stankiewicz uses Freudian theory to hypothesize why Eastern audiences are more inclined to find "truth" in Mrozek's plays: see Stankiewicz, Marketa Goetz. "The Metamorphosis of the Theatre of the Absurd or the Jobless Jester." *Pacific Coast Philology* 7 (1972): 54–64. Martin Esslin states that Western writers could "abstract themselves from an immediate political presence," while Europeans "confronted an existential anguish" in an "artificially distorted daily reality." See Esslin, Martin. "Mrozek, Beckett, and the Theatre of the Absurd." *New Theatre Quarterly* 10.40 (1994): 377–81. Barbara Kejna-Sharratt narrows the discussion to the Mrozek's Eastern absurd in particular, calling "the materialization of a metaphor" Mrozek's favorite technique. See Kejna-Sharratt, Barbara. "Slawomir Mrozek and the Polish Tradition of the Absurd." *New Zealand Slavonic Journal* 1 (1974): 75–86. For more on the separate East/West interpretation in Mrozek's writing, see Grabowski, Arthur, and Krempl, Renata. "One Table and Two Theatres: How to Produce a Polish Drama about Europe

for an American Audience, or What Use a Director Can Make of a Dramaturg." *Slavic and East European Performance* 26.3 (2006): 32–43, and Stankiewicz, Marketa Goetz. "Slawomir Mrozek: Two Forms of the Absurd." *Contemporary Literature* 12.2 (1971): 188–203.

20. Halina Filipowitz denotes *The Interrupted Act, Birth Rate,* and *The Guards* as a "post-modern trilogy," which "reflect both an awareness of the shortcomings of accepted dramatic conventions and an attempt to create a viable alternative," which according to her, "do not, as yet, have adequate notation." See Filipowicz, Halina. "Tadeusz Rozewicz's Postmodern Trilogy." *The Polish Review* 36.1 (1991): 83–102. For more on Rozewicz's method of re-constructing reality in theatre, see Filipowicz, Halina. "Theatrical Reality in the Plays of Tadeusz Rozewicz." *The Slavic and East European Journal* 26.4 (1982): 447–59. Correlative to this method of construction as described by Filipowicz is Daniel Gerould's proposed technique "collage and assemblage" in Rosewicz's work. See Gerould, Daniel C. "Tadeusz Rozewicz: Playwriting as Collage." *Performing Arts Journal* 1.2 (1976): 63–6.

21. Mark Tattenbaum claims "All Rozewicz's works ask the same question: is art possible after such cataclysmic events of the twentieth century?" See Tattenbaum, Mark F. "Rozewicz's Card Index Scattered in Its U.S. Premire: Recycling, Discarding, and Adding the Fragments." *Slavic and East European Performance: Drama, Theatre and Film* 27.2 (2007): 65–70. Edward Czerwinski provides a more refined version of this, pointing out the paradox and contradiction of modern man, stating, "man consciously assumes his role in a world half-asleep, half-awake, wherein beauty and ugliness exist contentedly and of necessity side by side." See Czerwinski, Edward J. "Tadeusz Rozewicz and the Jester-Priest Metaphor." *The Slavic and East European Journal* 13.2 (1969): 217–28.

22. Tadeusz Rozewicz, *The Card Index and Other Plays.* Trans. Adam Czerniawski (New York: Grove Press, 1969), 70.

23. R. B. Parker calls N. F. Simpson's work "solipsist fantasy," claiming his "comedy depends on conversations where monologues never quite meet, of private visions behind a façade of cliché." See Parker, R. B. "Farce and Society: The Range of Kingsley Amis." *Wisconsin Studies in Contemporary Literature* 2.3 (1961): 27–38. John Russell Taylor states plainly that "there seems nowadays little in any of his plays that is puzzling and difficult, but merely a lot that either you find funny or you don't." See Taylor, John Russell. "Ten Years of the English Stage Company." *The Tulane Drama Review* 11.2 (1966): 120–31. Charles Marowitz describes Simpson as something of an afterthought in English theatre; for more, see Marowitz, Charles, "State of Play." *The Tulane Drama Review* 11.2 (1966): 203–6. C. Z. Fothergill articulates this common thread of doubt, claiming "his plays are mostly a bundle of routines which can be easily relocated or omitted because there is little organizing plot or unifying philosophy," or in other words, "Simpson is interested in absurdity with a small 'a.'" See Fothergill, C.Z. "Echoes of A Resounding Tinkle: N.F. Simpson Reconsidered." *Modern Drama* 16.3–4 (1973): 299–306.

24. *Reality is an Illusion . . .* , BBC Radio 4, 5 April 2007.

25. "Neither gender can be completely free until both have been liberated from reiterations of oppressive historical norms. Because Stoppard doubts the possibility of such a

liberation, all of his passionate travellers must go on playing the circle game." See Barker, Roberta. "The Circle Game: Gender, Time, and 'Revolution' in Tom Stoppard's The Coast of Utopia." *Modern Drama* 48.4 (2005): 706–25. For more on the use of historical norms, see Innes, Christopher. "Allegories from the Past: Stoppard's Uses of History." *Modern Drama* 49.2 (2006): 223–37. Stoppard uses this historical context to provide commentary on the political condition concerning England (Rock 'n' Roll), Russia (The Coast of Utopia), and India (Indian Ink): See, respectively, Meerzon, Yana. "Dancing on the X-rays: On the Theatre of Memory, Counter-Memory, and Postmemory in the Post-1989 East-European Context." *Modern Drama* 54.4 (2011): 479–510, Zimmerman, Judith. "Tom Stoppard's Russian Thinkers." *New England Review: Middlebury Series* 28.3 (2007): 80–94, and Bhatia, Nandi. "Reinventing India through 'A Quite Witty Pastiche': Reading Tom Stoppard's Indian Ink." *Modern Drama* 52.2 (2009): 220–37.

26. Stoppard is notorious for his fascination with chaos theory and theatricalized, scientific thought experiments, which according to Moonyoung Chung, is Stoppard's true calling despite his appearance as a political commentator. See Chung, Moonyoung. "Stage as Hyperspace: Theatricality of Stoppard." *Modern Drama* 48.4 (2005): 689–705. Elizabeth Martin describes Stoppard's basic theory that art and love, human abstractions, make the repetitions of the universe impossible to predict despite their similarities. See Martin, Elizabeth. "Human Chaos and Arcadia's Hidden Twin." *Publications of the Mississippi Philological Association* (2010): 40–59. Martin Meisel provides multiple perspectives concerning language, highlighting the comedy of words being taken in a "mistaken" sense to symbolize these abstractions that differentiate the similar repetitions of the universe. See Meisel, Martin. "The Last Waltz: Tom Stoppard's Poetics of Science." *Wordsworth Circle* 38.1–2 (2007): 13–19 and Meisel, Martin. "Shaw, Stoppard and 'Audible Intelligibility'." *Shaw: The Annual of Bernard Shaw Studies* 27 (2007): 42–58. William W. Demastes explains Stoppard's attitude toward this incongruity in the universe, stating that "disorder for Stoppard is not only an inescapable condition; its presence is in many cases cause for celebration. He is a far cry from the ennui-ridden existentialism or absurdist despair that occupies the thoughts of many of his contemporaries." See Demastes, William W. "Portrait of an Artist as Proto-Chaotician: Tom Stoppard Working His Way to Arcadia." *Narrative* 19.2 (2011): 229–40.

Chapter 7. Post-absurdism?

1. Elsewhere, I argue that there is not just one, but that there are four interrogation scenes in Harold Pinter's *The Birthday Party* (Michael Y. Bennett, *Reassessing the Theatre of the Absurd: Camus, Beckett, Ionesco, Genet, and Pinter* [New York: Palgrave Macmillan, 2011], 53–69).

2. "It is hard to think of Eugene O'Neill's *Long Day's Journey Into Night* being a humorous play. But the Guthrie Theater's production of O'Neill's semiautobiographical classic produced not just occasional giggles but *laughter* – and a lot of it . . . The simultaneously comedic and tragic family drama became a staple of the theatre during the second half

of the twentieth century. Just as the family-room tragicomedies, like Edward Albee's *Who's Afraid of Virginia Woolf?* and Tracy Letts' *August: Osage County*, would not exist without *Long Day's Journey*, so the Guthrie Theater's production of O'Neill's masterpiece would not exist without the tragicomic sensibility of those plays." (Michael Y. Bennett, "Performance Review of *Long Day's Journey into Night*, by Eugene O'Neill," *Eugene O'Neill Review* 34.2 (2013): 273–5.)

3. Bennett, *Reassessing* 105.
4. Beth Henley, *Crimes of the Heart*.
5. Maria Irene Fornes, "Mud," *Maria Irene Fornes: Plays*.
6. *Reductio ad absurdum* works "to show the foolishness of a concept or idea by taking it to its apparent logical – and most outrageous – conclusion" (26). *Reductio ad absurdum* functions very well in satire because of satire's tendency to favor the general over the specific (27). Closely related to irony is signifying. Signifying has a number of definitions. I will give two of them. First, "It may describe a type of verbal jousting consisting of insults and trickery used to create a clever, often subtly devastating critique of a particular person, idea, or object" (28). Second, as Dickson-Carr quotes Claudia Mitchell-Kernan, signifying is "a way of encoding messages or meanings which involves, in most cases, an element of indirection" (28). Relying on a discursive community's shared understanding of certain terms, signifying is a way to critique without sounding vicious. In line with the rhetorical form of *reductio ad absurdum* is the presence of chaos in the African-American satire. The satirist must create a world that rivals the absurdity of the concept or idea that he or she is satirizing. Therefore, the grotesque or carnivalesque are present in many African-American satires (Dickson-Carr 31). John Clark, as Dickson-Carr quotes, explains the significance behind chaos: "All this clutter and disarray results from the fact that the satiric artist renders an 'imitation' of the excessive, the imperfect, and the negative . . . The apparent chaos of the satiric novel's scenery is but a pale imitation of the senselessness of racism" (31, 32). Though there are other ideological systems that are critiqued, racism is the major system examined in African American satire." (Michael Y. Bennett, ""Dominance and the Triumph of the White Trickster Over the Black Picaro in Amiri Baraka's *Great Goodness of Life: A Coon Show*." *Callaloo* 36.2 (Spring 2013): 316–17.)

Chapter 8. Absurd criticism

1. Martin Esslin, *The Theatre of the Absurd* (New York: Anchor Books, 1961, xix).
2. I first make this observation in a review essay, from which I have adapted and modified some of the material in this chapter: Michael Y. Bennett, "Away from the Absurd?: The Critical Response to Beckett at 100," *Kritikon Litterarum* 36.3/4 (December 2009): 230–8.
3. Edith Kern, "Drama Stripped for Inaction: Beckett's Godot," *Yale French Studies* 14 (1954): 45.
4. Kern 47.

5. Esslin xix.
6. David Carroll, "Rethinking the Absurd: *Le Mythe de Sisyphe,*" *The Cambridge Companion to Camus,* Ed. Edward J. Hughes (Cambridge University Press, 2007): 57.
7. Marc Blanchard, "Before Ethics: Camus' *Pudeur,*" *MLN* 112.4 (1997): 667.
8. Peter Royle, *The Sartre-Camus Controversy: A Literary and Philosophical Critique* (University of Ottawa Press, 1982): 87.
9. While discussing a different subject, I am indirectly drawing out some of my conclusion from Shannon Jackson, *Professing Performance: Theatre in the Academy from Philology to Performativity* (Cambridge University Press, 2004).
10. Bob Mayberry, *Theatre of Discord: Dissonance in Beckett, Albee, and Pinter* (London: Associated University Press, 1989); Enoch Brater and Ruby Cohen, eds., *Around the Absurd: Essays on Modern and Postmodern Drama* (Ann Arbor: The University of Michigan Press, 1990); and Deborah B. Gaensbauer, *The French Theater of the Absurd* (Boston: Twayne Publishers, 1991).
11. A "subject" search (accessed 30 January 2014) with the date range of the past ten years, from 2003 to 2013, on the *MLA International Bibliography* yields an amazing 238 results for "absurd" (with 179 of those just from 2006 – the year of Beckett's widely celebrated centenary birthday and the publication of Cornwell's *The Absurd in Literature* – to 2013; and with 50 of those from just 2011 – the year of the publication of my book, *Reassessing the Theatre of the Absurd* – to 2013). [Given that it takes a good amount of time for the *MLA International Bibliography* to record entries, it is very possible, and extremely likely, that the number of entries under the subject "absurd" will increase significantly for the year 2013.] This rising trend constitutes a very significant uptake in scholarly interest on the absurd, for example, if one compares it to the 47 results from the ten-year range of 1970 to 1980 (when, especially, almost no books were written about the absurd).
12. This constitutes at least seven doctoral dissertations on the absurd in just a two-year span (i.e., 2011–2013), versus a total of four doctoral dissertations on the absurd between 2001 and 2008.

Further reading

Absurd

Bennett, Michael Y. *Reassessing the Theatre of the Absurd: Camus, Beckett, Ionesco, Genet, and Pinter.* New York: Palgrave Macmillan, 2011.
Brater, Enoch and Ruby Cohn, eds. *Around the Absurd: Essays on Modern and Postmodern Drama.* Ann Arbor: The University of Michigan Press, 1990.
Cornwell, Neil. *The Absurd in Literature.* Manchester University Press, 2006.
Demastes, William W. *Theatre of Chaos: Beyond Absurdism, Into Orderly Disorder.* Cambridge University Press, 1998.
Esslin, Martin, ed. *Absurd Drama.* Middlesex: Penguin Books, 1965.
   The Theatre of the Absurd. New York: Anchor Books, 1961 [2nd edn. 1969; 3rd edn. 2004].
Gaensbauer, Deborah B. *The French Theater of the Absurd.* Boston: Twayne Publishers, 1991.
Gavins, Joanna. *Reading the Absurd.* Edinburgh: Edinburgh University Press, 2013.
Hinchcliffe, Arnold P. *The Absurd.* London: Methuen & Co Ltd, 1969.
Mayberry, Bob. *Theatre of Discord: Dissonance in Beckett, Albee, and Pinter.* Rutherford: Fairleigh Dickinson University Press, 1989.
Pronko, Leonard Cabell. *Avant-Garde: The Experimental Theater in France.* Berkeley: University of California Press, 1966.
Styan, J. L. *The Dark Comedy: The Development of Modern Comic Tragedy.* 2nd edn. Cambridge University Press, 1968.
Wellwarth, George. *The Theater of Protest and Paradox: Developments in the Avant-Guarde Drama.* Revised edn. New York University Press, 1971.

Albee

Primary sources
Albee, Edward. *The Collected Plays of Edward Albee: 1958–1965.* New York: Overlook Duckworth, 2007.
   The Collected Plays of Edward Albee: 1966–1977. New York: Overlook Duckworth, 2008.

The Collected Plays of Edward Albee: 1978–2003. New York: Overlook Duckworth, 2008.
Stretching My Mind. New York: Carroll & Graf Publishers, 2005.
"Which Theatre is the Absurd One?" *The New York Times.* 25 February 1962: SM11.

Secondary sources
Bottoms, Stephen, ed. *The Cambridge Companion to Edward Albee.* Cambridge University Press, 2005.
Gussow, Mel. *Edward Albee: A Singular Journey: A Biography.* New York: Simon & Schuster, 1999.
Kolin, Philip C., ed. *Conversations with Edward Albee.* Jackson: University Press of Mississippi, 1988.
Mann, Bruce J., ed. *Edward Albee: A Casebook.* New York: Routledge, 2003.
Paolucci, Anne. *From Tension to Tonic: The Plays of Edward Albee.* Carbondale: Southern Illinois University Press, 1972.

Beckett

Primary sources
Beckett, Samuel. *Collected Shorter Plays.* New York: Grove Press, 1984.
Disjecta: Miscellaneous Writings and a Dramatic Fragment. Ed. Ruby Cohn. New York: Grove Press, 1984.
Endgame. New York: Grove Press, 1956.
Happy Days. New York: Grove Press, 1961.
Murphy. New York: Grove Press, 1957.
Three Novels: Molloy, Malone Dies, The Unnamable. New York: Grove Press, 1958.
Waiting for Godot. New York: Grove Press, 1954.
Watt. New York: Grove Press, 1953.

Secondary sources
Ben-Zvi, Linda. *Samuel Beckett.* Boston: Twayne, 1986.
Beckett at 100: Revolving It All, eds. Linda Ben-Zvi and Angela Moorjani. Oxford University Press, 2008.
Brater, Enoch. *Beyond Minimalism: Beckett's Late Style in the Theatre.* New York: Oxford University Press, 1987.
The Drama in the Text: Beckett's Late Fiction. New York: Oxford University Press, 1994.
Why Beckett. London: Thames and Hudson, 1989.
Bryden, Mary. *Samuel Beckett and the Idea of God.* Basingstoke: Macmillan, 1998.
Cohen, Ruby. *A Beckett Canon.* Ann Arbor: University of Michigan Press, 2001.
ed. Samuel Beckett: *Waiting for Godot: A Casebook.* Houndmills: Macmillan, 1987.

Gontarski, S. E. *The Intent of Undoing Samuel Beckett's Dramatic Texts.*
    Bloomington: Indiana University Press, 1985.
Kern, Edith. "Drama Stripped for Inaction: Beckett's Godot." *Yale French Studies*
    14 (1954): pp. 56–62.
Knowlson, James. *Damned to Fame: The Life of Samuel Beckett.* London:
    Bloomsbury, 1996.
Le Juez, Brigette. *Beckett Before Beckett.* Trans. Ros Schwartz. London: Souvenir
    Press, 2008.
McDonald, Rónán. *The Cambridge Introduction to Samuel Beckett.* Cambridge
    University Press, 2006.
Oppenheim, Lois, ed. *Palgrave Advances in Samuel Beckett Studies.* New York:
    Palgrave Macmillan, 2004.
Pilling, John, ed. *The Cambridge Companion to Beckett.* Cambridge University
    Press, 1994.
Uhlmann, A. *Beckett and Poststructuralism.* Cambridge University Press, 1999.

Camus and absurdity

Primary sources
Camus, Albert. *The Fall.* Trans. Justin O'Brien. New York: Vintage International,
    1984.
    The Myth of Sisyphus: and Other Essays. Trans. Justin O'Brian. New York:
    Vintage Books, 1955.
    The Plague. Trans. Stuart Gilbert. New York: Vintage Books, 1972.
    The Rebel: An Essay on Man in Revolt. Trans. Anthony Bower. New York:
    Vintage Books, 1956.

Secondary sources
Blanchard, Marc. "Before Ethics: Camus's Pudeur." *MLN* 112.4 (1997): 666–82.
Brée, Germaine. *Camus and Sartre: Crisis and Commitment.* New York: Delacorte
    Press, 1972.
Carroll, David. "Rethinking the Absurd: Le Mythe de Sisyphe." *The Cambridge
    Companion to Camus.* Ed. Edward J. Hughes. Cambridge University
    Press, 2007, pp. 53–66.
Fotiade, Ramona. *Conceptions of the Absurd: From Surrealism to the Existential
    Thought of Chestov and Fondane.* Oxford: Legenda, 2001.
Hughes, Edward J., ed. *The Cambridge Companion to Camus.* Cambridge
    University Press, 2007.
Peter, Royle. *The Satre-Camus Controversy: A Literary and Philosophical Critique.*
    University of Ottawa Press, 1982.
Pollmann, Leo. *Sartre and Camus: Literature of Existence,* trans. Helen and Gregor
    Sebba. New York: Frederik Ungar Publishing Co., 1970.
Robinson, James E. "Sisyphus Happy: Beckett Beyond the Absurd." *Samuel
    Beckett Today/aujourd'hui* 6 (1997): 343–52.

Sagi, Avi. *Albert Camus and the Philosophy of the Absurd.* Amsterdam: Rodopi, 2002.

Vanborre, Emmanuelle Anne, ed., *The Originality and Complexity of Albert Camus's Writings.* New York: Palgrave Macmillan, 2012.

Zucker, Richard. "The Happiness of Sisyphus." *Kinesis* (1987): 41–65.

Genet

Primary sources

Genet, Jean. *The Balcony.* Trans. Bernard Frechtman. New York: Grove Press, 1966.

The Blacks: A Clown Show. Trans. Bernard Frechtman. New York: Grove Press, Inc., 1960.

The Maids and Deathwatch: Two Plays. Trans. Bernard Frechtman. New York: Grove Press, Inc., 1961.

Our Lady of the Flowers. Trans. Bernard Frechtman. Toronto: Bantam Books, 1964.

The Screens. Trans. Bernard Frechtman. New York: Grove Press, 1962.

The Thief's Journal. Trans. Bernard Frechtman. Middlesex: Penguin Books, 1967.

Secondary sources

Coe, Richard N. *The Vision of Genet.* New York: Grove Press, 1968.

Driver, Tom Faw. *Jean Genet.* New York: Columbia University Press, 1966.

Knapp, Bettina Liebowitz. *Jean Genet.* New York: Tw ayne, 1968.

McMahon, Joseph H. *The Imagination of Jean Genet.* New Haven: Yale University Press, 1963.

Oswald, Laura. *Jean Genet and the Semiotics of Performance.* Bloomington: Indiana University Press, 1989.

Savona, Jeannette L. *Jean Genet.* New York: Grove Press, 1983.

Styan, J. L. *Symbolism, Surrealism and the Absurd. Vol. 2 of Modern Drama in Theory and Practice.* Cambridge University Press, 1981.

Ionesco

Primary sources

Ionesco, Eugene. "Dans les armes de la ville." *Cahiers de la Companie Madeleine Renaud-Jean-Louis Barrault* 20 (October 1957): 2–5.

"Ionesco and the Critics: Eugene Ionesco Interviewed by Gabriel Jacobs." *Critical Inquiry* 1.3 (March 1975): 641–67.

Notes and Counter Notes. Trans. Donald Watson. New York: Grove Press, 1964.

"Notes on My Theatre." Trans. Leonard C. Pronko. *The Tulane Drama Review* 7 3 (Spring 1963): 126–59.
Rhinoceros and Other Plays. Trans. Derek Prouse. New York: Grove Press, Inc., 1960.
A Stroll in the Air, Frenzy for Two, Or More. Trans. Donald Watson. New York: Grove Press, 1965.
Three Plays: Amédée, The New Tenant, Victims of Duty. Trans. Donald Watson. New York: Grove Press, 1958.
Three Plays: Exit the King, The Killer, and Macbett. Trans. Charles Marowitz and Donald Watson. New York: Grove Press, 1985.
"Theaters of the Absurd." *Partisan Review* 56.1 (1989): 45–9.
"The Avant-Garde Theatre." *The Tulane Drama Review* 5.2 (December 1960): 44–53.
Four Plays: The Bald Soprano, The Lesson, Jack, or The Submission, The Chairs. Trans. Donald M. Allen. New York: Grove, 1958.
"The World of Ionesco." *The Tulane Drama Review* 3.1 (October 1958): 46–8.

Secondary sources

Gaensbauer, Deborah B. *Eugene Ionesco Revisited.* New York: Twayne Publishers, 1996.
Hayman, Ronald. *World Dramatists: Eugene Ionesco.* New York: Frederick Unger, 1976.
Lewis, Allan. *Ionesco.* New York: Twayne Publishers, Inc., 1972.

Pinter

Primary sources

Pinter, Harold. *Complete Works: One.* New York: Grove Press, 1976.
Complete Works: Two. New York: Grove Press, 1977.
Complete Works: Three. New York: Grove Press, 1978.
Complete Works: Four. New York: Grove Press, 1981.
The Dwarfs. New York: Grove Press, 1990.
"Letter to Peter Wood," *The Kenyon Review* 3.3 (Summer 1981): 1–5.

Secondary sources

Billington, Michael. *The Life and Work of Harold Pinter.* London: Faber and Faber, 1996.
Ford, Anna. *Pinter, Plays & Politics.* BBC Television Interview. 1988.
Gale, Steven H. *Butter's Going Up: A Critical Analysis of Harold Pinter's Work.* Durham: Duke University Press.
Raby, Peter, ed. *The Cambridge Companion to Harold Pinter,* 2nd edn. Cambridge University Press, 2009.

Miscellaneous Selected Reading

Adamov, Arthur. *Paolo Paoli.* Trans. Geoffrey Brereton. London: John Calder, 1959.
   Ping Pong: Two Plays by Arthur Adamov. Trans. Derek Prouse and Peter Meyer. London: John Calder, 1962.
Arrabal, Fernando. *Guernica and Other Plays.* New York: Grove Press, 1974.
Artaud, Antonin, *Collected Works: Volume One.* Trans. Victor Corti. London: John Calder, 1968.
   Collected Works: Volume Two. Trans. Victor Corti. London: John Calder, 1971.
   Collected Works: Volume Three. Trans. Alastair Hamilton. London: Calder & Boyars, 1972.
   The Theater and Its Double. Trans. Mary Caroline Richards. New York: Grove Press, 1958.
Dürrenmatt, Friedrich. *The Physicists.* Trans. James Kirkup. New York: Grove Press, 1964.
   The Visit: A Tragi-Comedy. Trans. Patrick Bowles. New York: Grove Press, 1962.
Gelber, Jack. *The Apple.* New York: Grove Press, 1960.
   The Connection. New York: Grove Press, 1960.
Havel, Václav. *The Garden Party and Other Plays.* New York: Grove Press, 1993.
Kimberly Jannarone, *Artaud and His Doubles.* Ann Arbor: University of Michigan Press, 2010.
Jarry, Alfred. *Ubu Roi.* Trans. Beverly Keith and G. Legman. Mineola: Dover Publications, Inc., 2003.
Kafka, Franz. *Metamorphosis and Other Stories.*
   The Trial.
Kennedy, Adrienne. *In One Act.* Minneapolis: University of Minnesota Press, 1988.
Kopit, Arthur. *Indians.* New York: The Noonday Press, 1969.
   Oh Dad, Poor Dad, Mamma's Hung You in the Closet and I'm Feelin' So Sad. New York: Pocket Books, 1966.
Mrozek, Slawomir. *Six Plays.* Trans. Nicholas Bethell. New York: Grove Press, 1967.
Ostashevsky, Eugene, ed. *OBERIU: An Anthology of Russian Absurdism.* Evanston: Northwestern University Press, 2006.
Rozewicz, Tadeusz. *The Card Index and Other Plays.* Trans. Adam Czerniawski. New York: Grove Press, 1969.
   Reading the Apocalypse in Bed: Selected Plays and Short Pieces. Trans. Adam Czerniawski, Barbara Plebanek, and Tony Howard. London: Marion Boyars, 1998.
Simpson, N. F. *One Way Pendulum: A Farce in a New Dimension.* New York: Grove Press, 1960.

Works Cited (Not Listed in Above Bibliographies)

Adler, Thomas P. "Public Faces, Private Graces: Apocalypse Postponed in Arthur Kopit's End of the World." *Studies in the Literary Imagination* 21.2 (1998): 107–18.

Barker, Roberta. "The Circle Game: Gender, Time, and 'Revolution' in Tom Stoppard's The Coast of Utopia." *Modern Drama* 48.4 (2005): 706–25.

Barnett, Claudia. "'An Evasion of Ontology': Being Adrienne Kennedy." *The Drama Review: A Journal of Performance Studies* 49.3 (2005): 157–86.

Bennett, Michael Y. "Away from the Absurd?: The Critical Response to Beckett at 100" *Kritikon Litterarum* 36.3/4 (December 2009): 230–8.

"The Cartesian Beckett: The Mind-Body Split in Murphy and Happy Days." *ANQ: A Quarterly Journal of Short Articles, Notes, and Reviews* 25.2 (May 2012): 118–22.

"Dominance and the Triumph of the White Trickster Over the Black Picaro in Amiri Baraka's Great Goodness of Life: A Coon Show." *Callaloo* 36.2 (Spring 2013)

"'The Essential Doesn't Change': Essence Precedes Experience and Cartesian Rationalism in Samuel Beckett's Waiting for Godot." *Notes on Contemporary Literature* 42.1 (January 2012): 5–7.

"Performance Review of Long Day's Journey into Night, by Eugene O'Neill," *Eugene O'Neill Review* 34.2 (2013): 273–5.

"Sartre's 'The Wall' and Beckett's Waiting for Godot: Existential and Non-Existential Nothingness." *Notes on Contemporary Literature* 39.5 (November 2009): 2–3.

Words, Space, and the Audience: The Theatrical Tension between Empiricism and Rationalism. New York: Palgrave Macmillan, 2012.

Ben-Zvi, Linda and Angela Moorjani, eds. *Beckett at 100: Revolving it All.* Oxford University Press, 2008.

Bhatia, Nandi. "Reinventing India through 'A Quite Witty Pastiche': Reading Tom Stoppard's Indian Ink." *Modern Drama* 52.2 (2009): 220–37.

Brayshaw, Richard and Burgoyne Dieckman, Suzanne. "Wings, Watchers, and Windows: Imprisonment in the Plays of Arthur Kopit." *Theatre Journal* 35.2 (1983): 195–211.

Camus, Albert. *Le mythe de Sisyphe: Essai sur L'Absurde.* Gallimard, 1942.

Carlson, Marvin. *Theories of the Theatre: A Historical and Critical Survey, from the Greeks to the Present.* Ithaca: Cornell University Press, 1984.

Carroll, David. "Rethinking the Absurd: Le Mythe de Sisyphe." *The Cambridge Companion to Camus.* Ed. Edward J. Hughes. Cambridge University Press, 2007, pp. 53–66.

Chung, Moonyoung. "Stage as Hyperspace: Theatricality of Stoppard." *Modern Drama* 48.4 (2005): 689–705.

Czerwinski, Edward J. "Tadeusz Rozewicz and the Jester-Priest Metaphor." *The Slavic and East European Journal* 13.2 (1969): 217–28.

Demastes, William W. *Beyond Naturalism: A New Realism in American Theatre.* New York: Greenwood Press, 1988.

"Portrait of an Artist as Proto-Chaotician: Tom Stoppard Working His Way to Arcadia." *Narrative* 19.2 (2011): 229–40.

Dietemann, Margaret. "Departure from the Absurd: Adamov's Last Plays." *Yale French Studies* 46 (1971): 48–59.

Diller, Edward. "Aesthetics and the Grotesque: Friedrich Durrenmatt." *Wisconsin Studies in Contemporary Literature* 7.3 (1966): 328–35.

"Friedrich Durrenmatt's Theological Concept of History." *The German Quarterly* 40.3 (1967): 363–71.

Donahue, Francis. "Arrabal: Organic Playwright." *Midwest Quarterly: A Journal of Contemporary Thought* 25 (1984): 187–200.

Doxtader, Erik W. "Characters in the Middle of Public Life: Consensus, Dissent, and Ethos." *Philosophy and Rhetoric* 33.4 (2000): 336–69.

Engler, Bernd. "Antidrama–Metadrama–Artistic Program? Arthur Kopit's The Hero in Context." *Connotations: A Journal for Critical Debate* 3.3 (1994): 279–90.

Esslin, Martin, ed. *Absurd Drama.* Middlesex: Penguin, 1965.

"Beckett and the Quest for Meaning," *Samuel Beckett Today* 11 (2001): 27–30.

"Beckett and the 'Theater of the Absurd.'" *Approaches to Teaching in Beckett's Waiting for Godot.* June Schlueter and Enoch Brater, eds. New York : Modern Language Association of America, 1991, pp. 42–7.

"Mrozek, Beckett, and the Theatre of the Absurd." *New Theatre Quarterly* 10.40 (1994): 377–81.

"The Theatre of the Absurd." *The Tulane Drama Review* 4.4 (May 1960): 3–15.

"What Beckett Teaches Me: His Minimalist Approach to Ethics," *Samuel Beckett Today* 2 (1993): 13–20.

Filipowicz, Halina. "Tadeusz Rozewicz's Postmodern Trilogy." *The Polish Review* 36.1 (1991): 83–102.

"Theatrical Reality in the Plays of Tadeusz Rozewicz." *The Slavic and East European Journal* 26.4 (1982): 447–59.

Fischler, Alexander. "The Absurd Professor in the Theater of the Absurd." *Modern Drama* 21 (1978): 137–52.

Fothergill, C. Z. "Echoes of a Resounding Tinkle: N.F. Simpson Reconsidered." *Modern Drama* 16.3–4 (1973): 299–306.

Gerould, Daniel C. "Tadeusz Rozewicz: Playwriting as Collage." *Performing Arts Journal* 1.2 (1976): 63–6.

Gillis, William. "Durrenmatt and the Detectives." *The German Quarterly* 35.1 (1962): 71–4.

Grabowski, Arthur and Krempl, Renata. "One Table and Two Theatres: How to Produce a Polish Drama about Europe for an American Audience, or What Use a Director Can Make of a Dramaturg." *Slavic and East European Performance* 26.3 (2006): 32–43.

Hurley, Paul J. "France and America: Versions of the Absurd." *College English* 26.8 (1965): 634–40.

Hurt, James. "Arthur Kopit's Wings and the Languages of the Theater." *American Drama* 8.1 (1998): 75–94.

Innes, Christopher. "Allegories from the Past: Stoppard's Uses of History." *Modern Drama* 49.2 (2006): 223–37.

"The Canon: The Theatre of the Absurd. By Martin Esslin," *Times Higher Education* 18 June 2009.

Jedrzekjo, Pawel and Baraka, Amiri. "Still a Revolutionary." *New Theatre Quarterly* 26.4 (2010): 340–50.

Jackson, Shannon. *Professing Performance: Theatre in the Academy from Philology to Performativity.* Cambridge University Press, 2004.

Juliet, Charles. *Conversations with Samuel Beckett and Bram van Velde.* Dalkey Archive Press, 1996.

Kampf, Louis. "The Permanence of Modernism." *College English* 28.1 (1966): 1–15.

Kejna-Sharratt, Barbara. "Slawomir Mrozek and the Polish Tradition of the Absurd." *New Zealand Slavonic Journal* 1 (1974): 75–86.

Kaufmann, Walter. *Existentialism: From Dostoevsky to Sartre.* New York: Plume, 1975.

Kumar, Nita N. "The Logic of Retribution: Amiri Baraka's Dutchman." *African American Review* 37.2 (2003): 271–9.

Marowitz, Charles. "State of Play." *The Tulane Drama Review* 11.2 (1966): 203–6.

Martin, Elizabeth. "Human Chaos and Arcadia's Hidden Twin." *Publications of the Mississippi Philological Association* (2010): 40–59.

Meerzon, Yana. "Dancing on the X-rays: On the Theatre of Memory, Counter-Memory, and Postmemory in the Post-1989 East-European Context." *Modern Drama* 54.4 (2011): 479–510.

Meisel, Martin. "Shaw, Stoppard and 'Audible Intelligibility'." *Shaw: The Annual of Bernard Shaw Studies* 27 (2007): 42–58.

"The Last Waltz: Tom Stoppard's Poetics of Science." *Wordsworth Circle* 38.1–2 (2007): 13–19.

Morfee, Adrian. *Antonin Artaud's Writing Bodies.* Oxford: Clarendon Press, 2005.

O'Connor, John. "Dancing with Freud: Slawomir Mrozek's Tango." *Studies in the Literary Imagination* 34.2 (2001): 1–11.

O'Neill, Michael C. "History as Dramatic Present: Arthur L. Kopit's 'Indians'." *Theatre Journal* 34.4 (1982): 493–504.

Parker, R. B. "Farce and Society: The Range of Kingsley Amis." *Wisconsin Studies in Contemporary Literature* 2.3 (1961): 27–38.

Piggford, George. "Looking into Black Skulls: Amiri Baraka's Dutchman and the Psychology of Race." *Modern Drama* 40.1 (1997): 74–85.

Plunka, Gene A., ed. *Antonin Artaud and the Modern Theater.* Rutherford: Fairleigh Dickinson University Press, 1994.

Podol, Peter L. "The Grotesque Mode in Contemporary Spanish Theater and Film." *Modern Language Studies* 15.4 (1985): 194–207.

Ross, Ciaran. *Beckett's Art of Absence: Rethinking the Void.* Houndsmills: Palgrave Macmillan, 2011.

Schryer, Stephen. "A Culture of Violence and Foodsmells: Amiri Baraka's The System of Dante's Hell and the War on Poverty." *Arizona Quarterly: A Journal of American Literature, Culture, and Theory* 66.1 (2010): 145–64.

Sell, Mike. "Jazz, Drama, and Drug War: The Living Theatre's Production of The Connection." *On-Stage Studies* 20 (1997): 28–47.

Sichert, Margit. "The Staging of Excessive Emotions; Adrienne Kennedy's Funnyhouse of a Negro." *The Yearbook of Research in English and American Literature* 16 (2000): 229–51.

Sikes, Alan W. "Politics and Pornography: Czech Performance in the International Arena." *Theatre Journal* 62.3 (2010): 373–87.

Sollors, Werner. "Owls and Rats in the American Funnyhouse: Adrienne Kennedy's Drama." *American Literature* 63.3 (1991): 507–32.

Spencer, Jenny S. "Emancipated Spectatorship in Adrienne Kennedy's Plays." *Modern Drama* 55.1 (2012): 19–39.

Stankiewicz, Marketa Goetz. "Slawomir Mrozek: Two Forms of the Absurd." *Contemporary Literature* 12.2 (1971): 188–203.

"The Metamorphosis of the Theatre of the Absurd or the Jobless Jester." *Pacific Coast Philology* 7 (1972): 54–64.

Tattenbaum, Mark F. "Rozewicz's Card Index Scattered in Its U.S. Premire: Recycling, Discarding, and Adding the Fragments." *Slavic and East European Performance: Drama, Theatre and Film* 27.2 (2007): 65–70.

Taylor, John Russell. "Ten Years of the English Stage Company." *The Tulane Drama Review* 11.2 (1966): 120–31.

Trensky, Paul I. "Vaclav Havel and the Language of the Absurd." *The Slavic and East European Journal* 13.1 (1969): 42–65.

Tsushima, Michiko. "On the Boundaries between Materiality and Immateriality: Words and Music and Cascando," Samuel Beckett Working Group, *IFTR 2011 Conference*, Osaka, Japan.

Zimmerman, Judith. "Tom Stoppard's Russian Thinkers." *New England Review: Middlebury Series* 28.3 (2007): 80–94.

Index

"Existential Front", 40
"The Great Quarrel", 44
"Three Dialogues", 65
"tragicomic pastoral", 51
"Whoroscope", 64
"Beats", 39
"fourth wall", 14
"In the Penal Colony", 29, 135
"Kafkaesque", 28
"parabolic drama", 17, 132
"psychotherapy", 33
"*questioning voice*", 30
"strange" situations, 19, 21, 57
"The Metamorphosis", 28
"The Theatre of Cruelty", 32

A Delicate Balance, 68, 70, 71, 72, 142
Act without Words I, 52, 53, 55, 57,
   86
Act without Words II, 52, 53, 55, 57
Adrian Marfee, 32
Adrienne Kennedy, 102
African-American Satire, 124
Alan S. Milward, 36, 37, 136
Albert Camus, vii, 1, 4, 5, 6, 9, 10, 14,
   15, 16, 19, 20, 30, 35, 40–44, 52,
   65, 75, 77, 78, 127, 128, 129, 132,
   133, 134, 136, 138, 139, 140, 142,
   147, 149, 150, 152, 153, 156
Alexander Vvedensky, 31
Alfred Jarry, 28
Amiri Baraka, viii, 25, 95, 96, 123, 125,
   143, 148, 156, 158, 159
analytic philosophy, 45
André Brenton, 13

Angela Moorjani, 131
Anthony Ulhmann, 131
Antonin Artaud, vii, 24, 32, 33, 135,
   136, 158
Aristotelian drama, 20, 61
Arnold P. Hinchcliffe, 130
Arthur Adamov, 93
Arthur Kopit, 103
audience response, 118

Baby Boomers, 39
Being and Nothingness, 40
Benjamin Fondane, 14, 15
Bertolt Brecht, 13, 14, 18, 26, 27, 28,
   79, 82, 93, 97, 98, 118, 121, 127
Bertrand Russell, 45
Beth Henley, 120
Betrayal, 91
Black Arts Movement, 101, 123, 125
Bread and Puppet Theater, 130
Breath, 52, 57
Brigitte Le Juez, 131

Caryl Churchill, 122
César Chávez, 40
Christopher Innes, 2, 3, 133
Christopher Murry, 131
Chuck Berry, 39
Ciaran Ross, 64
Cold War, 37, 39, 43, 137, 138
Come and Go, 54, 55
criticism of absurd label
   Edward Albee, 7
   Samuel Beckett, 6
Curb Your Enthusiasm, 127

Dadaism, 13
Daniil Kharms, 31, 32, 135
David Carroll, 128
David Drake, 40, 138

economy
    France, 37
    Great Britain, 38
    United States, 39
Edith Kern, 128
Edna O'Brien, 125
Edward Albee, 76
Elvis Presley, 39
Endgame, 52, 53, 55, 57, 151
Enoch Brater, 21, 22
Eugene Ionesco, 84
existentialism, 2, 9, 16, 41, 44, 45, 65,
    129, 138, 147
    "Existential Front", 2, 40
exposition, 20
expressionism, 13

Female Absurdists (Later), 122
Fernando Arrabal, 95
Francis Jeanson, 43
Franz Kafka, vii, 5, 24, 28, 31, 135
French Communist Party ("PCF"), 38,
    41, 44
Friedrich Dürrenmatt, 98

George Wellwarth, 130
Giraldi Cinthio, 11
Gottlob Frege, 45

Happy Days, 29, 52, 53, 54, 55, 56, 57,
    141, 151, 156
Harold Pinter, 91
Holocaust, 2, 9, 30, 35, 39, 90

J. L. Styan, 20, 118, 135
J. M. Coetzee, 125
Jack Gelber, 99
Jacques Derrida, 125
James Joyce, 1, 8, 17, 48
James Meredith, 40
James T. Patterson, 39, 137

Jean Genet, 81
Jean-Paul Sartre, vii, 1, 2, 5, 9, 10, 15,
    16, 19, 40, 41, 42, 43, 44, 45, 65,
    77, 129, 133, 134, 138, 139, 140,
    142, 149, 152, 156, 158
Jerzy Grotowski, 33
John Banville, 125
John Cage, 33
John F. Kennedy, 39
Julius Caesar Scaliger, 11

Korean War, 37, 106
Krapp's Last Tape, 48, 52, 53, 73

La MaMa, 130
Langston Hughes, 123
Lenny Bruce, 39
Léon Chestov, 14, 15
Leonard Cabell Pronko, 129
Les Temps modernes, 40, 42, 44, 138,
    140
Lewis Carroll, 12
Linda Ben-Zvi, 47, 131, 140, 151
Lorraine Hansberry, 123
Ludwig Wittgenstein, 45, 65
Luigi Pirandello, 13, 14, 26, 27, 28, 46,
    82

Malone Dies, 58, 59, 60, 66, 141, 151
Marc Blanchard, 128
Maria Irene Fornes, 122
Marshall Plan, 37
Martin Esslin, vii, 3, 4, 17, 23, 66, 92,
    94, 128, 129, 133, 143, 145, 148,
    158
Martin Heidegger, 65
meta-theatrical, 14
modernism, 116
modernism, comparison to, 7, 8, 12
Molloy, 58, 59, 60, 66, 141, 151
Multicultural Absurd, 124
Murphy, 18, 46, 55, 58, 59, 60, 61, 66,
    116, 141, 151, 156

N. F. Simpson, 113
Neil Cornwell, 12, 131

Nikolai Gogol, 12
Norman Mailer, 39
Not I, 52, 55

OBERIU, vii, 24, 31, 32, 34, 135, 155
Our Lady of the Flowers, 81

pataphysics, 25
Paul Muldoon, 125
Pauline Gregg, 38
Peter Royle, 129
Philosophical Investigations, 45
Plautus, 11
Poetics, 20
postmodernism, 116
postmodernism, comparison to, 7, 8,
    104

Reassessing the Theatre of the Absurd,
    16, 17, 132, 133, 135, 140, 142,
    147, 149, 150
reductio ad absurdum, 124, 148
René Descartes, 62, 63, 65
Rhinoceros, 83
ridiculousness, 10, 19
Ronan McDonald, 131
Ruby Cohen, 129

S. E. Gontarski, 131
Sam Shepard, 113
Samuel Beckett, i, viii, x, 1, 2, 4, 6, 17,
    18, 45, 47, 64, 66, 67, 68, 81, 92,
    94, 125, 129, 130, 131, 133, 135,
    140, 141, 151, 152, 156, 157, 158,
    159
  influence of, 18, 46, 125
  influence on, 48
  on music, 54
Seascape, 68, 72, 73, 142
Seinfeld's "The Chinese Restaurant,"
    126
Sesame Street's "Waiting for Elmo,"
    125
Sławomir Mrożek, 104
Soren Kierkegaard, 15

Søren Kierkegaard, 14
Sperone Speroni, 11
surreal, 19, 48, 56, 57, 61, 73, 101
Surrealism, 13

Tadeusz Różewicz, 105
The Absurd in Literature, 131, 132
The Balcony, 78
The Bald Soprano, 84
The Birthday Party, 88
The Blacks
  A Clown Show, 79
The Chairs, 84
The Dumb Waiter, 87
The Dwarfs, 90
The Goat, or Who Is Sylvia?, 68, 74, 75
The Homecoming, 90
The Living Theatre, 130
The Maids, 78
The Myth of Sisyphus, 4, 14, 15, 16, 30,
    41, 78, 128, 152
The Open Theater, 130
The Rebel, 41, 42, 134, 139, 152
The Room, 86
The Theatre and its Double, 32
The Theatre of the Absurd, 6
The Theatre of the Absurd, 3, 4, 6, 7, 48,
    129, 132, 150, 157, 158
The Thief's Jouranl, 80
The Tooth of Crime, 113
The Trial, 30, 46, 57, 85, 96, 155
The Unnamable, 59
The Zoo Story, 18, 35, 39, 67, 68, 69, 74,
    75
theatrical realism, 12
Three Tall Women, 68, 73, 74, 75
Tiny Alice, 68
Tom Lehrer, 39
Tom Stoppard, 114
Tractatus Logico-Philosophicus, 45
tragicomedy, 11, 60, 119
  "tragicomic pastoral", 12
  origins of, 11
tragicomic view, 35
Tristan Tzara, 13

Ubu Roi, 25, 26, 135, 155
United States
   post-war, 40

Václav Havel, 100

Waiting for Godot, viii, 4, 11, 20, 37, 45,
   47, 48, 49, 52, 54, 66, 81, 97, 101,
   120, 126, 128, 141, 142, 151, 156,
   157

Waiting for Guffman, 126
Walter Kaufmann, 2, 133
Watt, 62
Welfare State, 38
Who's Afraid of Virginia Woolf?, 68,
   69, 70, 74, 81, 90, 117, 142,
   148
William S. Burroughs, 125
WWII, vii, 2, 9, 16, 18, 30, 34, 35, 36,
   39, 43, 47, 50, 81

Cambridge Introductions to...

AUTHORS

Margaret Atwood Heidi Macpherson

Jane Austen (second edition) Janet Todd

Samuel Beckett Ronan McDonald

Walter Benjamin David Ferris

Lord Byron Richard Lansdown

Chaucer Alastair Minnis

Chekhov James N. Loehlin

J. M. Coetzee Dominic Head

Samuel Taylor Coleridge John Worthen

Joseph Conrad John Peters

Jacques Derrida Leslie Hill

Charles Dickens Jon Mee

Emily Dickinson Wendy Martin

George Eliot Nancy Henry

T. S. Eliot John Xiros Cooper

William Faulkner Theresa M. Towner

F. Scott Fitzgerald Kirk Curnutt

Michel Foucault Lisa Downing

Robert Frost Robert Faggen

Gabriel Garcia Marquez Gerald Martin

Nathaniel Hawthorne Leland S. Person

Zora Neale Hurston Lovalerie King

James Joyce Eric Bulson

Kafka Carolin Duttlinger

Thomas Mann Todd Kontje

Christopher Marlowe Tom Rutter

Herman Melville Kevin J. Hayes

Milton Stephen B. Dobranski

George Orwell John Rodden and John Rossi

Sylvia Plath Jo Gill

Edgar Allan Poe Benjamin F. Fisher

Ezra Pound Ira Nadel

Marcel Proust Adam Watt

Jean Rhys Elaine Savory

Edward Said Conor McCarthy

Shakespeare Emma Smith

Shakespeare's Comedies Penny Gay

Shakespeare's History Plays Warren Chernaik

Shakespeare's Poetry Michael Schoenfeldt

Shakespeare's Tragedies Janette Dillon

Tom Stoppard William W. Demastes

Harriet Beecher Stowe Sarah Robbins

Mark Twain Peter Messent

Edith Wharton Pamela Knights

Walt Whitman M. Jimmie Killingsworth

Virginia Woolf Jane Goldman

William Wordsworth Emma Mason

W. B. Yeats David Holdeman

TOPICS

American Literary Realism Phillip Barrish

The American Short Story Martin Scofield

Anglo-Saxon Literature Hugh Magennis

Comedy Eric Weitz

Creative Writing David Morley

Early English Theatre Janette Dillon

Early Modern Drama, 1576–1642 Julie Sanders

The Eighteenth-Century Novel April London

Eighteenth-Century Poetry John Sitter

English Theatre, 1660–1900 Peter Thomson

French Literature Brian Nelson

Francophone Literature Patrick Corcoran

German Poetry Judith Ryan

Literature and the Environment Timothy Clark

Modern British Theatre Simon Shepherd

Modern Irish Poetry Justin Quinn

Modernism Pericles Lewis

Modernist Poetry Peter Howarth

Narrative (second edition) H. Porter Abbott

The Nineteenth-Century American Novel Gregg Crane

The Novel Marina MacKay

Old Norse Sagas Margaret Clunies Ross

Postcolonial Literatures C. L. Innes

Postmodern Fiction Bran Nicol

Romantic Poetry Michael Ferber

Russian Literature Caryl Emerson

Scenography Joslin McKinney and Philip Butterworth

The Short Story in English Adrian Hunter

Theatre Directing Christopher Innes and Maria Shevtsova

Theatre Historiography Thomas Postlewait

Theatre and Literature of the Absurd Michael Y. Bennett

Theatre Studies Christopher B. Balme

Tragedy Jennifer Wallace

Victorian Poetry Linda K. Hughes